AN ESSAY

ON

Liberty and Slavery.

BY

ALBERT TAYLOR BLEDSOE, LL.D.

PROFESSOR OF MATHEMATICS IN THE UNIVERSITY OF VIRGINIA.

[1808 - 1877]

PHILADELPHIA:
J. B. LIPPINCOTT & CO.
1856.

CONTENTS.

INTRODUCTION.

THIS work has, for the most part, been thought out for several years, and various portions of it reduced to writing. Though we have long cherished the design of preparing it for the press, yet other engagements, conspiring with a spirit of procrastination, have hitherto induced us to defer the execution of this design. Nor should we have prosecuted it, as we have done, during a large portion of our last summer vacation, and the leisure moments of the first two months of the present session of the University, but for the solicitation of two intelligent and highly-esteemed friends. In submitting the work, as it now is, to the judgment of the truth-loving and impartial reader, we beg leave to offer one or two preliminary remarks.

We have deemed it wise and proper to notice only the more decent, respectable, and celebrated among the Abolitionists of the North. Those scurrilous writers, who deal in wholesale abuse of Southern character, we have deemed unworthy of notice. Their writings are, no doubt, adapted to the taste of their readers; but as it is certain that no educated gentleman will tolerate them, so we would not raise a finger to promote their downfall, nor to arrest their course toward the oblivion which so inevitably awaits them.

In replying to the others, we are conscious that we have often used strong language; for which, however, we have no apology to offer. We have dealt with their arguments and positions rather than with their motives and characters. If, in pursuing this course, we have often spoken strongly, we merely beg the reader to consider whether we have not also spoken justly. We have certainly not spoken without provocation. For even these men — the very lights and ornaments of abolitionism — have seldom condescended to argue the great question of Liberty and Slavery with us as with equals. On the contrary, they habitually address us as if nothing but a purblind ignorance of the very first elements of moral science could shield our minds against the force of their irresistible arguments. In the overflowing exuberance of their philanthropy, they take pity of our most lamentable moral darkness, and graciously condescend to teach us the very A B C of ethical philosophy! Hence, if we have deemed it a duty to lay bare their pompous inanities, showing them to be no oracles, and to strip their pitiful sophisms of the guise of a profound philosophy, we trust that no impartial reader will take offence at such vindication of the South against her accusers and despisers.

In this vindication, we have been careful throughout to distinguish between the abolitionists, our accusers, and the great body of the people of the North. Against these we have said nothing, and we could say nothing; since for these we entertain the most profound respect. We have only assailed those by whom we have been assailed; and we have held each and every man responsible only for what he himself has said and done. We should, indeed, despise ourselves if we could be guilty of the monstrous injustice of denouncing a whole people on account of the sayings and doings of a portion of them. We had infinitely rather suffer such injustice—as we have so long done—than practise it toward others.

We cannot flatter ourselves, of course, that the following work is without errors. But these, whatever else may be thought of them, are not the errors of haste and inconsideration. For if we have felt deeply on the subject here discussed, we have also thought long, and patiently endeavored to guard our minds against fallacy. How far this effort has proved successful, it is the province of the candid and impartial reader alone to decide. If our arguments and views are unsound, we hope he will reject them. On the contrary, if they are correct and well-grounded, we hope he will concur with us in the conclusion, that the institution of slavery, as it exists among us at the South, is founded in political justice, is in accordance with the will of GOD and the designs of his providence, and is conducive to the highest, purest, best interests of mankind.

LIBERTY AND SLAVERY.

CHAPTER I.

THE NATURE OF CIVIL LIBERTY.

FEW subjects, if any, more forcibly demand our attention, by their intrinsic grandeur and importance, than the great doctrine of human liberty. Correct views concerning this are, indeed, so intimately connected with the most profound interests, as well as with the most exalted aspirations, of the human race, that any material departure therefrom must be fraught with evil to the living, as well as to millions yet unborn. They are so inseparably interwoven with all that is great and good and glorious in the destiny of man, that whosoever aims to form or to propagate such views should proceed with the utmost care, and, laying aside all prejudice and passion, be guided by the voice of reason alone.

Hence it is to be regretted—deeply regretted—that the doctrine of liberty has so often been discussed with so little apparent care, with so little moral earnestness, with so little real energetic searching and longing after truth. Though its transcendent importance demands the best exertion of all our powers, yet has it been, for the most part, a theme for passionate declamation, rather than of severe analysis or of protracted and patient investigation. In the warm praises of the philosopher, no less than in the glowing inspirations of the poet, it often stands before us as a vague and ill-defined *something* which all men are required to worship, but which no man is bound to understand. It would seem, indeed, as if it were a mighty something not to be clearly seen, but only to be deeply felt. And felt it has been, too, by the ignorant as well as by the learned, by the simple as well as by the wise: felt as a fire in the blood, as a fever in the brain, and as a phantom in the imagination, rather than as a form of light and beauty in the intelligence. How often have the powers of darkness surrounded its throne, and desolation marked its path! How often from the altars of this *unknown idol* has the blood of human victims streamed! Even here, in this glorious land of ours, how often do the *too-religious* Americans seem to become deaf to the most appalling lessons of the past, while engaged in the frantic worship of this their tutelary deity! At this very moment, the highly-favored land in which we live is convulsed from its centre to its circumference by the agitations of these pious devotees of freedom; and how long ere scenes like those which called forth the celebrated exclamation of Madame Roland—"O Liberty, what crimes are perpetrated in thy name!" may be enacted among us, it is not possible for human sagacity or foresight to determine.

If no one would talk about liberty except those who had taken the pains to understand it, then would a perfect calm be restored, and peace once more bless a happy people. But there are so many who imagine they understand liberty as Falstaff knew the true prince, namely, by instinct, that all hope of such a consummation must be deferred until it may be shown that their instinct is a blind guide, and its oracles are false. Hence the necessity of a close study and of a clear analysis of the nature and conditions of civil liberty, in order to a distinct delineation of the great idol, which all men are so ready to worship, but which so few are willing to take the pains to understand. In the prosecution of such an inquiry, we intend to consult neither the pecuniary interests of the South nor the prejudices of the North; but calmly and immovably proceed to discuss, upon purely scientific principles, this great problem of our social existence and national prosperity, upon the solution of which the hopes and destinies of mankind in no inconsiderable measure depend. We intend no appeal to passion or to sordid interest, but only to the reason of the wise and good. And if justice, or mercy, or truth, be found at war with the institution of slavery, then, in the name of God, let slavery perish. But however guilty, still let it be tried, condemned, and executed according to law, and not extinguished by a despotic and lawless power more terrific than itself.

§ I. *The commonly-received definition of civil liberty.*

"Civil liberty," says Blackstone, "is no other than natural liberty so far restrained as is necessary and expedient for the general advantage." This definition seems to have been borrowed from Locke, who says that, when a man enters into civil society, "he is to part with so much of his *natural liberty*, in providing for himself, as the good, prosperity, and safety of the society shall require." So, likewise, say Paley, Berlamaqui, Rutherforth, and a host of others. Indeed, among jurists and philosophers, such seems to be the commonly-received definition of civil liberty. It seems to have become a political maxim that civil liberty is no other than a certain portion of our natural liberty, which has been carved therefrom, and secured to us by the protection of the laws.

But is this a sound maxim? Has it been deduced from the nature of things, or is it merely a plausible show of words? Is it truth—solid and imperishable truth—or merely one of those fair semblances of truth, which, through the too hasty sanction of great names, have obtained a currency among men? The question is not what Blackstone, or Locke, or Paley may have thought, but what is truth? Let us examine this point, then, in order that our decision may be founded, not upon the authority of man, but, if possible, in the wisdom of God.

§ II. *Examination of the commonly-received definition of civil liberty.*

Before we can determine whether such be the

2

origin of civil liberty, we must first ascertain the character of that natural liberty out of which it is supposed to be reserved. What, then, is natural liberty? What is the nature of the material out of which our civil liberty is supposed to be fashioned by the art of the political sculptor? It is thus defined by Locke: "To understand political power right, and derive it from its original, we must consider what state all men are naturally in; and that is a state of perfect freedom to order their actions and dispose of their possessions and persons as they think fit, *within the bounds of the law of nature*, without asking leave or depending upon the will of any other man."[a] In perfect accordance with this definition, Blackstone says: "This natural liberty consists in a power of acting as one thinks fit, without any restraint or control, unless by the laws of nature, being a right inherent in us by birth, and one of the gifts of God to man at his creation, when he endowed him with the faculty of free-will." Such, according to Locke and Blackstone, is that natural liberty, which is limited and abridged, as they suppose, when we enter into the bonds of civil society.

---

[a] Locke on Civil Government, chap. ii.

Now mark its features: it is the gift of God to man at his creation; the very top and flower of his existence; that by which he is distinguished from the lower animals and raised to the rank of moral and accountable beings. Shall we sacrifice this divine gift, then, in order to secure the blessings of civil society? Shall we abridge or mutilate the image of God, stamped upon the soul at its creation, by which we are capable of knowing and obeying his law, in order to secure the aid and protection of man? Shall we barter away any portion of this our glorious birthright for any poor boon of man's devising? Yes, we are told—and why? Because, says Blackstone, "Legal obedience and conformity is infinitely more valuable than *the wild and savage liberty which is sacrificed to obtain it.*"

But how is this? *Now* this natural liberty is a thing of light, and *now* it is a power of darkness. Now it is the gift of God, that moves within a sphere of light, and breathes an atmosphere of love; and anon, it is a wild and savage thing that carries terror in its train. It would be an angel of light, if it were not a power of darkness; and it would be a power of darkness, if it were not an angel of light. But as it is, it is both by turns, and neither long, but runs through its Protean changes, according to the exigencies of the flowing discourse of the learned author. Surely such inconsistency, so glaring and so portentous, and all exhibited on one and the same page, is no evidence that the genius of the great commentator was as steady and profound as it was elegant and classical.

The source of this vacillation is obvious. With Locke, he defines natural liberty to be a power of acting as one thinks fit, *within the limits prescribed by the law of nature;* but he soon loses sight of this all-important limitation, from which natural liberty derives its form and beauty. Hence it becomes in his mind a power to act as one pleases, without the restraint or control of any law whatever, either human or divine. The sovereign will and pleasure of the individual becomes the only rule of conduct, and lawless anarchy the condition which it legitimates. Thus, having loosed the bonds and marred the beauty of natural liberty, he was prepared to see it, now become so "wild and savage," offered up as a sacrifice on the altar of civil liberty.

This, too, was the great fundamental error of Hobbes. What Blackstone thus did through inadvertency, was knowingly and designedly done by the philosopher of Malmesbury. In a state of nature, says he, all men have a right to do as they please. Each individual may set up a right to all things, and consequently to the same things. In other words, in such a state there is no law, except that of force. The strong arm of power is the supreme arbiter of all things. Robbery and outrage and murder are as lawful as their opposites. That is to say, there is no such thing as a law of nature; and consequently all things are, in a state of nature, equally allowable. Thus it was that Hobbes delighted to legitimate the horrors of a state of nature, as it is called, in order that mankind might, without a feeling of indignation or regret, see the wild and ferocious liberty of such a state sacrificed to despotic power. Thus it was that he endeavoured to recommend the "Leviathan," by contrasting it with the huger monster called Natural Liberty.

This view of the state of nature, by which all law and the great Fountain of all law are shut out of the world, was perfectly agreeable to the atheistical philosophy of Hobbes. From one who had extinguished the light of nature, and given dominion to the powers of darkness, no better could have been expected; but is it not

B 2*

deplorable that a Christian jurist should, even
for a moment, have forgotten the great central
light of his own system, and drawn his arguments from such an abyss of darkness?

Blackstone has thus lost sight of truth, not
only in regard to his general propositions, but
also in regard to particular instances. "The
law," says he, "which restrains a man from
doing mischief to his fellow-citizens diminishes
the natural liberty of mankind." Now, is this
true? The doing of mischief is contrary to the
law of nature, and hence, according to the
definition of Blackstone himself, the perpetration
of it is not an exercise of any natural right.
As no man possesses a natural right to do mischief, so the law which forbids it does not
diminish the natural liberty of mankind. The
law which forbids mischief is a restraint not
upon the *natural liberty*, but upon the *natural
tyranny*, of man.

Blackstone is by no means alone in the error
to which we have alluded. By one of the clearest thinkers and most beautiful writers of the
present age,* it is argued, "that as government
implies restraint, it is evident we give up a cer-

---

* Robert Hall.

tain portion of our liberty by entering into it."
This argument would be valid, no doubt, if
there were nothing in the world beside liberty
to be restrained; but the evil passions of men,
from which proceed so many frightful tyrannies
and wrongs, are not to be identified with their
rights or liberties. As government implies
restraint, it is evident that something is restrained when we enter into it; but it does not
follow that this something must be our natural
liberty. The argument in question proceeds
on the notion that government can restrain
nothing, unless it restrain the natural liberty of
mankind; whereas, we have seen, the law which
forbids the perpetration of mischief, or any other
wrong, is a restriction, not upon the *liberty*, but
upon the *tyranny*, of the human will. It sets a
bound and limit, not to any right conferred on
us by the Author of nature, but upon the evil
thoughts and deeds of which we are the sole
and exclusive originators. Such a law, indeed,
so far from restraining the natural liberty of
man, recognises his natural rights, and secures
his freedom, by protecting the weak against the
injustice and oppression of the strong.

The way in which these authors show that
natural liberty is, and of right ought to be,

abridged by the laws of society, is, by identify-
ing this natural freedom, not with a power to act
as God wills, but with a power in conformity
with our own sovereign will and pleasure. The
same thing is expressly done by Paley.* "To
do what we will," says he, "is natural liberty."
Starting from this definition, it is no wonder
that he should have supposed that natural liberty
is restrained by civil government. In like manner, Burke first says, "That the effect of liberty
to individuals is, *that they may do what they
please;*" and then concludes, that in order to
"secure some liberty," we make "a surrender
in trust of the whole of it."† Thus the natural
rights of mankind are first caricatured, and then
sacrificed.

If there be no God, if there be no difference
between right and wrong, if there be no moral
law in the universe, then indeed would men
possess a natural right to do mischief or to act
as they please. Then indeed should we be fet-
tered by no law in a state of nature, and liberty
therein would be coextensive with power.
Right would give place to might, and the least

---

* Political Phil., chap. v.

† Reflections on the Revolution in France.

restraint, even from the best laws, would impair our natural freedom. But we subscribe to no such philosophy. That learned authors, that distinguished jurists, that celebrated philosophers, that pious divines, should thus deliberately include the enjoyment of our natural rights and the indulgence of our evil passions in one and the same definition of liberty, is, it seems to us, matter of the most profound astonishment and regret. It is to confound the source of all tyranny with the fountain of all freedom. It is to put darkness for light, and light for darkness. And it is to inflame the minds of men with the idea that they are struggling and contending for liberty, when, in reality, they may be only struggling and contending for the gratification of their malignant passions. Such an offence against all clear thinking, such an outrage against all sound political ethics, becomes the more amazing when we reflect on the greatness of the authors by whom it is committed, and the stupendous magnitude of the interests involved in their discussions.

Should we, then, exhibit the fundamental law of society, and the natural liberty of mankind, as antagonistic principles? Is not this the way to prepare the human mind, at all times so pas-

sionately, not to say so madly, fond of freedom,
for a repetition of those tremendous conflicts
and struggles beneath which the foundations of
society have so often trembled, and some of its
best institutions been laid in the dust? In one
word, is it not high time to raise the inquiry,
Whether there be, in reality, any such opposition
as is usually supposed to exist between the law
of the land and the natural rights of mankind?
Whether such opposition be real or imaginary?
Whether it exists in the nature of things, or
only in the imagination of political theorists?

§ III. *No good law ever limits or abridges the
natural liberty of mankind.*

By the two great leaders of opposite schools,
Locke and Burke, it is contended that when we
enter into society the natural right of self-defence is surrendered to the government. If any
natural right, then, be limited or abridged by
the laws of society, we may suppose the right
of self-defence to be so; for this is the instance
which is always selected to illustrate and confirm
the reality of such a surrender of our natural
liberty. It has, indeed, become a sort of maxim,
that when we put on the bonds of civil society,
we give up the natural right of self-defence.

But what does this maxim mean? Does it mean that we transfer the right to repel force by force? If so, the proposition is not true; for this right is as fully possessed by every individual after he has entered into society as it could have been in a state of nature. If he is assailed, or threatened with immediate personal danger, the law of the land does not require him to wait upon the strong but slow arm of government for protection. On the contrary, it permits him to protect himself, to repel force by force, in so far as this may be necessary to guard against injury to himself; and the law of nature allows no more. Indeed, if there be any difference, the law of the land allows a man to go farther in the defence of self than he is permitted to go by the law of God. Hence, in this sense, the maxim under consideration is not true; and no man's natural liberty is abridged by the State.

Does this maxim mean, then, that in a state of nature every man has a right to redress his own wrongs by the *subsequent* punishment of the offender, which right the citizen has transferred to the government? It is clear that this must be the meaning, if it have any correct meaning at all. But neither in this sense is the maxim or proposition true. The right to punish an

offender must rest upon the one or the other
of two grounds: either upon the ground that
the offender deserves punishment, or that his
punishment is necessary to prevent similar offences. Now, upon neither of these grounds
has any man, even in a state of nature, the
right to punish an offence committed against
himself.

First, he has no right to punish such an
offence on the ground that it deserves punishment. No man has, or ever had, the right to
wield the awful attribute of retributive justice;
that is, to inflict so much pain for so much guilt
or moral turpitude. This is the prerogative of
God alone. To his eye, all secrets are known,
and all degrees of guilt perfectly apparent; and
to him alone belongs the vengeance which is
due for moral ill-desert. His law extends over
the state of nature as well as over the state of
civil society, and calls all men to account for
their evil deeds. It is evident that, in so far as
the intrinsic demerit of actions is concerned, it
makes no difference whether they be punished
here or hereafter. And besides, if the individual had possessed such a right in a state
of nature, he has not transferred it to society; for society neither has nor claims any

such right. Blackstone but utters the voice of
the law when he says: "The end or final cause
of human punishment is not by way of atone-
ment or expiation, for that must be left to the
just determination of the supreme Being, but
as a precaution against future offences of the
same kind." The exercise of retributive justice
belongs exclusively to the infallible Ruler of the
world, and not to frail, erring man, who himself
so greatly stands in need of mercy. Hence, the
right to punish a transgressor on the ground
that such punishment is deserved, has not been
transferred from the individual to civil society:
first, because he had no such natural right to
transfer; and, secondly, because society possesses
no such right.

In the second place, if we consider the other
ground of punishment, it will likewise appear
that the right to punish never belonged to the
individual, and consequently could not have
been transferred by him to society. For, by the
law of nature, the individual has no right to
punish an offence against himself *in order to
prevent future offences of the same kind*. If the
object of human punishment be, as indeed it is,
to prevent the commission of crime, by holding
up examples of terror to evil-doers, then it is

3

evidently no more the natural right of the party injured to redress the wrong, than it is the right of others. All men are interested in the prevention of wrongs, and hence all men should unite to redress them. All men are endowed by their Creator with a sense of justice, in order to impel them to secure its claims, and throw the shield of its protection around the weak and oppressed.

The prevention of wrong, then, is clearly the natural duty, and consequently the natural right, of all men.

This duty should be discharged by others, rather than by the party aggrieved. For it is contrary to the law of nature itself, as both Locke and Burke agree, that any man should be "judge in his own case;" that any man should, by an *ex post facto* decision, determine the amount of punishment due to his enemy, and proceed to inflict it upon him. Such a course, indeed, so far from preventing offences, would inevitably promote them; instead of re-dressing injuries, would only add wrong to wrong; and instead of introducing order, would only make confusion worse confounded, and turn the moral world quite upside down.

On no ground, then, upon which the right to

punish may be conceived to rest, does it appear that it was ever possessed, or could ever have been possessed, by the individual. And if the individual never possessed such a right, it is clear that he has never transferred it to society. Hence, this view of the origin of government, however plausible at first sight, or however generally received, has no real foundation in the nature of things. It is purely a creature of the imagination of theorists; one of the phantoms of that manifold, monstrous, phantom deity called Liberty, which has been so often invoked by the *pseudo* philanthropists and reckless reformers of the present day to subvert not only the law of capital punishment, but also other institutions and laws which have received the sanction of both God and man.

The simple truth is, that we are all bound by the law of nature and the law of God to love our neighbor as ourselves. Hence it is the duty of every man, in a state of nature, to do all in his power to protect the rights and promote the interests of his fellow-men. It is the duty of all men to consult together, and concert measures for the general good. Right here it is, then, that the law of man, the constitution of civil society, comes into contact with the law of God and rests upon it. Thus, civil society arises, not from a surrender of individual rights, but from a right originally possessed by all; nay, from a solemn duty originally imposed upon all by God himself—a duty which must be performed, whether the individual gives his consent or not. The very law of nature itself requires, as we have seen, not only the punishment of the offender, but also that he be punished according to a pre-established law, and by the decision of an impartial tribunal. And in the enactment of such law, as well as in the administration, the collective wisdom of society, or its agents, moves in obedience to the law of God, and not in pursuance of rights derived from the individual.

§ IV. *The distinction between rights and liberty.*

In the foregoing discussion we have, in conformity to the custom of others, used the terms *rights* and *liberty* as words of precisely the same import. But, instead of being convertible terms, there seems to be a very clear difference in their signification. If a man be taken, for example, and without cause thrown into prison, this deprives him of his *liberty*, but not of his *right*, to go where he pleases. The right still exists;

and his not being allowed to enjoy this right, is precisely what constitutes the oppression in the case supposed. If there were no right still subsisting, then there would be no oppression. Hence, as the *right* exists, while the *liberty* is extinguished, it is evident they are distinct from each other. The liberty of a man in such a case, as in all others, would consist in an opportunity to enjoy his right, or in a state in which it might be enjoyed if he so pleased.

This distinction between rights and liberty is all-important to a clear and satisfactory discussion of the doctrine of human freedom. The great champions of that freedom, from a Locke down to a Hall, firmly and passionately grasping the natural rights of man, and confounding these with his liberty, have looked upon society as the restrainer, and not as the author, of that liberty. On the other hand, the great advocates of despotic power, from a Hobbes down to a Whewell, seeing that there can be no genuine liberty—that is, no secure enjoyment of one's rights—in a state of nature, have ascribed, not only our liberty, but all our existing rights also, to the State.

But the error of Locke is a noble and generous sentiment when compared with the odious

3*

dogma of Hobbes and Whewell. These learned authors contend that we derive all our existing rights from society. Do we, then, live and move and breathe and think and worship God only by rights derived from the State? No, certainly. We have these rights from a higher source. God gave them, and all the powers of earth combined cannot take them away. But as for our liberty, this we freely own is, for the most part, due to the sacred bonds of civil society. Let us render unto Cæsar the things that are Cæsar's, and unto God the things that are God's.

§ V. *The relation between the state of nature and of civil society.*

Herein, then, consists the true relation between the *natural* and the *social* states. Civil society does not abridge our natural rights, but secures and protects them. She does not assume our right of self-defence,—she simply discharges the duty imposed by God to defend us. The original right is in those who compose the body politic, and not in any individual. Hence, civil society does not impair our natural liberty, as actually existing in a state of nature, or as it might therein exist; for, in such a state, there would be no real liberty, no real enjoyment of natural rights.

Mr. Locke, as we have seen, defines the state of nature to be one of "perfect freedom." Why then should we leave it? "If man, in the state of nature, be so free," says he, "why will he part with his freedom? To which it is obvious to answer," he continues, "that though, in the state of nature, he hath such a right, *yet the enjoyment of it is very uncertain,* and constantly exposed to the invasion of others; for all being kings as much as he, every man his equal, and the greater part not strict observers of equity and justice, the enjoyment of the property he has in this state is very unsafe, very insecure. This makes him willing to quit a condition which, *however free,* is *full of fears and continual dangers;* and it is not without reason that he seeks out, and is willing to join in society with, others who are already united, or have a mind to unite, *for the mutual preservation of their lives, liberties, and estates,* which I call by the general name *property.*"* What! can that be a state of perfect freedom which is subject to fears and perpetual dangers? In one word, can a

---

* Locke on Civil Government, chap. ix.

reign of terror be the reign of liberty? It is evident, we think, that Locke has been betrayed into no little inaccuracy and confusion of thought from not having distinguished between rights and liberty.

The truth seems to be that, in a state of nature, we would possess rights, but we could not enjoy them. That is to say, notwithstanding all our rights, we should be destitute of freedom or liberty. Society interposes the strong arm of the law to protect our rights, to secure us in the enjoyment of them. She delivers us from the alarms, the dangers, and the violence of the natural state. Hence, under God, she is the mother of our peace and joy, by whose sovereign rule anarchy is abolished and liberty established. Liberty and social law can never be dissevered. Liberty, robed in law, and radiant with love, is one of the best gifts of God to man. But liberty, despoiled of law, is a wild, dark, fierce spirit of licentiousness, which tends "to uproar the universal peace."

Hence it is a frightful error to regard the civil state or government as antagonistic to the natural liberty of mankind; for this is, indeed, the author of the very liberty we enjoy. Good government it is that restrains the elements of tyranny and oppression, and introduces liberty into the world. Good government it is that shuts out the reign of anarchy, and secures the dominion of equity and goodness. He who would spurn the restraints of law, then, by which pride, and envy, and hatred, and malice, ambition, and revenge, are kept within the sacred bounds of eternal justice—he, we say, is not the friend of human liberty. He would open the flood-gates of tyranny and oppression; he would mar the harmony and extinguish the light of the world. Let no such man be trusted.

If the foregoing remarks be just, it would follow that the state of nature, as it is called, would be one of the most unnatural states in the world. We may conceive it to exist, for the sake of illustration or argument; but if it should actually exist, it would be at war with the law of nature itself. For this requires, as we have seen, that men should unite together, and frame such laws as the general good demands.

Not only the law, but the very necessities of nature, enjoin the institution of civil government. God himself has thus laid the foundations of civil society deep in the nature of man.

c

It is an ordinance of heaven, which no human decree can reverse or annul. It is not a thing of compacts, bound together by promises and paper, but is itself a law of nature as irreversible as any other. Compacts may give it one form or another, but in one form or another it must exist. It is no accidental or artificial thing, which may be made or unmade, which may be set up or pulled down, at the mere will and pleasure of man. It is a decree of God; the spontaneous and irresistible working of that nature, which, in all climates, through all ages, and under all circumstances, manifests itself in social organizations.

§ VI. *Inherent and inalienable rights.*

Much has been said about inherent and in-alienable rights, which is either unintelligible or rests upon no solid foundation. "The inalien-able rights of men" is a phrase often brandished by certain reformers, who aim to bring about "the immediate abolition of slavery." Yet, in the light of the foregoing discussion, it may be clearly shown that the doctrine of inalienable rights, if properly handled, will not touch the institution of slavery.

An inalienable right is either one which the

possessor of it himself cannot alienate or transfer, or it is one which society has not the power
to take from him. According to the import
of the terms, the first would seem to be what
is meant by an inalienable right; but in this
sense it is not pretended that the right to either
life or liberty has been transferred to society
or alienated by the individual. And if, as we
have endeavored to show, the right, or power,
or authority of society is not derived from a
transfer of individual rights, then it is clear
that neither the right to life nor liberty is transferred to society. That is, if no rights are transferred, than these particular rights are still un-
transferred, and, if you please, untransferable.
Be it conceded, then, that the individual has
never transferred his right to life or liberty to
society.

But it is not in the above sense that the
abolitionist uses the expression, *inalienable rights*.
According to his view, an inalienable right is
one of which society itself cannot, without doing wrong, deprive the individual, or deny the
enjoyment of it to him. This is evidently his
meaning; for he complains of the injustice of
society, or civil government, in depriving a certain portion of its subjects of civil freedom, and

consigning them to a state of servitude. "Such an act," says he, "is wrong, because it is a violation of the inalienable rights of all men." But let us see if his complaint be just or well founded.

It is pretended by no one that society has the right to deprive any subject of either life or liberty, *without good and sufficient cause or reason.* On the contrary, it is on all hands agreed that it is only for good and sufficient reasons that society can deprive any portion of its subjects of either life or liberty. Nor can it be denied, on the other side, that a man may be deprived of either, or both, by a preordained law, in case there be a good and sufficient reason for the enactment of such law. For the crime of murder, the law of the land deprives the criminal of life: *à fortiori*, might it deprive him of liberty. In the infliction of such a penalty, the law seeks, as we have seen, not to deal out so much pain for so much guilt, nor even to deal out pain for guilt at all, but simply to protect the members of society, and *secure the general good.* The general good is the sole and sufficient consideration which justifies the state in taking either the life or the liberty of its subjects.

Hence, if we would determine in any case

whether society is justified in depriving any of its members of civil freedom by law, we must first ascertain whether the general good demands the enactment of such a law. If it does, then such a law is just and good—as perfectly just and good as any other law which, for the same reason or on the same ground, takes away the life or liberty of its subjects. All this talk about the inalienable rights of men may have a very admirable meaning, if one will only be at the pains to search it out; but is it not evident that, when searched to the bottom, it has just nothing at all to do with the great question of slavery? But more of this hereafter.*

This great problem, as we have seen, is to be decided, not by an appeal to the inalienable rights of men, but simply and solely by a reference to the general good. It is to be decided, not by the aid of abstractions alone; a little good sense and *practical sagacity* should be allowed to assist in its determination. There are inalienable rights, we admit—inalienable both because the individual cannot transfer them, and because society can never rightfully deprive any man of their enjoyment. But life and

---

* Chap. ii. § x.

4

liberty are *not* "among these." There are inalienable rights, we admit, but then such abstractions are the edge-tools of political science, with which it is dangerous for either men or children to play. They may inflict deep wounds on the cause of humanity; they can throw no light on the great problem of slavery.

One thing seems to be clear and fixed; and that is, that the rights of the individual are subordinate to those of the community. *An inalienable right is a right coupled with a duty; a duty with which no other obligation can interfere.* But, as we have seen, it is the *duty*, and consequently, the *right*, of society to make such laws as the general good demands. This inalienable right is conferred, and its exercise enjoined, by the Creator and Governor of the universe. All individual rights are subordinate to this inherent, universal, and inalienable right. It should be observed, however, that in the exercise of this paramount right, this supreme authority, no society possesses the power to contravene the principles of justice. In other words, it should be observed that no unjust law can ever promote the public good. Every law, then, which is not unjust, and which the public good demands, should be enacted by society.

But we have already seen and shall still more fully see, that the law which ordains slavery is not unjust in itself, or, in other words, that it interferes with none of the inalienable rights of man. Hence, if it be shown that the public good, and especially the good of the slave, demands such a law, then the question of slavery will be settled. We purpose to show this before we have done with the present discussion. And if, in the prosecution of this inquiry, we should be so fortunate as to throw only one steady ray of light on the great question of slavery, by which the very depths of society have been so fearfully convulsed, we shall be more than rewarded for all the labour which, with no little solicitude, we have felt constrained to bestow upon an attempt at its solution.

§ VII. *Conclusion of the first chapter.*

In conclusion, we shall merely add that if the foregoing remarks be just, it follows that the great problem of political philosophy is not precisely such as it is often taken to be by statesmen and historians. This problem, according to Mackintosh and Macaulay, consists in finding such an adjustment of the antagonistic principles of public order and private liberty, that neither shall overthrow or subvert the other, but each be confined within its own appropriate limits. Whereas, if we are not mistaken, these are not *antagonistic*, but *co-ordinate*, principles. The very law which institutes public order is that which introduces private liberty, since no secure enjoyment of one's rights can exist where public order is not maintained. And, on the other hand, unless private liberty be introduced, public order cannot be maintained, or at least such public order as should be established; for, if there be not private liberty, if there be no secure enjoyment of one's rights, then the highest and purest elements of our nature would have to be extinguished, or else exist in perpetual conflict with the surrounding despotism. As license is not liberty, so despotism is not order, nor even friendly to that enlightened, wholesome order, by which the good of the public and the individual are at the same time introduced and secured. In other words, what is taken from the one of these principles is not given to the other; on the contrary, every additional element of strength and beauty which is imparted to the one is an accession of strength and beauty to the other. Private liberty, indeed, lives and moves and has its very being in the bosom of public order. On the other hand, that public order alone which cherishes the true liberty of the individual is strong in the approbation of God and in the moral sentiments of mankind. All else is weakness, and death, and decay.

The true problem, then, is, not how the conflicting claims of these two principles may be adjusted, (for there is no conflict between them,) but how a real public order, whose claims are identical with those of private liberty, may be introduced and maintained. The practical solution of this problem, for the heterogeneous population of the South imperatively demands, as we shall endeavor to show, the institution of slavery; and that without such an institution it would be impossible to maintain either a sound public order or a decent private liberty. We shall endeavor to show, that the very laws or institution which is supposed by fanatical declaimers to shut out liberty from the Negro race among us, really shuts out the most frightful *license* and disorder from society. In one word, we shall endeavor to show that in preaching up liberty *to and for* the slaves of the South, the abolitionist is "casting pearls before swine," that can neither comprehend the nature, nor

4*

enjoy the blessings, of the freedom which is so officiously thrust upon them. And if the Negro race should be moved by their fiery appeals, it would only be to rend and tear in pieces the fair fabric of American liberty, which, with all its shortcomings and defects, is by far the most beautiful ever yet conceived or constructed by the genius of man.

CHAPTER II.

THE ARGUMENTS AND POSITIONS OF ABOLITIONISTS.

HAVING in the preceding chapter discussed and defined the nature of civil liberty, as well as laid down some of the political conditions on which its existence depends, we shall now proceed to examine the question of slavery. In the prosecution of this inquiry, we shall, in the first place, consider the arguments and positions of the advocates of immediate abolition; and, in the second, point out the reasons and grounds on which the institution of slavery is based and its justice vindicated. The first branch of the investigation, or that relating to the arguments and positions of the abolitionist, will occupy the remainder of the present chapter.

It is insisted by abolitionists that the institution of slavery is, in all cases and under all circumstances, morally wrong, or a violation of the law of God. Such is precisely the ground assumed by the one side and denied by the other.

Thus says Dr. Wayland: "I have wished to make it clear that slavery, or the holding of men in bondage, and 'obliging them to labor for our benefit, without their contract or consent,' is always and everywhere, or, as you well express it, *semper et ubique*, a moral wrong, a violation of the obligations under which we are created to our fellow-men, and a transgression of the law of our Creator."

Dr. Fuller likewise: "The simple question is, Whether it *is necessarily, and amid all circumstances, a crime to hold men in a condition where they labor for another without their consent or contract?* and in settling this matter all impertinences must be retrenched."

In one word, Dr. Wayland insists that slavery is condemned by the law of God, by the moral law of the universe. We purpose to examine the arguments which he has advanced in favor of this position. We select his arguments for examination, because, as a writer on moral and political science, he stands so high in the northern portion of the Union. His work on these subjects has indeed long since passed the fiftieth thousand; a degree of success which, in his own estimation, authorizes him to issue his letters on slavery over the signature of " THE

AUTHOR OF THE MORAL SCIENCE." But the very fact that his popularity is so great, and that he is *the* author of *the* Moral Science, is a reason why his arguments on a question of such magnitude should be subjected to a severe analysis and searching scrutiny, in order that, under the sanction of so imposing a name, no error may be propagated and no mischief done.

Hence we shall hold Dr. Wayland amenable to all the laws of logic. Especially shall we require him to adhere to the point he has undertaken to discuss, and to retrench all irrelevancies. If, after having subjected his arguments to such a process, it shall be found that every position which is assumed on the subject is directly contradicted by himself, we shall not make haste to introduce anarchy into the Southern States, in order to make it answer to the anarchy in his views of civil and political freedom. But whether this be the case or not, it is not for us to determine; we shall simply proceed to examine, and permit the impartial reader to decide for himself.

§ I. *The first fallacy of the abolitionist.*

The abolitionists do not hold their passions in subjection to reason. This is not merely the judgment of a Southern man: it is the opinion of the more decent and respectable abolitionists themselves. Thus says Dr. Channing, censuring the conduct of the abolitionists: "They have done wrong, I believe; nor is their wrong to be winked at because done fanatically or with good intentions; for how much mischief may be wrought with good designs! They have fallen into the common error of enthusiasts—that of exaggerating their object, of feeling as if no evil existed but that which they opposed, and as if no guilt could be compared with that of countenancing or upholding it."* In like manner, Dr. Wayland says: "I unite with you and the late lamented Dr. Channing in the opinion that the tone of the abolitionists at the North has been frequently, I fear I must say generally, 'fierce, bitter, and abusive.' The abolitionist press has, I believe, from the beginning, too commonly indulged in *exaggerated statement*, in violent denunciation, and in coarse and lacerating invective. At our late Missionary Convention in Philadelphia, I heard many things from men who claim to be the exclusive friends of the slave, which pained me more than I can

* Channing's Works, vol. ii., p. 126.

express. It seemed to me that the spirit which many of them manifested was very different from the spirit of Christ. I also cheerfully bear testimony to the general courtesy, the Christian urbanity, and the calmness under provocation which, in a remarkable degree, characterized the conduct of the members from the South."

In the flood of sophisms which the abolitionists usually pour out in their explosions of passion, none is more common than what is technically termed by logicians the *ignoratio elenchi*, or a mistaking of the point in dispute. Nor is this fallacy peculiar to the more vulgar sort of abolitionists. It glares from the pages of Dr. Wayland, no less than from the writings of the most fierce, bitter, and vindictive of his associates in the cause of abolitionism. Thus, in one of his letters to Dr. Fuller, he says: "To present this subject in a simple light. Let us suppose that your family and mine were neighbors. We, our wives and children, are all human beings in the sense that I have described, and, in consequence of that common nature, and by the will of our common Creator, are subject to the law, *Thou shalt love thy neighbor as thyself*. Suppose that I should set fire to your house, shoot you as you came out of it, and seizing

your wife and children, 'oblige them to labor
for my benefit without their contract or consent.'
Suppose, moreover, aware that I could not thus
oblige them, unless they were inferior in intellect to myself, I should forbid them to read,
and thus consign them to intellectual and moral
imbecility. Suppose I should measure out to
them the knowledge of God on the same principle. Suppose I should exercise this dominion
over them and their children as long as I lived,
and then do all in my power to render it certain
that my children should exercise it after me.
*The question before us I suppose to be simply this :
Would I, in so doing, act at variance with the relations existing between us as creatures of God?*
Would I, in other words, violate the supreme
law of my Creator, Thou shalt love thy neighbor
as thyself? or that other, Whatsoever ye would
that men should do unto you, do ye even so
unto them? I do not see how any intelligent
creature can give more than one answer to this
question. Then I think that every intelligent
creature must affirm that to do this is wrong, or,
in the other form of expression, that it is a great
moral evil. Can we conceive of any greater?"

It was surely very kind in Dr. Wayland to
undertake, with so much pains, to instruct us

poor, benighted sons of the South in regard to
the difference between right and wrong. We
would fain give him full credit for all the kindly
feeling he so freely professes for his "Southern
brethren;" but if he really thinks that the
question, whether arson, and murder, and
cruelty are offences against the "supreme law
of the Creator," is still open for discussion
among us, then we beg leave to inform him
that he labors under a slight hallucination.
If he had never written a word, we should
have known, perhaps, that it is wrong for a man
to set fire to his neighbor's house, and shoot
him as he came out, and reduce his wife and
children to a state of ignorance, degradation,
and slavery. Nay, if we should find his house
already burnt, and himself already shot, we
should hardly feel justified in treating his wife
and children in so cruel a manner. Not even
if they were "guilty of a skin," or ever so degraded, should we deem ourselves justified in
reducing them to a state of servitude. This is
NOT "the question before us." We are quite
satisfied on all such points. The precept, too,
Thou shalt love thy neighbor as thyself, was not
altogether unknown in the Southern States before his letters were written. A committee of

very amiable philanthropists came all the way
from England, as the agents of some abolition
society there, and told us all that the law of God
requires us to love our neighbor as ourselves.
In this benevolent work of enlightenment they
were, if we mistake not, several months in advance of Dr. Wayland. We no longer need to
be enlightened on such points. Being sufficiently instructed, we admit that we should
love our neighbor as ourselves, and also that
arson, murder, and so forth are violations of
this law. But we want to know whether, *semper
et ubique*, the institution of slavery is morally
wrong. *This is the question*, and to this we
intend to hold the author.

§ II. *The second fallacy of the abolitionist.*

Lest we should be suspected of misrepresentation, we shall state the position of Dr. Wayland in his own words. In regard to the
institution of slavery, he says: "I do not see
that it does not sanction the whole system
of the slave-trade. *If I have a right to a
thing after I have gotten it, I have a natural right
to the means necessary for getting it.* If this
be so, I should be as much justified in sending
a vessel to Africa, murdering a part of the

inhabitants of a village, and making slaves of the rest, as I should be in hunting a herd of wild animals, and either slaying them or subjecting them to the yoke."

Now mark the principle on which this most wonderful argument is based: "If I have a right to a thing after I have gotten it, I have a natural right to the means for getting it." That is to say, If I have the right to a slave, now that I have got him, then I may rightfully use all necessary means to reduce other men to slavery! I may shoot, burn, or murder, if by this means I can only get slaves! Was any consequence ever more wildly drawn? Was any *non sequitur* ever more glaring?

Let us see how this argument would apply to other things. If I have a right to a watch after I have gotten it, no matter how, then I have a right to use the means necessary to get watches; I may steal them from my neighbors! Or, if I have a right to a wife, provided I can get one, then may I shoot my friend and marry his widow! Such is the argument of one who seeks to enlighten the South and reform its institutions!

§ III. *The third fallacy of the abolitionist.*

Nearly allied to the foregoing argument is that of the same author, in which he deduces from the right of slavery, supposing it to exist, another retinue of monstrous rights. "This right also," says Dr. Wayland, referring to the right to hold slaves, "as I have shown, involves the right to use all the means necessary to its establishment and perpetuity, and *of course the right to crush his intellectual and social nature,* and to stupefy his conscience, in so far as may be necessary to enable me to enjoy this right with the least possible peril." This is a compound fallacy, a many-sided error. But we will consider only two phases of its absurdity.

In the first place, if the slaveholder should reason in this way, no one would be more ready than the author himself to condemn his logic. If any slaveholder should say, That because I have a right to my slaves, therefore I have the right to crush the intellectual and moral nature of men, in order to *establish* and perpetuate their bondage,—he would be among the first to cry out against such reasoning. This is evident from the fact that he everywhere commends those slaveholders who deem it their duty, as a return for the service of their slaves, to promote both their temporal and eternal good. He everywhere insists that such is the duty of slaveholders; and if such be their duty, they surely have no right to violate it, by crushing the intellectual and moral nature of those whom they are bound to elevate in the scale of being. If the slaveholder, then, should adopt such an argument, his logic would be very justly chargeable by Dr. Wayland with evidencing not so much the existence of a clear head as of a bad heart.

In the second place, the above argument overlooks the fact that the Southern statesman vindicates the institution of slavery on the ground that it finds the Negro race already so degraded as to unfit it for a state of freedom. He does not argue that it is right to seize those who, by the possession of cultivated intellects and pure morals, are fit for freedom, and debase them in order to prepare them for social bondage. He does not imagine that it is ever right to shoot, burn, or corrupt, in order to reduce any portion of the enlightened universe to a state of servitude. He merely insists that those only who are already unfit for a higher and

5*

nobler state than one of slavery, should be
held by society in such a state. This position,
although it is so prominently set forth by every
advocate of slavery at the South, is almost in-
variably overlooked by the Northern abolitionists. They talk, and reason, and declaim, indeed, just as if we had caught a bevy of black
angels as they were winging their way to some
island of purity and bliss here upon earth, and
reduced them from their heavenly state, by the
most diabolical cruelties and oppressions, to one
of degradation, misery, and servitude. They
forget that Africa is not yet a paradise, and
that Southern servitude is not quite a hell.
They forget — in the heat and haste of their
argument they forget — that the institution of
slavery is designed by the South not for the
enlightened and the free, but only for the ignorant and the debased. They need to be constantly reminded that the institution of slavery
is not the mother, but the daughter, of ignorance and degradation. It is, indeed, the legitimate offspring of that intellectual and moral
debasement which, for so many thousand years,
has been accumulating and growing upon the
African race. And if the abolitionists at the
North will only invent some method by which

all this frightful mass of degradation may be blotted out *at once*, then will we most cheerfully consent to "the *immediate* abolition of slavery." On this point, however, we need not dwell, as we shall have occasion to recur to it again when we come to consider the grounds and reasons on which the institution of slavery is vindicated.

Having argued that the right of slavery, if it exist, implies the right to shoot and murder an enlightened neighbor, with a view to reduce his wife and children to a state of servitude, as well as to crush their intellectual and moral nature in order to keep them in such a state, the author adds, "If I err in making these inferences, I *err innocently*." We have no doubt of the most perfect and entire innocence of the author. But we would remind him that innocence, however perfect or *childlike*, is not the only quality which a great reformer should possess.

§ IV. *The fourth fallacy of the abolitionist.*

He is often guilty of a *petitio principii*, in taking it for granted that the institution of slavery is an injury to the slave, which is the very point in dispute. Thus says Dr. Wayland:

"If it be asked when, [slavery must be abandoned,] I ask again, when shall a man begin
to cease doing wrong? Is not the answer *immediately?* If a man is injuring us, do we doubt
as to the *time when* he ought to cease? There
is, then, no doubt in respect to the time when
we ought to cease inflicting injury upon others."*
Here it is assumed that slavery is an *injury*
to the slave: but this is the very point which
is denied, and which he should have discussed.
If a state of slavery be a greater injury to the
slave than a state of freedom would be, then
are we willing to admit that it should be
abolished. But even in that case, not *immediately,* unless it could be shown that the
remedy would not be worse than the evil. If, on
the whole, the institution of slavery be a curse
to the slave, we say let it be abolished; not
suddenly, however, as if by a whirlwind, but
by the counsels of wise, cautious, and far-seeing
statesmen, who, capable of looking both before
and after, can comprehend in their plans of reform all the diversified and highly-complicated
interests of society.

"But it may be said," continues the author,

---

* Elements of Moral Science, Part ii. chap. i. sec. 11.

"immediate abolition would be the greatest possible injury to the slaves themselves. They are not competent to self-government." True: this is the very thing which may be, and which is, said by every Southern statesman in his advocacy of the institution of slavery. Let us see the author's reply. "This is a question of fact," says he, "*which is not in the province of moral philosophy to decide.* It very likely may be so. So far as I know, the facts are not sufficiently known to warrant a full opinion on the subject. We will, therefore, suppose it to be the case, and ask, What is the duty of masters *under these circumstances?*" In the discussion of this question, the author comes to the conclusion that a master may hold his slaves in bondage, provided his intentions be good, and with a view to set them at liberty as soon as they shall be qualified for such a state.

Moral philosophy, then, it seems, when it closes its eyes upon facts, pronounces that slavery should be *immediately* abolished; but if it consider facts, which, instead of being denied, are admitted to be "very likely" true, it decides against its immediate abolition! Or, rather, moral philosophy looks at the fact that slavery is an *injury*, in order to see that it should be forthwith abolished; but closes its eyes upon the fact that its abolition may be a still greater injury, lest this foregone conclusion should be called in question! Has moral philosophy, then, an eye only for the facts which lie one side of the question it proposes to decide?

Slavery is an *injury*, says Dr. Wayland, and therefore it should be *immediately* abolished. But its abolition would be a still greater *injury*, replies the objector. This may be true, says Dr. Wayland: it is highly probable; but then this question of injury is one of fact, which it is not in the province of moral philosophy to decide! So much for the consistency and even-handed justice of the author.

The position assumed by him, that questions of fact are not within the province of moral philosophy, is one of so great importance that it deserves a separate and distinct notice. Though seldom openly avowed, yet is it so often tacitly assumed in the arguments and declamations of abolitionists, that it shall be more fully considered in the following section.

§ V. *The fifth fallacy of the abolitionist.*

"Suppose that A has a right to use the body of B according to his—that is, A's—will. Now if this be true, it is true universally; and hence, A has the control over the body of B, and B has control over the body of C, C of D, &c., and Z again over the body of A: that is, every separate will has the right of control over some other body besides its own, and has no right of control over its own body or intellect."* Now, if men were cut out of pasteboard, all exactly alike, and distinguished from each other only by the letters of the alphabet, then the reasoning of the author would be excellent. But it happens that men are not cut out of pasteboard. They are distinguished by differences of character, by diverse habits and propensities, which render the reasonings of the political philosopher rather more difficult than if he had merely to deal with or arrange the letters of the alphabet. In one, for example, the intellectual and moral part is almost wholly eclipsed by the brute; while, in another, reason and religion have gained the ascendancy, so as to maintain a steady empire over the whole man. The first, as the author himself admits, is incompetent to self-government, and should therefore be held by the law of society in a state

* Moral Science, Part ii. chap, i. sec. 2.

of servitude. But does it follow that " if this be true, it is true *universally?*" Because one man who cannot govern himself may be governed by another, does it follow that every man should be governed by others? Does it follow that the one who has acquired and maintained the most perfect self-government, should be subjected to the control of him who is wholly incompetent to control himself? Yes, certainly, if the reasoning of Dr. Wayland be true; but, according to every sound principle of political ethics, the answer is, emphatically, No!

There is a difference between a Hottentot and a Newton. The first should no more be condemned to astronomical calculations and discoveries, than the last should be required to follow a plough. Such differences, however, are overlooked by much of the reasoning of the abolitionist. In regard to the question of fact, whether a man is really a man and not a mere thing, he is profoundly versed. He can discourse most eloquently upon this subject: he can prove, by most irrefragable arguments, that a Hottentot is a man as well as a Newton. But as to the differences among men, such nice distinctions are beneath his philosophy! It is true that one may be sunk so low in the scale of being that civil freedom would be a curse to him; yet, whether this be so or not, is a question of fact which his philosophy does not stoop to decide. He merely wishes to know what rights A can possibly have, either by the law of God or man, which do not equally belong to B? And if A would feel it an injury to be placed under the control of B, then "there is no doubt" that it is equally wrong to place B under the control of A? In plain English, if it would be injurious and wrong to subject a Newton to the will of a Hottentot, then it would be equally injurious and wrong to subject a Hottentot to the will of a Newton! Such is the inevitable consequence of his very profound political principles! Nay, such is the identical consequence which he draws from his own principles!

If questions of fact are not within the province of the moral philosopher, then the moral philosopher has no business with the science of political ethics. This is not a pure, it is a mixed science. Facts can no more be overlooked by the political architect, than magnitude can be disregarded by the mathematician. The man, the political dreamer, who pays no attention to them, may be fit, for aught we know, to frame a government out of moonshine for the inhabitants of Utopia; but, if we might choose our own teachers in political wisdom, we should decidedly prefer those who have an eye for facts as well as abstractions. If we may borrow a figure from Mr. Macaulay, the legislator who sees no difference among men, but proposes the same kind of government for all, acts about as wisely as a tailor who should measure the Apollo Belvidere to cut clothes for all his customers—for the pigmies as well as for the giants.

§ VI. *The sixth fallacy of the abolitionist.*

It is asserted by Dr. Wayland that the institution of slavery is condemned as "a violation of the plainest dictates of natural justice," by "the natural conscience of man, from at least as far back as the time of Aristotle." If any one should infer that Aristotle himself condemned the institution of slavery, he would be grossly deceived; for it is known to every one who has read the Politics of Aristotle that he is, under certain circumstances, a strenuous advocate of the natural justice, as well as of the political wisdom, of slavery. Hence we shall suppose that Dr. Wayland does not mean to include Aristotle in his broad assertion, but

only those who came after him. Even in this
sense, or to this extent, his positive assertion
is so diametrically opposed to the plainest facts
of history, that it is difficult to conceive how
he could have persuaded himself of its truth.
It is certain that, on other occasions, he was
perfectly aware of the fact that the natural conscience of man, from the time of Aristotle down
to that of the Christian era, was in favor of the
institution of slavery; for as often as it has
served his purpose to assert this fact, he has not
hesitated to do so. Thus, "the universal existence of slavery at the time of Christ," says
he, "took its origin from the moral darkness
of the age. The immortality of the soul was
unknown. Out of the Hebrew nation not a
man on earth had any true conception of the
character of the Deity or of our relations and
obligations to him. The law of universal love
to man had never been heard of."* No wonder
he here argues that *slavery received the universal
sanction of the heathen world*, since so great was
the moral darkness in which they were involved.
This darkness was so great, if we may believe
the author, that the men of one nation esteemed

---

* Letters on Slavery, p. 89.

those of another "as by nature foes, whom they had a right" not only "to subdue or enslave, but also to murder "whenever and in what manner soever they were able."* The sweeping assertion, that such was the moral darkness of the heathen world, is wide of the truth; for, at the time of Christ, no civilized nation "esteemed it right to murder or enslave, whenever and in what manner soever they were able," the people of other nations. There were some ideas of natural justice, even then, among men; and if there were not, why does Dr. Wayland appeal to their ideas of natural justice as one argument against slavery? If the heathen world "esteemed it right" to make slaves, how can it be said that its conscience condemned slavery? Is it not evident that Dr. Wayland is capable of asserting either the one thing or its opposite, just as it may happen to serve the purpose of his anti-slavery argument? Whether facts lie within the province of moral philosophy or not, it is certain, we think, that the moral philosopher who may be pleased to set facts at naught has no right to substitute fictions in their stead.

---

* Letters on Slavery, p. 92.

§ VII. *The seventh fallacy of the abolitionist.*

"Thou shalt love thy neighbor as thyself," is the rule of action which, in the estimation of abolitionists, should at once and forever decide every good man against the institution of slavery. But when we consider the stupendous interests involved in the question, and especially those of an intellectual and moral nature, we dare not permit ourselves to be carried away by any form of mere words. We *must* pause and investigate. The fact that the dexterous brandishing of the beautiful precept in question has made, and will no doubt continue to make, its thousands of converts or victims, is a reason why its real import should be the more closely examined and the more clearly defined. The havoc it makes among those whose philanthropy is stronger than their judgment—or, if you please, whose judgment is weaker than their philanthropy—flows not from the divine precept itself, but only from human interpretations thereof. And it should ever be borne in mind that he is the real enemy of the great cause of philanthropy who, by absurd or overstrained applications of this sublime precept, lessens that profound respect to which it is so

E   6*

justly entitled from every portion of the rational universe.

It is repeatedly affirmed by Dr. Wayland that every slaveholder lives in the habitual and open violation of the precept which requires us to love our neighbor as ourselves. "The moral precepts of the Bible," says he, "are diametrically opposed to slavery. These are, 'Thou shalt love thy neighbor as thyself,' and 'All things whatsoever ye would that men should do unto you, do ye even so unto them.' Now, were this precept obeyed," he continues, "it is manifest that slavery could not in fact exist for a single instant. The principle of the precept is absolutely subversive of the principle of slavery." If strong assertion were argument, we should no doubt be overwhelmed by the irresistible logic of Dr. Wayland. But the assertion of no man can be accepted as sound argument. We want to know the very meaning of the words of the great Teacher, and to be guided by *that*, rather than by the fallible authority of an earthly oracle. What, then, is the meaning, the real meaning, of his inspired words?

Do they mean that whatsoever we might, in any relation of life, desire for ourselves, we should be willing to grant to others in the like relation or condition? This interpretation, we are aware, has been put upon the words by a very celebrated divine. If we may believe that divine, we cannot do as we would be done by, unless, when we desire the estate of another, we forthwith transfer our estate to him! If a poor man, for example, should happen to covet the estate of his rich neighbor, then he is bound by this golden rule of benevolence to give his little all to him, without regard to the necessities or wants of his own family! But this interpretation, though seriously propounded by a man of undoubted genius and piety, has not, so far as we know, made the slightest possible impression on the plain good sense of mankind. Even among his most enthusiastic admirers, it has merely excited a good-natured smile at what they could not but regard as the strange hallucination of a benevolent heart.

A wrong desire in one relation of life is not a reason for a wrong act in another relation thereof. A man may desire the estate, he may desire the man-servant, or the maid-servant, or the wife of his neighbor, but this is no reason why he should abandon his own man-servant, or his maid-servant, or his wife to the will of another. The criminal who trembles at the bar of justice may desire both judge and jury to acquit him, but this is no reason why, if acting in the capacity of either judge or juror, he should bring in a verdict of acquittal in favor of one justly accused of crime. If we would apply the rule in question aright, we should consider, not what we might wish or desire if placed in the situation of another, but what we *ought* to wish or desire.

If a man were a child, he might wish to be exempt from the wholesome restraint of his parents; but this, as every one will admit, is no reason why he should abandon his own children to themselves. In like manner, if he were a slave, he might most vehemently desire freedom; but this is no reason why he should set his slaves at liberty. The whole question of right turns upon what he *ought* to wish or desire if placed in such a condition. If he were an intelligent, cultivated, civilized man,—in one word, if he were fit for freedom,—then his desire for liberty would be a rational desire, would be such a feeling as he *ought* to cherish; and hence, he should be willing to extend the same blessing to all other intelligent, cultivated, civilized men, to all such as are prepared for its enjoyment. Such is the sentiment which he should entertain, and such is precisely the sentiment entertained at the South. No one here proposes to reduce any one to slavery, much less those who are qualified for freedom; and hence the inquiry so often propounded by Dr. Wayland and other abolitionists, how we would like to be subjected to bondage, is a grand impertinence. We should like it as little as themselves; and in this respect we shall do as we would be done by.

But suppose we were veritable slaves—slaves in character and in disposition as well as in fact —and as unfit for freedom as the Africans of the South—what *ought* we then to wish or desire? Ought we to desire freedom? We answer, no; because on that supposition freedom would be a curse and not a blessing. Dr. Wayland himself admits that "it is very likely" freedom would be "the greatest possible injury" to the slaves of the South. Hence, we cannot perceive that if we were such as they, we ought to desire so great an evil to ourselves. It would indeed be to desire "the greatest possible injury" to ourselves; and though, as ignorant and blind slaves, we might cherish so foolish a desire, especially if instigated by abolitionists, yet this is no reason why, as enlightened citizens, we should be willing to inflict the same great evil upon others. *A foolish desire, we repeat, in one relation of life, is not a good reason for a foolish or injurious act in another relation thereof.*

The precept which requires us to do as we would be done by, was intended to enlighten the conscience. It is used by abolitionists to hoodwink and deceive the conscience. This precept directs us to conceive ourselves placed in the condition of others, in order that we may the more clearly perceive what is due to them. The abolitionist employs it to convince us that, because we desire liberty for ourselves, we should extend it to all men, even to those who are not qualified for its enjoyment, and to whom it would prove "the greatest possible injury." He employs it not to show us what is due to others, but to persuade us to injure them! He may deceive himself; but so long as we believe what even he admits as highly probable—namely, that the "abolition of slavery would be the greatest possible injury to the slaves themselves"—we shall never use the divine precept as an instrument of delusion and of wrong. What! inflict the greatest injury on our neighbor, and that, too, out of pure Christian charity?

But we need not argue with the abolitionist

upon his own admissions. We have infinitely stronger ground to stand on. The precept, "Thou shalt love thy neighbor as thyself," is to be found in the Old Testament as well as in the New. Thus, in the nineteenth chapter of Leviticus, it is said, "Thou shalt love thy neighbor as thyself;" and no greater love than this is anywhere inculcated in the New Testament. Yet in the twenty-fifth chapter of the same book, it is written, "Of the children of the strangers that do sojourn among you, of them shall ye buy, and of their families that are with you, which they begat in your land: and they shall be your possession. And ye shall take them as an inheritance for your children after you, to inherit them for a possession; they shall be your bondsmen forever." This language is too plain for controversy. In regard to this very passage, in which the Hebrews are commanded to enter upon and take possession of the land of the Canaanites, Dr. Wayland himself is constrained to admit—"The authority to take them as slaves seems to be a part of this original, peculiar, and I may perhaps say, anomalous grant."* Now, if the prin-

---

* Letters, p. 50.

ciple of slavery, and the principle of the precept, Thou shalt love thy neighbor as thyself, be as Dr. Wayland boldly asserts, *always and everywhere* at war with each other, how has it happened that both principles are so clearly and so unequivocally embodied in one and the same code by the Supreme Ruler of the world? Has this discrepancy escaped the eye of Omniscience, and remained in the code of laws from heaven, to be detected and exposed by "the author of the Moral Science"?

We do not mean that Dr. Wayland sees any discrepancy among the principles of the divine legislation. It is true he sees there the precept, "Thou shalt love thy neighbor as thyself," and also this injunction, "Thou shalt buy them for a possession," and "They shall be your bondmen forever;" but although this looks very "anomalous" to him, he dare not pronounce it absurd or self-contradictory. It is true, he declares, that slavery is condemned *always and everywhere* by "the plainest dictates of natural justice;" but yet, although, according to his own admission,* it was instituted by Heaven, he has found out a method to save

---

* Letters, p. 50.

the character of the Almighty from the disgrace of such a law. He says, "I know the word 'shalt' is used when speaking of this subject, but it is clearly used as *prophetic*, and not as *mandatory*." Ay, the words "thou shalt" are used in regard to the buying and holding of slaves, just as they are used in the commands which precede and follow this injunction. There is no change in the form of the expression. There is not, in any way, the slightest intimation that the Lawgiver is about to prophesy; all seems to be a series of commands, and is clothed in the same language of authority—"*thou shalt.*" Yet in one particular instance, and in one instance only, this language seems "clearly" *prophetic* to Dr. Wayland, and not *mandatory*. Now, I submit to the candid and impartial reader, if this be not egregious trifling with the word of God.

Dr. Wayland forgets that he had himself admitted that the very passage in question clothed the Hebrews with "the authority to take slaves."* He now, in the face of his own admission, declares that this language "is clearly prophetic," and tells what *would* or what *might* be, and not

---

* Letters, p. 50.
7

what *should* or what *must* be." The poor Hebrews, however, when they took slaves by the
authority of a *"thou shalt"* from the Lord, never
imagined that they were merely fulfilling a pro-
phecy, and committing an abominable sin.

This is clear to Dr. Wayland, if we may trust
the last expression of his opinion. But it is
to be regretted, that either the clearness of his
perceptions, or the confidence of his assertions,
is so often disproportioned to the evidence before him. Thus, he says with the most admirable modesty, "It *seems to me* that the soul is
the most important part of a human being;"*
and yet he peremptorily and positively declares
that the very strongest language of authority
ever found in Scripture "is *clearly* used as prophetic and not mandatory!" He may, however,
well reserve the tone of dogmatic authority for
such propositions, since, if they may not be carried by assertion, they must be left wholly without the least shadow of support. But one would
suppose that strength of assertion in such cases
required for its unembarrassed utterance no
little strength of countenance.

"If any one doubts," says Dr. Wayland, "re-

---

* Letters, p. 113.

specting the bearing of the Scripture precept upon this case, a few plain questions may throw additional light upon the subject."* Now, if we mistake not, the few plain questions which he deems so unanswerable may be answered with the most perfect ease. "Would the master be willing," he asks, "that another person should subject him to slavery, for the same reasons and on the same grounds that he holds his slave in bondage?" We answer, No. If any man should undertake to subject Southern masters to slavery, on the ground that they are intellectually and morally sunk so low as to be unfit for freedom or self-control, we should certainly not like the compliment. It may argue a very great degree of self-complacency in us, but yet the plain fact is, that we really do believe ourselves competent to govern ourselves, and to manage our affairs, without the aid of masters. And as we are not willing to be made slaves of, especially on any such humiliating grounds, so we are not willing to see any other nation or race of men, whom we may deem qualified for the glorious condition of freedom, subjected to servitude.

---

* Moral Science, Part ii. chap. i. § 2.

"Would the gospel allow us," he also asks, "if it were in our power, to reduce our fellow-citizens of our own color to slavery?" Certainly not. Nor do we propose to reduce any one, either white or black, to a state of slavery. It is amazing to see with what an air of confidence such questions are propounded. Dr. Channing, no less than Dr. Wayland, seems to think they must carry home irresistible conviction to the heart and conscience of every man who is not irremediably blinded by the detestable institution of slavery. "Now, let every reader," says he, "ask himself this plain question: Could I, can I, be rightfully seized and made an article of property?" And we, too, say, Let every reader ask himself this plain question, and then, if he please, answer it in the negative. But what, then, should follow? Why, if you please, he should refuse to seize any other man or to make him an article of property. He should be opposed to the crime of kidnapping. But if, from such an answer, he should conclude that the institution of slavery is "everywhere and always wrong," then surely, after what has been said, not another word is needed to expose the ineffable weakness and futility of the conclusion.

This golden rule, this divine precept, requires us to conceive ourselves placed in the condition of our slaves, and then to ask ourselves, How should we be treated by the master? in order to obtain a clear and impartial view of our duty to them. This it requires of us; and this we can most cheerfully perform. We can conceive that we are poor, helpless, dependent beings, possessing the passions of men and the intellects of children. We can conceive that we are by nature idle, improvident, and, without a protector and friend to guide and control us, utterly unable to take care of ourselves. And, having conceived all this, if we ask ourselves, How should we be treated by the masters whom the law has placed over us, what is the response? Is it that they should turn us loose to shift for ourselves? Is it that they should abandon us to ourselves, only to fall a prey to indolence, and to the legion of vices and crimes which ever follow in its train? Is it that they should set us free, and expose us, without protection, to the merciless impositions of the worst portions of a stronger and more sagacious race? Is it, in one word, that we should be free from the dominion of men who, as a general thing, are humane and wise in their management of us,

7*

only to become the victims—the most debased and hopeless victims—of every evil way? We answer, No! Even the spirit of abolitionism itself has, in the person of Dr. Wayland, declared that such treatment would, in all probability, be the greatest of calamities. We feel sure it would be an infinite and remediless curse. And as we believe that, if we were in the condition of slaves, such treatment would be so great and so withering a curse, so we cannot, out of a feeling of love, proceed to inflict this curse upon our slaves. On the contrary, *we would do as we so clearly see we ought to be done by,* if our conditions were changed.

Is it not amazing, as well as melancholy, that learned divines, who undertake to instruct the benighted South in the great principles of duty, should entertain such superficial and erroneous views of the first, great, and all-comprehending precept of the gospel? If their interpretation of this precept were correct, then the child might be set free from the authority of the father, and the criminal from the sentence of the judge. All justice would be extinguished, all order overthrown, and boundless confusion introduced into the affairs of men. Yet, with unspeakable self-complacency, they come with such miserable interpretations of the plainest truths to instruct those whom they conceive to be blinded by custom and the institution of slavery to the clearest light of heaven. They tell us, "Thou shouldst love thy neighbor as thyself;" and they reiterate these words in our ears, just as if we had never heard them before. If this is all they have to say, why then we would remind them that the *meaning* of the precept is the precept. It is not a mere *sound*, it is *sense*, which these glorious words are intended to convey. And if they can only repeat the words for us, why then they might just as well send a host of free negroes with good, strong lungs to be our instructors in moral science.

§ VIII. *The eighth fallacy of the abolitionist.*

An argument is drawn from the divine attributes against the institution of slavery. One would suppose that a declaration from God himself is some little evidence as to what is agreeable to his attributes; but it seems that moral philosophers have, now-a-days, found out a better method of arriving at what is implied by his perfections. Dr. Wayland is one of those who, setting aside the word of God, appeal to his attributes in favor of the immediate and universal abolition of slavery. If slavery were abolished, says he, "the laborer would then work in conformity with the conditions which God has appointed, whereas he now works at variance with them; in the one case, we should be attempting to accumulate property under the blessing of God, whereas now we are attempting to do it under *his special and peculiar malediction.* How can we expect to prosper, when there is not, as Mr. Jefferson remarks, 'an attribute of the Almighty that can be appealed to in our favor'?"* If we may rely upon his own words, rather than upon the confident assertions of Dr. Wayland, we need not fear the curse of God upon the slaveholder. The readiness with which Dr. Wayland points the thunders of the divine wrath at our heads, is better evidence of the passions of his own heart than of the perfections of the Almighty.

Again he says: "If Jefferson trembled for his country when he remembered that God is just, and declared that, 'in case of insurrection, the Almighty has no attribute that can take part with us in the contest,' surely it becomes a *disciple of Jesus Christ* to pause and reflect." Now let it

---

* Letters, p. 119, 120.

be borne in mind that all this proceeds from a man, from a professed disciple of Jesus Christ, who, in various places, has truly, as well as emphatically, said, " *The duty of slaves* is also explicitly made known in the Bible. They are bound to *obedience, fidelity, submission,* and respect to their masters,"* &c. &c.

Such, then, according to Dr. Wayland himself, is the clear and unequivocal teaching of revelation. And such being the case, shall the *real* "disciple of Jesus Christ" be made to believe, on the authority of Mr. Jefferson or of any other man, that the Almighty has no attribute which could induce him to take sides with his own law? If, instead of submission to that law, there should be rebellion,—and not only rebellion, but bloodshed and murder,—shall we believe that the Almighty, the supreme Ruler of heaven and earth, would look on well pleased? Since such is the express declaration of God himself respecting the duty of slaves, it surely becomes a disciple of Christ to pause and reflect whether he will follow his voice or the voice of man.

We owe at least one benefit to the Northern

---

* Moral Science, Part ii. chap. i. sec. 2.

F

abolitionists. Ere the subject of slavery was agitated by them, there were many loose, floating notions among us, as well as among themselves, respecting the nature of liberty, which were at variance with the institution of slavery. But since this agitation began, we have looked more narrowly into the grounds of slavery, as well as into the character of the arguments by which it is assailed, and we have found the first as solid as adamant, the last as unsubstantial as moonshine. If Mr. Jefferson had lived till the present day, there can be no doubt, we think, that he would have been on the same side of this great question with the Calhouns, the Clays, and the Websters of the country. We have known many who, at one time, fully concurred with Mr. Jefferson on this subject, but are now firm believers in the perfect justice and humanity of negro slavery.

§ IX. *The ninth fallacy of the abolitionist.*

We have already seen that the abolitionist argues the question of slavery as if Southerners were proposing to catch freemen and reduce them to bondage. He habitually overlooks the fact, that slavery results, not from the action of the individual, but from an ordinance of the State. He forgets that it is a civil institution, and proceeds to argue as if it were founded in individual wrong. And even when he rises—as he sometimes does—to a contemplation of the real question in dispute, he generally takes a most narrow and one-sided view of the subject. For he generally takes it for granted that the legislation which ordains the institution of slavery is *intended* solely and exclusively for the benefit of the master, without the least regard to the interests of the slave

Thus says Dr. Wayland: "Domestic slavery proceeds upon the principle that the master has a right to control the actions — physical and intellectual — of the slave for his own (that is, the master's) individual benefit,"* &c. And again: "It supposes that the Creator intended one human being to govern the physical, intellectual, and moral actions of as many other human beings as, by purchase, he can bring within his physical power; and that *one human being may thus acquire a right to sacrifice the happiness of any number of other human beings, for the purpose of promoting his*

* Moral Science, Part ii. chap. i. sec. 2.

own."* Now, surely, if this representation be just, then the institution of slavery should be held in infinite abhorrence by every man in Christendom.

But we can assure Dr. Wayland that, however ignorant or heathenish he may be pleased to consider the people of the Southern States, we are not so utterly lost to all reverence for the Creator as to suppose, even for a moment, that he *intended any one human being to possess the right of sacrificing the happiness of his fellow-men to his own*. We can assure him that we are not quite so dead to every sentiment of political justice, as to imagine that any legislation which intends to benefit the one at the expense of the many is otherwise than unequal and iniquitous in the extreme. There is some little sense of justice left among us yet; and hence we approve of no institution or law which proceeds on the monstrous principle that any one man has, or can have, the "*right to sacrifice the happiness of any number of other human beings for the purpose of promoting his own*." We recognise no such right. It is as vehemently abhorred

---

* Moral Science, Part ii. chap. i. sec. 2.

and condemned by us as it can be abhorred and condemned by the author himself.

In thus taking it for granted, as Dr. Wayland so coolly does, that the institution in question is "intended" to sacrifice the happiness of the slaves to the selfish interests of the master, he incontinently begs the whole question. Let him establish this point, and the whole controversy will be at an end. But let him not hope to establish any thing, or to satisfy any one, by assuming the very point in dispute, and then proceed to demolish what every man at the South condemns no less than himself. Surely, no one who has looked at both sides of this great question can be ignorant that the legislation of the South proceeds on the principle that slavery is beneficial, not to the master only, but also and *especially* to the slave. Surely, no one who has either an eye or an ear for facts can be ignorant that the institution of slavery is based on the ground, or principle, that it is beneficial, not only to the parts, but also to the whole, of the society in which it exists. This ground, or principle, is set forth in every defence of slavery by the writers and speakers of the South; it is so clearly and so unequivocally set forth, that he who runs may read. Why, then, is it overlooked by Dr. Wayland? Why is he pleased to imagine that he is combatting Southern principles, when, in reality, he is merely combatting the monstrous figment, the distorted conception of his own brain,—namely, the right of one man to sacrifice the happiness of multitudes to his own will and pleasure? Is it because facts do not lie within the province of the moral philosopher? Is it because fiction alone is worthy of his attention? Or is it because a blind, partisan zeal has so far taken possession of his very understanding, that he finds it impossible to speak of the institution of slavery, except in the language of the grossest misrepresentation?

§ X. *The tenth, eleventh, twelfth, thirteenth, fourteenth, fifteenth, and sixteenth fallacies of the abolitionist; or his seven arguments against the right of a man to hold property in his fellow-man.*

"This claim of property in a human being," says Dr. Channing, "is altogether false, groundless. No such right of man in man can exist. A human being cannot be justly owned." The only difficulty in maintaining this position is, according to Dr. Channing, "on account of its exceeding obviousness. It is too plain for proof. To defend it is like trying to confirm a self-evident truth," &c. &c. Yet he advances no less than seven "arguments," as he calls them, in order to establish this self-evident position. We shall examine these seven arguments, and see if his great confidence be not built on a mere abuse of words.

"The consciousness of our humanity," says he, "involves the persuasion that we cannot be owned as a tree or a brute." This, as everybody knows, is one of the hackneyed commonplaces of the abolitionist. He never ceases to declaim about the injustice of slavery, because it regards, as he is pleased to assert, a man as a mere thing or a brute. Now, once for all, we freely admit that it were monstrously unjust to regard or treat a man otherwise than as a man. We freely admit that a human being "cannot be owned as a tree or a brute."

A tree may be *absolutely* owned. That is to say, the owner of a tree may do what he pleases with his own, provided he do no harm or injury with it. He may cut it down; and, if he please, he may beat it as long as he has the power to raise an arm. He may work it into a house or into a piece of furniture, or he may lay it on the fire, and reduce it to ashes. He may, we repeat, do just exactly what he pleases with his own, if his own be such a thing as a tree, *for a tree has no rights*.

It is far otherwise with a brute. The owner of a horse, for example, may not do what he pleases with his own. Here his property is not *absolute;* it is *limited*. He may not beat his horse without mercy, "for a good man is merciful to his beast." He may not cut his horse to pieces, or burn him on the fire. For the horse has rights, which the owner himself is bound to respect. The horse has a right to food and kind treatment, and the owner who refuses these is a tyrant. Nay, the very worm that crawls beneath our feet has his rights as well as the monarch on his throne; and just in so far as these rights are disregarded by a man is that man a tyrant.

Hence even the brute may not be regarded or treated as a mere thing or a tree. He can be owned and treated no otherwise than as a brute. The horse, for example, may not be left, like a tree, without food and care; but he may be saddled and rode as a horse; or he may be hitched to the plough, and compelled to do his master's work.

In like manner, a man cannot be owned or treated as a horse. He cannot be saddled or rode, nor hitched to the plough and be made to do the work of a horse. On the contrary, he should be treated as a man, and required to perform only the work of a man. The right to such work is all the ownership which any one man can rightfully have in another; and this is all which any slaveholder of the South needs to claim.

The real question is, *Can one man have a right to the personal service or obedience of another without his consent?* We do not intend to let the abolitionist throw dust in our eyes, and shout victory amid a clamor of words. We intend to hold him to the point. Whether he be a learned divine, or a distinguished senator, we intend he shall speak to the point, or else his argument shall be judged, not according to the eloquent noise it makes or the excitement it produces, but according to the *sense* it contains.

Can a man, then, have a right to the labor or obedience of another without his consent? Give us this right, and it is all we ask. We lay no claim to the soul of the slave. We grant

8*

to the abolitionist, even more freely than he can assert, that the "soul of the slave is his own." Or, rather, we grant that his soul belongs exclusively to the God who gave it. The master may use him not as a tree or a brute, but only as a rational, accountable, and immortal being may be used. He may not command him to do any thing which is wrong; and if he should so far forget himself as to require such service of his slave, he would himself be guilty of the act. If he should require his slave to violate any law of the land, he would be held not as a *particeps criminis* merely, but as a criminal in the first degree. In like manner, if he should require him to violate the law of God, he would be guilty—far more guilty than the slave himself — in the sight of heaven. These are truths which are just as well understood at the South as they are at the North.

The master, we repeat, lays no claim to the soul of the slave. He demands no spiritual service of him, he exacts no divine honors. With his own soul he is fully permitted to serve his own God. With this soul he may follow the solemn injunction of the Most High, "Servants, obey your masters;" or he may listen to the voice of the tempter, "Servants,

fly from your masters." Those only who instigate him to violate the law of God, whether
at the North or at the South, are the men who
seek to deprive him of his rights and to exercise
an infamous dominion over his soul.

Since, then, the master claims only a right to
the labor and lawful obedience of the slave, and
no right whatever to his soul, it follows that the
argument, which Dr. Channing regards as the
strongest of his seven, has no real foundation.
Since the master claims to have no property in
the "rational, moral, and immortal" part of his
being, so all the arguments, or rather all the
empty declamation, based on the false supposition of such claim, falls to the ground. So the
passionate appeals, proceeding on the supposition of such a monstrous claim, and addressed
to the religious sensibilities of the multitude,
are only calculated to deceive and mislead their
judgment. It is a mere thing of words; and,
though "full of sound and fury," it signifies
nothing. "The traffic in human souls," which
figures so largely in the speeches of the divines
and demagogues, and which so fiercely stirs up
the most unhallowed passions of their hearers,
is merely the transfer of a right to labor.

Does any one doubt whether such a right may

exist? The master certainly has a right to the labor of his apprentice for a specified period of time, though he has no right to his soul even for a moment. The father, too, has a right to the personal service and obedience of his child until he reach the age of twenty-one; but no one ever supposed that he owned the soul of his child, or might sell it, if he pleased, to another. Though he may not sell the soul of his child, it is universally admitted that he may, for good and sufficient reasons, transfer his right to the labor and obedience of his child. Why, then, should it be thought impossible that such a right to service may exist for life? If it may exist for one period, why not for a longer, and even for life? If the good of both parties and the good of the whole community require such a relation and such a right to exist, why should it be deemed so unjust, so iniquitous, so monstrous? This whole controversy turns, we repeat, not upon any consideration of abstract rights, but solely upon the highest good of all— upon the highest good of the slave as well as upon that of the community.

"It is plain," says Dr. Channing, in his first argument, "that if any one man may be held as property, then any other man may be so held."

This sophism has been already sufficiently refuted. It proceeds on the supposition that if
one man, however incapable of self-government,
may be placed under the control of another,
then all men may be placed under the control
of others! It proceeds on the idea that all men
should be placed in precisely the same condition,
subjected to precisely the same authority, and
required to perform precisely the same kind of
labor. In one word, it sees no difference and
makes no distinction between a Negro and a
Newton. But as an overstrained and false idea
of equality lies at the foundation of this argument, so it will pass under review again, when
we come to consider the great demonstration
which the abolitionist is accustomed to deduce
from the axiom that "all men are created equal."

The third argument of Dr. Channing is, like
the first, "founded on the essential equality of
men." Hence, like the first, it may be post-
poned until we come to consider the true meaning and the real political significancy of the
natural equality of all men. We shall barely
remark, in passing, that two arguments cannot
be made out of one by merely changing the
mode of expression.

The second argument of the author is as follows: "A man cannot be seized and held as property, because he has rights. . . . A being having rights cannot justly be made property, *for this claim over him virtually annuls all his rights.*" This argument, it is obvious, is based on the arbitrary idea which the author has been pleased to attach to the term *property*. If it proves any thing, it would prove that a horse could not be held as property, for a horse certainly has rights. But, as we have seen, a limited property, or a right to the labor of a man, does not deny or annul all his rights, nor necessarily any one of them. This argument needs no further refutation. For we acknowledge that the slave has rights; and the limited or qualified property which the master claims in him, extending merely to his personal human labor and his lawful obedience, touches not one of these rights.

The fourth argument of Dr. Channing is identical with the second. "That a human being," says he, "cannot be justly held as property, is apparent from *the very nature of property*. Property is an exclusive right. It shuts out all claim but that of the possessor. What one man owns cannot belong to another." The only difference between the two arguments is this: in one the "*nature of* property" is said "to annul all rights;" and in the other it is said "to exclude all rights!" Both are based on the same idea of property, and both arrive at the same conclusion, with only a very slight difference in the mode of expression!

And both are equally unsound. True; "what one man owns cannot belong to another." But may not one man have a right to the labor of another, as a father to the labor of his son, or a master to the labor of his apprentice; and yet that other a right to food and raiment, as well as to other things? May not one man have a right to the service of another, without annulling or excluding all the rights of that other? This argument proceeds, it is evident, on the false supposition that if any being be held as property, then he has no rights: a supposition which, if true, would exclude and annul the right of property in every living creature.

Dr. Channing's fifth argument is deduced from "the universal indignation excited toward *a man* who makes another his slave." "Our laws," says he, "know no higher crime than that of reducing a man to slavery. To steal or to buy an African on his own shores is piracy." "To

steal a man," we reply, is one thing; and, by
the authority of the law of the land, to require
him to do certain labor, is, one would think,
quite another. The first may be as high a crime
as any known to our laws; the last is recognised
by our laws themselves. Is it not wonderful
that Dr. Channing could not see so plain a distinction, so broad and so glaring a difference?
The father of his country held slaves; *he did
not commit the crime of man-stealing.*

The sixth argument of Dr. Channing, "against
the right of property in man," is "drawn from
a very obvious principle of moral science. It
is a plain truth, universally received, that every
right supposes or involves a corresponding obligation. If, then, a man has a right to another's
person or powers, the latter is under obligation
to give himself up as a chattel to the former."
Most assuredly, if one man has a right to the
service or obedience of another, then that other
is under obligation to render that service or
obedience to him. But is such an obligation
absurd? Is it inconsistent with the inherent,
the inalienable, the universal rights of man
that the "servant should obey his master?" If
so, then we fear the rights of man were far
better understood by Dr. Channing than by the

Creator of the world and the Author of revelation.

Such are the seven arguments adduced by Dr. Channing to show that no man can rightfully hold property in his fellow-man. But before we quit this branch of the subject, we shall advert to a passage in the address of the Hon. Charles Sumner, before the people of New York, at the Metropolitan Theatre, May 9, 1855. "I desire to present this argument," says he, "on grounds above all controversy, impeachment, or suspicion, even from slave-masters themselves. Not on triumphant story, not even on indisputable facts, do I now accuse slavery, but on its character, as revealed in its own simple definition of itself. Out of its own mouth do I condemn it." Well, and why does he condemn it? Because, "by the law of slavery, man, created in the image of God, is *divested of his human character* and declared to be a *mere* chattel. That the statement may not seem to be put forward without precise authority, I quote the law of two different slave States." That is the accusation. It is to be proved by the law of slavery itself. It is to be proved beyond "all controversy," by an appeal to "indisputable facts." Now let us have the facts: here they are. "The law of another polished slave State," says Mr. Sumner, "gives this definition : 'Slaves shall be delivered, sold, taken, reputed, and adjudged in law to be chattels personal, in the hands of their owners and possessors, and their executors, administrators, and assignees, to all intents, constructions, and purposes whatsoever.'"

Now, *mark;* the learned Senator undertook to prove, beyond all doubt and controversy, that slavery *divests the slave of his human character,* and declares him to be a *mere* chattel. But he merely proves that it declares him to be a "chattel personal." He merely proves that the law of a Southern State regards the slave, not as real estate or landed property, but as a "chattel personal." Does this divest him of his human character? does this make him a *mere* chattel? May the slave, in consequence of such law, be treated as a brute or a tree? May he be cut in pieces or worked to death at the will and pleasure of the master?

We think that a learned Senator, especially when he undertakes to demonstrate, should distinguish between declaring a man to be "a chattel personal," and a *mere* chattel. No one doubts that a man is a thing; but is he therefore a *mere* thing, or nothing more than

a thing? In like manner, no one doubts that
a man is an animal; does it follow, therefore,
that he is a *mere* animal, or nothing but an
animal? It is clear, that to declare a man
may be held as a "chattel personal," is a very
different thing from declaring that he is a *mere*
chattel. So much for his honor's "precise
authority."

In what part of the law, then, is the slave
"divested of his human character?" In no
part whatever. If it had declared him to be
a *mere* thing, or a *mere* chattel, or a *mere* animal, it would have denied his human character,
we admit; but the law in question has done
no such thing. Nor is any such declaration
contained in the other law quoted by the learned
Senator from the code of Louisiana. It is
merely by the interpolation of this little word
mere, that the Senator of Massachusetts has
made the law of South Carolina dives. immortal being of his "human character." He
is welcome to all the applause which this may
have gained for him in the "Metropolitan
Theatre."

The learned Senator adduces another authority. "A careful writer," says he, "Judge
Stroud, in a work of juridical as well as phi-

lanthropic merit, thus sums up the law: 'The cardinal principle of slavery—that the slave is not to be ranked among *sentient** beings, but among *things*—as an article of property—a chattel personal—obtains as undoubted law in all these (the slave) States.'" We thus learn from this very "careful writer" that slaves among us are "not ranked among *sentient* beings," and that this is "the cardinal principle of slavery." No, they are not fed, nor clothed, nor treated as sentient beings! They are left without food and raiment, just as if they were stocks and stones! They are not talked to, nor reasoned with, as if they were rational animals, but only driven about, like dumb brutes beneath the lash! No, no, not the lash, for that would recognise them as "sentient beings!" They are only thrown about like stones, or boxed up like chattels; they are not set, like men, over the lower animals, required to do the work of men; the precise work which, of all others, in the grand and diversified economy of *human* industry, they are the best qualified to perform! So far, indeed, is this from being "the cardinal principle of slavery,"

---

* The *Italics* are his own.

that it is no principle of slavery at all. It bears not the most distant likeness or approximation to any principle of slavery, with which we of the South have any the most remote acquaintance.

That man may, in certain cases, be held as property, is a truth recognised by a higher authority than that of senators and divines. It is, as we have seen, recognised by the word of God himself. In that word, the slave is called the "possession"* of the master, and even "his money."† Now, is not this language as strong, if not stronger, than that adduced from the code of South Carolina? It certainly calls "the bondman" his master's "money." Why, then, did not the Senator from Massachusetts denounce this language, as divesting "a man of his human character," and declaring him to be *mere* money? Why did he not proceed to condemn the legislation of Heaven, as well as of the South, out of its own mouth? Most assuredly, if his principles be correct, then is he bound to pronounce the law of God itself manifestly unjust and iniquitous. For that law as clearly recognises the

---

* Lev. chap. xxv.　　　† Exod. chap. xxi.

9*

right of property in man as it could possibly be recognised in words. But it nowhere commits the flagrant solecism of supposing that this right of the master annuls or excludes all the rights of the slave. On the contrary, the rights of the slave are recognised, as well as those of the master. For, according to the law of God, though "a possession," and an "inheritance," and "a bondman forever," yet is the slave, nevertheless, a man; and, as a man, is he protected in his rights; in his rights, not as defined by abolitionists, but as recognised by the word of God.

§ XI. *The seventeenth fallacy of the abolitionist; or the argument from the Declaration of Independence.*

This argument is regarded by the abolitionists as one of their great strongholds; and no doubt it is so in effect, for who can bear a superior? Lucifer himself, who fell from heaven because he could not acknowledge a superior, seduced our first parents by the suggestion that in throwing off the yoke of subjection, they should become "as gods." We need not wonder, then, if it should be found, that an appeal to the absolute equality of all

men is the most ready way to effect the ruin
of States. We can surely conceive of none
better adapted to subvert all order among us
of the South, involving the two races in a servile war, and the one or the other in utter
extinction. Hence we shall examine this argument from the equality of all men, or rather
this appeal to all men's abhorrence of infe-
riority. This appeal is usually based on the
Declaration of Independence: " We hold these
truths to be self-evident: that all men are created equal; that they are endowed by their
Creator with certain inalienable rights; that
among these are life, liberty, and the pursuit
of happiness." We do not mean to play upon
these words; we intend to take them exactly
as they are understood by our opponents. As
they are not found in a metaphysical document
or discussion, so it would be unfair to suppose—as is sometimes done—that they inculcate the wild dream of Helvetius, that all men
are created with equal natural capacities of
mind. They occur in a declaration of independence; and as the subject is the doctrine
of human rights, so we suppose they mean to
declare that all men are created equal with
respect to natural rights.

Nor do we assert that there is no truth in this celebrated proposition or maxim; for we believe that, if rightly understood, it contains most important and precious truth. It is not on this account, however, the less dangerous as a maxim of political philosophy. Nay, falsehood is only then the more dangerous, when it is so blended with truth that its existence is not suspected by its victims. Hence the unspeakable importance of dissecting this pretended maxim, and separating the precious truth it contains from the pernicious falsehood by which its followers are deceived. Its truth is certainly very far from being self-evident, or rather its truth is self-evident to some, while its falsehood is equally self-evident to others, according to the side from which it is viewed. We shall endeavor to throw some light both upon its truth and its falsehood, and, if possible, draw the line which divides them from each other.

This maxim does not mean, then, that all men have, by nature, an equal right to political power or to posts of honor. No doubt the words are often understood in this sense by those who, without reflection, merely echo the Declaration of Independence; but, in this

sense, they are utterly untenable. If all men
had, by nature, an equal right to any of the
offices of government, how could such rights
be adjusted? How could such a conflict be
reconciled? It is clear that all men could not
be President of the United States; and if all
men had an equal natural right to that office,
no one man could be elevated to it without a
wrong to all the rest. In such case, all men
should have, at least, an equal chance to occupy the presidential chair. Such equal chance
could not result from the right of all men to
offer themselves as candidates for the office;
for, at the bar of public opinion, vast multitudes would not have the least shadow of a
chance. The only way to effect such an object
would be by resorting to the lot. We might
thus determine who, among so many equally
just claimants, should actually possess the power
of the supreme magistrate. This, it must be
confessed, would be to recognise in deed, as
well as in word, the equal rights of all men.
But what more absurd than such an equality of
rights? It is not without example in history;
but it is to be hoped that such example will
never be copied. The democracy of Athens,
it is well known, was, at one time, so far car-

ried away by the idea of equal rights, that her generals and orators and poets were elected by the lot. This was an equality, not in theory merely, but in practice. Though the lives and fortunes of mankind were thus intrusted to the most ignorant and depraved, or to the most wise and virtuous, as the lot might determine, yet this policy was based on an equality of rights. It is scarcely necessary to add that this idea of equality prevailed, not in the better days of the Athenian democracy, but only during its imbecility and corruption.

If all men, then, have not a natural right to fill an office of government, who has this right? Who has the natural right, for example, to occupy the office of President of the United States? Certainly some men have no such right. The man, for example, who has no capacity to govern himself, but needs a guardian, has no right to superintend the affairs of a great nation. Though a citizen, he has no more right to exercise such power or authority than if he were a Hottentot, or an African, or an ape. Hence, in bidding such a one to stand aside and keep aloof from such high office, no right is infringed and no injury done. Nay, right is secured, and injury prevented.

Who has such a right, then?—such natural right, or right according to the law of nature or reason? The man, we answer, who, all things considered, is the best qualified to discharge the duties of the office. The man who, by his superior wisdom, and virtue, and statesmanship, would use the power of such office more effectually for the good of the whole people than would any other man. If there be one such man, and only one, he of *natural right* should be our President. And all the laws framed to regulate the election of President are, or should be, only so many means designed to secure the services of that man, if possible, and thereby secure the rights of all against the possession of power by the unworthy or the less worthy. This object, it is true, is not always attained, these means are not always successful; but this is only one of the manifold imperfections which necessarily attach to all human institutions; one of the melancholy instances in which natural and legal right run in different channels. All that can be hoped, indeed, either in the construction or in the administration of human laws, is an approximation, more or less close, to the great principles of natural justice.

What is thus so clearly true in regard to the

office of President, is equally true in regard to all the other offices of government. It is contrary to reason, to natural right, to justice, that either fools, or knaves, or demagogues should occupy seats in Congress; yet all of these classes are sometimes seen there, and by the law of the land are entitled to their seats. Here, again, that which is right and fit in itself is different from that which exists under the law.

The same remarks, it is evident, are applicable to governors, to judges, to sheriffs, to constables, and to justices of the peace. In every instance, he who is best qualified to discharge the duties of an office, and who would do so with greatest advantage to all concerned, has the natural right thereto. And no man who would fill any office, or exercise any power so as to injure the community, has any right to such office or power.

There is precisely the same limitation to the exercise of the elective franchise. Those only should be permitted to exercise this power who are qualified to do so with advantage to the community; and all laws which regulate or limit the possession of this power should have in view, not the equal rights of all men, but solely and exclusively the public good. It is on this principle that foreigners are not allowed to vote as soon as they land upon our shores, and that native Americans can do so only after they have reached a certain age. And if the public good required that any class of men, such as free blacks or slaves, for example, should be excluded from the privilege altogether, then no doubt can remain the law excluding them would be just. It might not be equal, but would be *just*. Indeed, in the high and holy sense of the word, it would be equal; for, if it excluded some from a privilege or power which it conferred upon others, this is because they were not included within the condition on which alone it should be extended to any. Such is not an equality of rights and power, it is true; but it is an equality of justice, like that which reigns in the divine government itself. In the light of that justice, it is clear that no man, and no class of men, can have a natural right to exercise a power which, if intrusted to them, would be wielded for harm, and not for good.

This great truth, when stripped of the manifold sophistications of a false logic, is so clear and unquestionable, that it has not failed to secure the approbation of abolitionists themselves. Thus, after all his wild extravagancies about inherent, inalienable, and equal rights, Dr. Channing has, in one of his calmer moods, recognised this great fundamental truth. "The slave," says he, "cannot rightfully, and should not, be owned by the individual. But, like every citizen, *he is subject to the community*, AND THE COMMUNITY HAS A RIGHT AND IS BOUND TO CONTINUE ALL SUCH RESTRAINTS AS ITS OWN SAFETY AND THE WELL-BEING OF THE SLAVE DEMANDS." Now this is all we ask in regard to the question of equal rights. All we ask is, that each and every individual may be in such wise and so far restrained as the public good demands and no farther. All we ask is, as may be seen from the first chapter of this Essay, that the right of the individual, whether real or imaginary, may be held in subjection to the undoubted right of the community to protect itself and to secure its own highest good. This solemn right, so inseparably linked to a sacred duty, is paramount to the rights and powers of the individual. Nay, as we have already seen,* the individual can have no right that conflicts with this; because it is his *duty* to co-operate in

---

* In the first chapter.

the establishment of the general good. Surely he can have no right which is adverse to duty. Indeed, if for the general good, he would not cheerfully lay down both liberty and life, then both may be rightfully taken from him. We have, it is true, inherent and *inalienable rights*, but among these is neither liberty nor life. For these, upon our country's altar, may be sacrificed; but conscience, truth, honor may not be touched by man.

Has the community, then, after all, the right to compel "a man," a "rational and immortal being," to work? Let Dr. Channing answer: "If he (the slave) cannot be induced to work by rational and natural motives, *he should be obliged to labor, on the same principle on which the vagrant in other communities is confined and compelled to earn his bread*." Now, if a man be "confined, and compelled" to work in his confinement, what becomes of his "inalienable right to liberty?" We think there must be a slight mistake somewhere. Perhaps it is in the Declaration of Independence itself. Nay, is it not evident, indeed, that if all men have an inalienable right to liberty," then is this sacred right trampled in the dust by every government on earth? Is it not as really disregarded by the enlightened Commonwealth of Massachusetts, which "confines and compels" vagrants to earn their bread, as it is by the Legislature of Virginia, which has taken the wise precaution to prevent the rise of a swarm of vagrants more destructive than the locusts of Egypt? The plain truth is, that although this notion of the "inalienable right" of all to liberty may sound very well in a declaration of independence, and may be most admirably adapted to stir up the passions of men and produce fatal commotions in a commonwealth, yet no wise nation ever has been or ever will be guided by it in the construction of her laws. It may be a brand of discord in the hands of the abolitionist and the demagogue. It will never be an element of light, or power, or wisdom, in the bosom of the statesman.

"The gift of liberty," continues Dr. Channing, "would be a mere name, and worse than nominal, were he (the slave) to be let loose on society under circumstances driving him to commit crimes, for which he would be condemned to severer bondage than he had escaped." If then, after all, liberty may be worse than a mere name, is it not a pity that all men should have an "inalienable right" to it? If it may be a curse, is it not a pity that all men should be required to embrace it, and to be even ready to die for it, as an invaluable blessing? We trust that "no man," that "no rational and immortal being," will ever be so ungrateful as to complain of those who have withheld from him that which is "worse than nominal," and a curse. For if such, and such only, be his inalienable birthright, were it not most wisely exchanged for a mess of potage? The vagrant, then, should not be consulted whether he will work or not. He should be "confined and compelled" to work, says Dr. Channing. Nor should the idle and the vicious, those who cannot be induced to work by rational motives, be asked whether they will remain pests to society, or whether they will eat their bread in the sweat of their brow. "For they, too," says Dr. Channing, "should be compelled to work." But how? "The slave should not have an owner," says Dr. Channing, "but he should have a guardian. He needs authority, to supply the lack of that discretion which he has not yet attained; but it should be the authority of a friend, an official authority, conferred by the State, and for which there should be responsibility to the State." Now,

H   10*

if all this be true, is not the doctrine of equal rights, as held by Dr. Channing, a mere dream? If one man may have "a guardian," "an official authority," appointed by the State, to compel him to work, why may not another be placed under the same authority, and subjected to the same servitude? Are not all equal? Have not all men an equal right to liberty and to a choice of the pursuits of happiness? Let these questions be answered by the admirers of Dr. Channing; and it will be found that they have overthrown all the plausible logic, and blown away all the splendid rhetoric, which has been reared, on the ground of equal rights, against the institution of slavery at the South.

We are agreed, then, that men may be compelled to work. We are also agreed that, for this purpose, the slaves of the South should be placed under guardians and friends by the authority of the State. Dr. Channing thinks, however, that the owner is not the best guardian or the best friend whom the State could place over the slave. On the contrary, he thinks his best friend and guardian would be an official overseer, bound to him by no ties of interest, and by no peculiar feelings of affection. In all this, we think Dr. Channing greatly mistaken; and mistaken because he is an utter stranger to the feelings usually called forth by the relation of master and slave. But, be this as it may, since such are the concessions made by Dr. Channing, it is no longer necessary to debate the question of slavery with him, on the high ground of abstract inalienable rights. It is brought down to one of practical utility, of public expediency.

And such being the nature of the question, we, as free citizens of the South, claim the right to settle the matter for ourselves. We claim the right to appoint such guardians and friends for this class of our population as we believe will be most advantageous to them, as well as to the whole community. We claim the right to impose such restraints, and such only, as the well-being of our own society seems to us to demand. This claim may be denied. The North may claim the right to think for us in regard to this question of expediency. But it cannot be denied that if liberty may be a curse, then no man can, in such case, have a right to it as a blessing.

If liberty would be an equal blessing to all men, then, we freely admit, all men would have an equal right to liberty. But to concede, as Dr. Channing does, that it were a curse to some men, and yet contend that all men have an equal right to its enjoyment, is sheer absurdity and nonsense. But Dr. Channing, as we have seen, sometimes speaks a better sense. Thus, he has even said, "It would be cruelty, not kindness, to the latter (to the slave) to give him a freedom which he is unprepared to understand or enjoy. It would be cruelty to strike the fetters from a man whose first steps would infallibly lead him to a precipice." So far, then, according to the author himself, are all men from having an "inalienable right" to liberty, that some men have no right to it at all.

In like manner, Dr. Wayland, by his own admission, has overthrown all his most confident deductions from the notion of equal rights. He, too, quotes the Declaration of Independence, and adds, "That the equality here spoken of is not of the means of happiness, but in the right to use them as one wills, is too evident to need illustration." If this be the meaning, then the meaning is not so evidently true. On the contrary, the vaunted maxim in question, as understood by Dr. Wayland, appears to be pure and unmixed error. Power, for example, is one means of happiness; and so great a means, too, that without it all other means would be of no avail. But has any man a right to use this means of happiness as he wills? Most assuredly not. He has no right to use the power he may possess, nor any other means of happiness, as he will, but only as lawful authority has willed. If it be a power conferred by man, for example, such as that of a chief magistrate, or of a senator, or of a judge, he may use it no otherwise than as the law of the land permits, or in pursuance of the objects for which it was conferred. In like manner, if it proceed from the Almighty, it may be used only in conformity with his law. So far, then, is it from being true that all men possess an equal right to use the means of happiness as they please, that no man ever has, or ever will, possess any such right at all. And if such be the meaning of the Declaration of Independence, then the Declaration of Independence is too evidently erroneous to need any further refutation. Unless, indeed, man may put forth a declaration of independence which shall annul and destroy the immutable obligations of the moral law, and erect *one's will* as the rule of right. But is an equal exemption from the restraints of that law liberty, or is it universal anarchy and confusion?

It were much nearer the truth to say that all men have an equal right, not to act as "one wills," but to have their wills restrained by law. No greater want is known to man, indeed, than the restraints of law and government. Hence, all men have an equal right to these, but not to the same restraints, to the same laws and governments. All have an equal right to that government which is the best for them. But the same government is not the best for all. A despotism is best for some; a limited monarchy is best for others; while, for a third people, a representative republic is the best form of government.

This proposition is too plain for controversy. It has received the sanction of all the great teachers of political wisdom, from an Aristotle down to a Montesquieu, and from a Montesquieu down to a Burke. It has become, indeed, one of the commonplaces of political ethics; and, however strange the conjunction, it is often found in the very works which are loudest in proclaiming the universal equality of human

rights. Thus, for example, says Dr. Wayland:
"The best form of government for any people
*is the best that its present moral condition renders
practicable. A people may be so entirely surrendered to the influence of passion, and so feebly
influenced by moral restraints, that a government
which relied upon moral restraint could not exist
for a day.* In this case, a subordinate and
inferior principle yet remains—*the principle of
fear, and the only resort is to a government of
force* or a military despotism. And such do we
see to be the fact." What, then, becomes of
the equal and inalienable right of all men to
freedom? Has it vanished with the occasion
which gave it birth?

But this is not all. "Anarchy," continues
Wayland, "always ends in this form of government. [A military despotism.] After this has
been established, and habits of subordination
have been formed, while the moral restraints
are too feeble for self-government, an hereditary
government, which addresses itself to the imagination, and strengthens itself by the influence
of domestic connections, may be as good a form
as a people can sustain. As they advance in
intellectual and moral cultivation, it may ad-
vantageously become more and more elective,

and, in a suitable moral condition, it may be wholly so. For beings who are willing to govern themselves by moral principles, there can be no doubt that a government relying upon moral principle is the true form of government. There is no reason why a man should be oppressed by taxation and subjected to fear who is willing to govern himself by the law of reciprocity. It is surely better for an intelligent and moral being to do right from his own will, than *to pay another to force him to do right*. And yet, as it is better that he should do right than wrong, even though he be forced to do it, it is well that he should pay others to force him, if there be no other way of insuring his good conduct. God has rendered the blessing of freedom inseparable from moral restraint to the individual; and hence it is vain for a people to expect to be free unless they are first willing to be virtuous." Again, "There is no self-sustaining power in any form of social organization. The only self-sustaining power is in individual virtue.

"And the form of a government will always adjust itself to the moral condition of a people. A virtuous people will, by their own moral power, frown away oppression, and, under any form of constitution, become essentially free. A people surrendered up to their own licentious passions must be held in subjection by force; for every one will find that force alone can protect him from his neighbors; and he will submit to be oppressed, if he can only be protected. Thus, in the feudal ages, the small independent landholders frequently made themselves slaves of one powerful chief to shield themselves from the incessant oppression of twenty."

Now all this is excellent sense. One might almost imagine that the author had been reading Aristotle, or Montesquieu, or Burke. It is certain he was not thinking of equal rights. It is equally certain that his eyes were turned away from the South; for he could see how even "independent landholders" might rightfully make "slaves" of themselves. After such concessions, one would think that all this clamor about inherent and *inalienable* rights ought to cease.

In a certain sense, or to a certain extent, all men have equal rights. All men have an equal right to the air and light of heaven; to the same air and the same light. In like manner, all men have an equal right to food and raiment, though not to the same food and

11

raiment. That is, all men have an equal right
to food and raiment, provided they will earn
them. And if they will not earn them, choosing
to remain idle, improvident, or nuisances to
society, then they should be placed under a
goverment of force, and compelled to earn
them.

Again, all men have an equal right to serve
God according to the dictates of their own
consciences. The poorest slave on earth possesses this right—this inherent and inalienable
right; and he possesses it as completely as the
proudest monarch on his throne. He may
choose his own religion, and worship his own
God according to his own conscience, provided
always he seek not in such service to interfere
with the rights of others. But neither the slave
nor the freeman has any right to murder, or
instigate others to murder, the master, even
though he should be ever so firmly persuaded
that such is a part of his religious duty. He has,
however, the most absolute and perfect right to
worship the Creator of all men in all ways not
inconsistent with the moral law. And wo be
to the man by whom such right is denied or
set at naught! Such a one we have never
known; but whosoever he may be, or where-

soever he may be found, let all the abolitionists, we say, hunt him down. He is not fit to be a man, much less a Christian master.

But, it will be said, the slave has also a right to religious instruction, as well as to food and raiment. So plain a proposition no one doubts. But is this right regarded at the South? No more, we fear, than in many other portions of the so-called Christian world. Our children, too, and our poor, destitute neighbors, often suffer, we fear, the same wrong at our remiss hands and from our cold hearts. Though we have done much and would fain do more, yet, the truth must be confessed, this sacred and imperious claim has not been fully met by us.

It may be otherwise at the North. There children and poor neighbors, too, may all be trained and taught to the full extent of the moral law. This godlike work may be fully done by our Christian brethren of the North. They certainly have a large surplus of bene-volence to bestow on us. But if this glorious work has not been fully done by them, then let him who is without sin cast the first stone. This simple thought, perhaps, might call in doubt their right to rail at us, at least with such malignant bitterness and gall. This simple thought, perhaps, might save us many a pitiless pelting of philanthropy.

But here lies the difference—here lies our peculiar sin and shame. This great, primordial right is, with us, denied by law. The slave shall not be taught to read. Oh! that he might be taught! What floods of sympathy, what thunderings and lightnings of philanthropy, would then be spared the world! But why, we ask, should the slave be taught to read? That he might read the Bible, and feed on the food of eternal life, is the reply; and the reply is good.

Ah! if the slave would only read his Bible, and drink its very spirit in, we should rejoice at the change; for he would then be a better and a happier man. He would then know his duty, and the high ground on which his duty rests. He would then see, in the words of Dr. Wayland, that *"The duty of slaves is explicitly made known in the Bible.* They are bound to obedience, fidelity, submission, and respect to their masters—not only to the good and kind, but also to the unkind and froward; not, however, on the ground of duty to man, but *on the ground of duty to God."* But, with all, we have some little glimpse of our dangers, as well as some little sense of our duties.

The tempter is not asleep. His eye is still, as ever of old, fixed on the forbidden tree; and thither he will point his hapless victims. Like certain senators, and demagogues, and doctors of divinity, he will preach from the Declaration of Independence rather than from the Bible. He will teach, not that submission, but that *resistance*, is a duty. To every evil passion his inflammatory and murder-instigating appeals will be made. Stung by these appeals and maddened, the poor African, it is to be feared, would have no better notions of equality and freedom, and no better views of duty to God or man, than his teachers themselves have. Such, then, being the state of things, ask us not to prepare the slave for his own utter undoing. Ask us not—O most kind and benevolent Christian teacher!—ask us not to lay the train beneath our feet, that *you* may no longer hold the blazing torch in vain!

Let that torch be extinguished. Let all incendiary publications be destroyed. Let no conspiracies, no insurrections, and no murders be instigated. Let the pure precepts of the gospel and its sublime lessons of peace be everywhere set forth and inculcated. In one word, let it be seen that in reality the eternal good of the slave is aimed at, and, by the co-operation of all, may be secured, and then may we be asked to teach him to read. But until then we shall refuse to head a conspiracy against the good order, the security, the morals, and against the very lives, of both the white and the black men of the South.

We might point out other respects in which men are essentially equal, or *have equal rights*. But our object is not to write a treatise on the philosophy of politics. It is merely to expose the errors of those who push the idea of equality to an extreme, and thereby unwisely deny the great differences that exist among men. For if the scheme or the political principles of the abolitionists be correct, then there is no difference among men, not even among the different races of men, that is worthy the attention of the statesman.

There is one difference, we admit, which the abolitionists have discovered between the master and the slave at the South. Whether this discovery be entirely original with them, or whether they received hints of it from others, it is clear that they are now fully in possession of it. The dazzling idea of equality itself has not been able to exclude it from their vision. For, in spite of this idea, they have discovered that between the Southern master and slave there is a difference of color! Hence, as if this were the only difference, in their political harangues, whether from the stump or from the pulpit, they seldom fail to rebuke the Southern statesman in the words of the poet: "He finds his fellow guilty of a skin not colored like his own;" and "for such worthy cause dooms and devotes him as his lawful prey." Shame and confusion seize the man, we say, who thus dooms and devotes his fellow-man, because he finds him "guilty of a skin!" If his sensibilities were only as soft as his philosophy is shallow, he would certainly cry, "Down with the institution of slavery!" For how could he tolerate an institution which has no other foundation than a difference of color? Indeed, if such were the only difference between the two races among us, we should ourselves unite with Mr. Seward of New York, and most "affectionately advise all men to be born white." For thus, the only difference having been abolished, all men would be equal in fact, and consequently entitled to become equal in political rights, and power, and position. But if such be not the only difference between the white and the black man of the South, then neither philosophy nor paint can establish an equality between them.

Every man, we admit, is a man. But this profound aphorism is not the only one to which the political architect should give heed. An equality of conditions, of political powers and privileges, which has no solid basis in an equality of capacity or fitness, is one of the wildest and most impracticable of all Utopian dreams. If in the divine government such an equality should prevail, it is evident that all order would be overthrown, all justice extinguished, and utter confusion would reign. In like manner, if in human government such equality should exist, it would be only for a moment. Indeed, to aim at an equality of conditions, or of rights and powers, except by first aiming at an equality of intelligence and virtue, is not to reform—it is to demolish—the governments of society. It is, indeed, to war against the eternal order of divine Providence itself, in which an immutable justice ever reigns. "It is this aiming after an equality," says

Aristotle, "which is the cause of seditions." But though seditions it may have stirred up, and fierce passions kindled, yet has it never led its poor deluded victims to the boon after which they have so fondly panted.

Equality is not liberty. "The French," said Napoleon, "love equality: they care little for liberty." Equality is plain, simple, easily understood. Liberty is complex, and exceedingly difficult of comprehension. The most illiterate peasant may, at a glance, grasp the idea of equality; the most profound statesman may not, without much care and thought, comprehend the nature of liberty. Hence it is that equality, and not liberty, so readily seizes the mind of the multitude, and so mightily inflames its passions. The French are not the only people who care but little for liberty, while they are crazy for equality. The same blind passion, it is to be feared, is possible even in this enlightened portion of the globe. Even here, perhaps, a man may rant and rave about equality, while, really, he may know but little more, and consequently care but little more, about that complicated and beautiful structure called civil liberty, than a horse does about the mechanism of the heavens.

I

Thus, for example, a Senator* of the United States declares that the democratic principle is "Equality of natural rights, guaranteed and secured to all by the laws of a just, popular government. For one, I desire to see that principle applied to every subject of legislation, no matter what that subject may be—to the great question involved in the resolution now before the Senate, and to every other question." Again, this principle is "the element and guarantee of liberty."

Apply this principle, then, to every subject, to every question, and see what kind of government would be the result. All men have an equal right to freedom from restraint, and consequently all are made equally free. All have an equal right to the elective franchise, and to every political power and privilege. But suppose the government is designed for a State in which a large majority of the population is without the character, or disposition, or habits, or experience of freemen? No matter: the equal rights of all are natural; and hence they should be applied in all cases, and to every possible "subject of legislation." The principle

---

* Mr. Chase, of Ohio.

of equality should reign everywhere, and mould every institution. Surely, after what has been said, no comment is necessary on a scheme so wild, on a dream so visionary. "As distant as heaven is from earth," says Montesquieu, "so is the true spirit of equality from that of extreme equality." And just so distant is the Senator in question, with all his adherents, from the true idea of civil and political freedom.

The Senator thinks the conduct of Virginia "singular enough," because, in presenting a bill of rights to Congress, she omitted the provision of "her own bill of rights," "that all men are born* equally free and independent." We think she acted wisely. For, in truth and in deed, all men are born absolutely dependent, and utterly devoid of freedom. What right, we ask, has the new-born infant? Has he the right to go where he pleases? He has no power to go at all; and hence he has no more a right to go than he has to fly. Has he the right to think for himself? The power of thought is as yet wholly undeveloped. Has he the right to worship God according to his own conscience? He has no idea of God, nor of the

---

* "By nature," in the Original Bill of Rights.

duties due to him. The plain truth is, that no human being possesses a right until the power or capacity on which the enjoyment of that right depends is suitably developed or acquired. The child, for instance, has no right to think for himself, or to worship God according to the dictates of conscience, until his intellectual and moral powers are suitably developed. He is certainly not born with such rights. Nor has he any right to go where he pleases, or attempt to do so, until he has learned to walk. Nor has he the right then, for, according to the laws of all civilized nations, he is subject to the control of the parent until he reaches the lawful age of freedom. The truth is, that all men are born not equally free and independent, but equally without freedom and without independence. "All men are born equal," says Montesquieu; but he does not say they "are born equally free and independent." The first proposition is true: the last is diametrically opposed to the truth.

Another Senator* seems to entertain the same passion for the principle of equality. In his speech on the Compromise Bill of 1850, he says

---

* Mr. Seward, of New York.

that "a statesman or a founder of States" should adopt as an axiom the declaration, "That all men are created equal, and have inalienable rights of life, liberty, and choice of pursuits of happiness." Let us suppose, then, that this distinguished statesman is himself about to establish a constitution for the people of Mississippi or Louisiana, in which there are more blacks than whites. As they all have a natural and "inalienable right" to liberty, of course he would make them all free. But would he confer upon all, upon black as well as upon white, the power of the elective franchise? Most certainly. For he has said, "We of New York are guilty of slavery still by withholding the *right of suffrage* from the race we have emancipated." Surely, if he had to found a State himself, he would not thus be guilty of slavery—of the one odious thing which his soul abhors. All would then be invested with the right of suffrage. A black legislature would be the consequence. The laws passed by such a body would, we fear, be no better than the constitution provided by the Senator—by the statesman—from New York.

"All men are born equal," says Montesquieu; but in the hands of such a thinker no danger

12

need be apprehended from such an axiom. For having drank deeply of the true spirit of law, he was, in matters of government, ever ready to sacrifice abstract perfection to concrete utility. Neither the principle of equality, nor any other, would he apply in all cases or to every subject. He was no dreamer. He was a profound thinker and a real statesman. "Though real equality," says he, "be the very soul of a democracy, *it is so difficult to establish, that an extreme exactness in this respect is not always convenient.*"

Again, he says: "All inequalities in democracies ought to be derived from the nature of the government, and even from the principle of equality. For example, it may be apprehended that people who are obliged to live by labor would be too much impoverished by public employment, or neglect the duties of attending to it; that artisans would grow insolent; and that *too great a number of freemen would overpower the ancient citizens.* IN THIS CASE, THE EQUALITY IN A DEMOCRACY MAY BE SUPPRESSED FOR THE GOOD OF THE STATE."

Thus to give all men equal power where the majority is ignorant and depraved, would be indeed to establish equality, but not liberty.

On the contrary, it would be to establish the most odious despotism on earth,—the reign of ignorance, passion, prejudice, and brutality. It would be to establish a mere nominal equality, and a real inequality. For, as Montesquieu says, by introducing "too great a number of freemen," the "ancient citizens" would be oppressed. In such case, the principle of equality, even in a democracy, should be " suppressed for the good of the State." It should be suppressed, in order to shut out a still greater and more tremendous inequality. The legislator, then, who aims to introduce an extreme equality, or to apply the principle of equality to every question, would really bring about the most frightful of all inequalities, especially in a commonwealth where the majority are ignorant and depraved.

Hence the principle of equality is merely a standard toward which an approximation may be made—an approximation always limited and controlled by the public good. This principle should be applied, not to every question, but only to such as the general good permits. For this good it "may be suppressed." Nay, it must be suppressed, if, without such suppression, the public order may not be sustained;

for, as we have abundantly seen, it is only in the bosom of an enlightened public order that liberty can live, or move, or have its being. Thus, as Montesquieu advises, we deduce an inequality from the very principle of equality itself; since, if such inequality be not deduced and established by law, a still more terrific inequality would be forced upon us. Blind passion would dictate the laws, and brute force would reign, while innocence and virtue would be trampled in the dust. Such is the inequality to which the honorable senators would invite us; and that, too, by an appeal to our love of equality! If we decline the invitation, this is not because we are the enemies, but because we are the friends, of human freedom. It is not because we love equality less, but liberty more.

The legislators of the North may, if they please, choose the principle of equality as the very "element and guarantee" of their liberty; and, to make that liberty perfect, they may apply it to every possible "subject of legislation," and to "every question" under the sun. But, if we may be permitted to choose for ourselves, we should beg to be delivered from such an extreme equality. We should reject it as the very worst "element," and the very surest "guarantee," of an unbounded licentiousness and an intolerable oppression. As the "element and guarantee" of freedom for ourselves, and for our posterity, we should decidedly prefer the principle of an enlightened public order.

12*

CHAPTER III.

THE ARGUMENT FROM THE SCRIPTURES.

IN discussing the arguments of the abolitionists, it was scarcely possible to avoid intimating,
to a certain extent, the grounds on which we
intend to vindicate the institution of slavery, as
it exists among us at the South. But these
grounds are entitled to a more distinct enun-
ciation and to a more ample illustration. In
the prosecution of this object we shall first
advert to the argument from revelation; and,
if we mistake not, it will be found that in the
foregoing discussion we have been vindicating
against aspersion not only the peculiar institution of the Southern States, but also the very
legislation of Heaven itself.

§ I. *The argument from the Old Testament.*

The ground is taken by Dr. Wayland and
other abolitionists, that slavery is always and
everywhere, *semper et ubique*, morally wrong,
and should, therefore, be instantly and univer-

sally swept away. We point to slavery among the Hebrews, and say, There is an instance in which it was not wrong, because there it received the sanction of the Almighty. Dr. Wayland chooses to overlook or evade the bearing of that case upon his fundamental position; and the means by which he seeks to evade its force is one of the grossest fallacies ever invented by the brain of man.

Let the reader examine and judge for himself. Here it is: "Let us reduce this argument to a syllogism, and it will stand thus: Whatever God sanctioned among the Hebrews he sanctions for all men and at all times. God sanctioned slavery among the Hebrews; therefore God sanctions slavery for all men and at all times."

Now I venture to affirm that no man at the South has ever put forth so absurd an argument in favor of slavery,—not only in favor of slavery for the negro race so long as they may remain unfit for freedom, but in favor of slavery for all men and for all times. If such an argument proved any thing, it would, indeed, prove that the white man of the South, no less than the black, might be subjected to bondage. But no one here argues in favor of the subjection of the white man, either South or North, to a state of servitude. No one here contends for the subjection to slavery of any portion of the civilized world. We only contend for slavery in certain cases; in opposition to the thesis of the abolitionist, we assert that it is not always and everywhere wrong. For the truth of this assertion we rely upon the express authority of God himself. We affirm that since slavery has been ordained by him, it cannot be always and everywhere wrong. And how does the abolitionist attempt to meet this reply? Why, by a little legerdemain, he converts this reply from an argument against his position, that slavery is always and everywhere wrong, into an argument in favor of the monstrous dogma that it is always and everywhere right! If we should contend that, in some cases, it is right to take the life of a man, he might just as fairly insist that we are in favor of having every man on earth put to death! Was any fallacy ever more glaring? was any misrepresentation ever more flagrant?

Indeed we should have supposed that Dr. Wayland might have seen that his representation is not a fair one, if he had not assured us of the contrary. We should have supposed that he might have distinguished between an argument in favor of slavery for the lowest grade of the ignorant and debased, and an argument in favor of slavery for all men and all times, if he had not assured us that he possesses no capacity to make it. For after having twisted the plea of the most enlightened statesmen of the South into an argument in favor of the universal subjection of mankind to slavery, he coolly adds, "I believe that in these words I express the argument correctly. If I do not, it is solely because I do not know how to state it more correctly." Is it possible Dr. Wayland could not distinguish between the principle of slavery for some men and the principle of slavery for all men? between the proposition that the ignorant, the idle, and the debased may be subjected to servitude, and the idea that all men, even the most enlightened and free, may be reduced to bondage? If he had not positively declared that he possessed no such capacity, we should most certainly have entertained a different opinion.

It will not be denied, we presume, that the very best men, whose lives are recorded in the Old Testament, were the owners and holders of slaves. "I grant at once," says Dr. Way-

land, "that the Hebrews held slaves from the
time of the conquest of Canaan, and that Abraham and the patriarchs held them many centuries before. I grant also that Moses enacted
laws with special reference to that relation. . . . .
I wonder that any should have had the hardihood to deny so plain a matter of record. I
should almost as soon deny the delivery of the
ten commandments to Moses."

Now, is it not wonderful that directly in
the face of "so plain a matter of record," a
pious Presbyterian pastor should have been
arraigned by abolitionists, not for holding
slaves, but for daring to be so far a freeman
as to express his convictions on the subject of
slavery? Most abolitionists must have found
themselves a little embarrassed in such a proceeding. For *there* was the fact, staring them
in the face, that Abraham himself, "the friend
of God" and the "father of the faithful," was
the owner and holder of more than a thousand
slaves. How, then, could these professing
Christians proceed to condemn and excommu-
nicate a poor brother for having merely approved what Abraham had practised? Of all
the good men of old, Abraham was the most
eminent. The sublimity of his faith and the

fervor of his piety has, by the unerring voice of inspiration itself, been held up as a model for the imitation of all future ages. How, then, could a parcel of poor common saints presume, without blushing, to try and condemn one of their number because he was no better than "Father Abraham?" This was the difficulty; and, but for a very happy discovery, it must have been an exceedingly perplexing one. But "Necessity is the mother of invention." On this trying occasion she conceived the happy thought that the plain matter of record "was all a mistake;" that Abraham never owned a slave; that, on the contrary, he was "a prince," and the "men whom he bought with his money" were "his subjects" merely! If, then, we poor sinners of the South should be driven to the utmost extremity,—all honest arguments and pleas failing us,—may we not escape the unutterable horrors of civil war, by calling our masters princes, and our slaves subjects?

We shall conclude this topic with the pointed and powerful words of Dr. Fuller, in his reply to Dr. Wayland: "Abraham," says he, "was 'the friend of God,' and walked with God in the closest and most endearing intercourse; nor can any thing be more exquisitely touching than those words, 'Shall I hide from Abraham that thing which I do?' It is the language of a friend who feels that concealment would wrong the confidential intimacy existing. The love of this venerable servant of God in his promptness to immolate his son has been the theme of apostles and preachers for ages; and such was his faith, that all who believe are called 'the children of faithful Abraham.' This Abraham, you admit, held slaves. Who is surprised that Whitefield, with this single fact before him, could not believe slavery to be a sin? Yet if your definition of slavery be correct, holy Abraham lived all his life in the commission of one of the most aggravated crimes against God and man which can be conceived. His life was spent in outraging the rights of hundreds of human beings, as moral, intellectual, immortal, fallen creatures, and in violating their relations as parents and children, and husbands and wives. And God not only connived at this appalling iniquity, but, in the covenant of circumcision made with Abraham, expressly mentions it, and confirms the patriarch in it, speaking of those 'bought with his money,' and requiring him to circumcise them.

Why, at the very first blush, every Christian will cry out against this statement. To this, however, you must come, or yield your position; and this is only the first utterly incredible and monstrous corollary involved in the assertion that slavery is essentially and always 'a sin of appalling magnitude.'"

Slavery among the Hebrews, however, was not left merely to a tacit or implied sanction. It was thus sanctioned by the express legislation of the Most High: "Both thy bondmen and thy bondmaids, which thou shalt have, shall be of the heathen that are round about you; of them shall ye buy bondmen and bondmaids. Moreover, of the children of the strangers that do sojourn among you, of them shall ye buy, and of their families that are with you, which they begat in your land; and they shall be your possession. And ye shall take them as an inheritance for your children after you, to inherit them for a possession; they shall be your bondmen forever."* Now these words are so perfectly explicit, that there is no getting around them. Even Dr. Wayland, as we have seen, admits that the authority to take slaves *seems*

---

* Lev. xxv. 44, 45, 46.

to be a part of "this original, peculiar," and perhaps "anomalous grant." No wonder it appeared *peculiar* and *anomalous*. The only wonder is, that it did not appear impious and absurd. So it has appeared to some of his co-agitators, who, because they could not agree with Moses, have denied his mission as an inspired teacher, and joined the ranks of infidelity.

Dr. Channing makes very light of this and other passages of Scripture. He sets aside this whole argument from revelation with a few bold strokes of the pen. "In this age of the world," says he, "and amid the light which has been thrown on the true interpretation of the Scriptures, such reasoning hardly deserves notice." Now, even if not for our benefit, we think there are two reasons why such passages as the above were worthy of Dr. Channing's notice. In the first place, if he had condescended to throw the light in his possession on such passages, he might have saved Dr. Wayland, as well as other of his admirers, from the necessity of making the very awkward admission that the Almighty had authorized his chosen people to buy slaves, and hold them as "bondmen forever." He might have enabled them to see through the great difficulty, that God has authorized his people to commit "a sin of appalling magnitude," to perpetrate as "great a crime as can be conceived;" which seems so clearly to be the case, if their views of slavery be correct. Secondly, he might have enabled his followers to espouse the cause of abolition without deserting, as so many of them have openly done, the armies of the living God. For these two reasons, if for no other, we think Dr. Channing owed it to the honor of his cause to notice the passages of Scripture bearing on the subject of slavery.

The Mosaic Institutes not only recognise slavery as lawful; they contain a multitude of minute directions for its regulation. We need not refer to all of them; it will be sufficient for our purpose if we only notice those which establish some of the leading characteristics of slavery among the people of God.

1. Slaves were regarded as property. They were, as we have seen, called a "possession" and an "inheritance."* They were even called the "money" of the master. Thus, it is said, "if a man smite his servant or his

---

* Lev. xxv. 44, 45, 46.

maid with a rod, and he die under his hand, he shall surely be punished. Notwithstanding, if he continue a day or two, he shall not be punished, for he is his money."* In one of the ten commandments this right of property is recognised: "Thou shalt not covet thy neighbor's house, thou shalt not covet thy neighbor's wife, nor *his* man-servant, nor *his* maid-servant, nor his ox, nor his ass, nor any thing that is thy neighbor's."

2. They might be sold. This is taken for granted in all those passages in which, for particular reasons, the master is forbidden to sell his slaves. Thus it is declared: "Thou shalt not make merchandise of her, because thou hast humbled her." And still more explicitly: "If a man sell his daughter to be a maid-servant, she shall not go out as the men-servants do. If she please not her master who hath betrothed her to himself, then shall he let her be redeemed: to sell her to a strange nation, he shall have no power, seeing he hath dealt deceitfully with her."†

3. The slavery thus expressly sanctioned was hereditary and perpetual: "Ye shall take them

---

* Exod. xxi. 20, 21.   † Exod. xxi. 7, 8.

as an inheritance for your children after you, to inherit them for a possession; they shall be your bondmen forever." Even the Hebrew servant might, by his own consent, become in certain cases a slave for life: "If thou buy a Hebrew servant, six years shall he serve; and in the seventh shall he go out free for nothing. If he came in by himself, he shall go out by himself: if he were married, then his wife shall go out with him. If his master have given him a wife, and she have borne him sons or daughters, the wife and the children shall be her master's, and he shall go out by himself. And if the servant shall plainly say, I love my master, my wife, and my children; I will not go out free: then his master shall bring him unto the judges: he shall also bring him to the door or unto the door-post, and his master shall bore his ear through with an awl, and *he shall serve him forever.*"

Now it is evident, we think, that the legislator of the Hebrews was not inspired with the sentiments of an abolitionist. The principles of his legislation are, indeed, so diametrically opposed to the political notions of the abolitionist, that the latter is sadly perplexed to dispose of them. While some deny

13*

the authority of these principles altogether, and of the very book which contains them, others are content to evade their force by certain ingenious devices of their own. We shall now proceed to examine some of the more remarkable of these cunningly-devised fables.

It is admitted by the inventors of these devices, that God expressly permitted his chosen people to buy and hold slaves. Yet Dr. Wayland, by whom this admission is made, has endeavored to weaken the force of it by alleging that God has been pleased to enlighten our race progressively. If, he argues, the institution of slavery among His people appears so very "peculiar and anomalous," this is because he did not choose to make known his whole mind on the subject. He withheld a portion of it from his people, and allowed them, by express grant, to hold slaves until the fuller revelation of his will should blaze upon the world. Such is, perhaps, the most plausible defence which an abolitionist could possibly set up against the light of revelation.

But to what does it amount? If the views of Dr. Wayland and his followers, respecting slavery, be correct, it amounts to this: The Almighty has said to his people, you may commit "a sin of appalling magnitude;" you may perpetrate "as great an evil as can be conceived;" you may persist in a practice which consists in "outraging the rights" of your fellow-men, and in "crushing their intellectual and moral" nature. They have a natural, inherent, and inalienable right to liberty as well as yourselves, but yet you may make slaves of them, and they may be your bondmen forever. In one word, *you*, my chosen people, may degrade "rational, accountable, and immortal beings" to the "rank of brutes." Such, if we may believe Dr. Wayland, is the first stage in the divine enlightenment of the human race! It consists in making known a part of God's mind, not against the monstrous iniquity of slavery, but in its favor! It is the utterance, not of a partial truth, but of a monstrous falsehood! It is the revelation of his will, not against sin, but in favor of as great a sin "as can be conceived." Now, we may fearlessly ask if the cause which is reduced to the necessity of resorting to such a defence may not be pronounced desperate indeed, and unspeakably forlorn?

It is alleged that polygamy and divorce, as well as slavery, are permitted and regulated in the Old Testament. This, we reply, proves, in regard to polygamy and divorce, exactly what it proves in regard to slavery,—namely, that neither is in itself sinful, that neither is *always* and *everywhere* sinful. In other words, it proves that neither polygamy nor divorce, as permitted in the Old Testament, is "*malum in se*," is inconsistent with the eternal and unchangeable principles of right. They are forbidden in the New Testament, not because they are in themselves absolutely and immutably wrong, but because they are inconsistent with the best interests of society; especially in civilized and Christian communities. If they had been wrong in themselves, they never could have been permitted by a holy God, who is of purer eyes than to behold iniquity, except with infinite abhorrence.

Again, it is contended by Dr. Wayland that "Moses intended to abolish slavery," because he forbade the Jews "to deliver up a fugitive slave." The words are these: "Thou shalt not deliver unto his master the servant that is escaped from his master unto thee: He shall dwell with thee, even among you, in that place which he shall choose in one of the gates where it liketh him best: thou shalt not oppress him."*

---

* Deut. xxiii. 15,16.

"This precept, I think," says Dr. Wayland, "clearly shows that Moses intended to abolish slavery. How could slavery long continue in a country where every one was forbidden to deliver up a fugitive slave? How different would be the condition of slaves, and how soon would slavery itself cease, were this the law of compulsory bondage among us!"

The above passage of Scripture is a precious morsel with those who are opposed to a fugitive slave law. A petition from Albany, New York, from the enlightened seat of empire of the Empire State itself, signed, if we recollect right, by one hundred and fifty persons, was presented to the United States Senate by Mr. Seward, praying that no bill in relation to fugitive slaves might be passed, which should not contain that passage. Whether Mr. Seward was enlightened by his constituents, or whether he made the discovery for himself, it is certain that he holds an act for the reclamation of fugitive slaves to be "contrary to the divine law." It is certain that he agrees with his constituents, who, in the petition referred to, pronounced every such act "immoral," and contrary to the law of God. But let us look at this passage a little, and see if these abolitionists, who thus plant themselves so confidently upon "a higher law," even upon "the divine law" itself, be not as hasty and rash in their interpretation of this law as they are accustomed to be in their judgment respecting the most universal and long-established institutions of human society.

In the first place, if their interpretation be correct, we are at once met by a very serious difficulty. For we are required to believe that one passage of Scripture grants an "authority to take slaves," while another passage is designed to annul this authority. We are required to believe that, in one portion of the divine law, the right of the master to hold his slaves as "bondsmen" is recognised, while another part of the same law denies the existence of such right. In fine, we are required to believe that the legislator of the Jews intended, in one and the same code, both to establish and to abolish slavery; that with one hand he struck down the very right and institution which he had set up with the other. How Dr. Channing and Mr. Sumner would have disposed of this difficulty we know full well, for they carry within their own bosoms a higher law than this higher law itself. But how Dr. Wayland, as an enlightened member of the good old orthodox Baptist Church, with whom the Scripture is really and in truth the inspired word of God, would have disposed of it, we are at some loss to conceive.

We labor under no such difficulty. The words in question do not relate to slaves owned by Hebrew masters. They relate to those slaves only who should escape from heathen masters, and seek an asylum among the people of God. "The first inquiry of course is," says a learned divine,* "in regard to those very words, 'Where does his master live?' Among the Hebrews, or among foreigners? The language of the passage fully develops this and answers the question. 'He has escaped from his master unto the Hebrews; (the text says—*thee, i. e.* Israel;) *he shall dwell with thee, even among you . . . in one of thy gates.*' Of course, then, he is an *immigrant,* and did *not* dwell *among them* before his flight. If he had been a Hebrew servant, belonging to a Hebrew, the whole face of the thing would be changed. Restoration, or restitution, if we may judge by the tenor of other

---

* Moses Stewart, a divine of Massachusetts, who had devoted a long and laborious life to the interpretation of Scripture, and who was by no means a friend to the institution of slavery.

property-laws among the Hebrews, would have surely been enjoined. But, be that as it may, the language of the text puts it beyond a doubt that the servant is a *foreigner*, and has fled from a *heathen master*. This entirely changes the complexion of the case. The Hebrews were God's chosen people, and were the only nation on earth which worshipped the only living and true God. . . . . In case a slave escaped from them (the heathen) and came to the Hebrews, two things were to be taken into consideration, according to the views of the Jewish legislator. The first was that the treatment of slaves among the heathen was far more severe and rigorous than it could lawfully be under the Mosaic law. The heathen master possessed the power of life and death, of scourging or imprisoning, or putting to excessive toil, even to any extent that he pleased. Not so among the Hebrews. *Humanity* pleaded there for the protection of the fugitive. The second and most important consideration was, that only among the Hebrews could the fugitive slave come to the knowledge and worship of the only living and true God."

Now this view of the passage in question harmonizes one portion of Scripture with another, and removes every difficulty. It shows, too, how greatly the abolitionists have deceived themselves in their rash and blind appeal to "the divine law" in question. "The reason of the law," says my Lord Coke, "is the law." It is applicable to those cases, and to those cases only, which come within the reason of the law. Hence, if it be a fact, and if our Northern brethren really believe that we are sunk in the darkness of heathen idolatry, while the light of the true religion is with them alone, why, then, we admit that the reason and principle of the divine law in question is in their favor. Then we admit that the return of our fugitive slaves is "contrary to the divine law." But if we are not heathen idolaters, if the God of the Hebrews be also the God of Southern masters, then the Northern States do not violate the precept in question—they only discharge a solemn constitutional obligation—in delivering up our "fugitives from labor."

§ II. *The argument from the New Testament.*

The New Testament, as Dr. Wayland remarks, was given, "not to one people, but to the whole race; not for one period, but for all time." Its lessons are, therefore, of uni-

14

versal and perpetual obligation. If, then, the
Almighty had undertaken to enlighten the
human race by degrees, with respect to the
great sin of slavery, is it not wonderful that,
in the very last revelation of his will, he has
uttered not a single syllable in disapprobation
thereof? Is it not wonderful, that he should
have completed the revelation of his will,—that
he should have set his seal to the last word he
will ever say to man respecting his duties, and
yet not one word about the great obligation of
the master to emancipate his slaves, nor about
the "appalling sin" of slavery? Such silence
must, indeed, appear exceedingly peculiar and
anomalous to the abolitionist. It would have
been otherwise had he written the New Testament. He would, no doubt, have inserted at
least one little precept against the sin of
slavery.

As it is, however, the most profound silence
reigns through the whole word of God with
respect to the sinfulness of slavery. "It must
be granted," says Dr. Wayland, "that the New
Testament contains no *precept* prohibitory of
slavery." Marvellous as such silence must
needs be to the abolitionist, it cannot be more
so to him than his attempts to account for it

are to others. Let us briefly examine these attempts:

"You may give your child," says Dr. Wayland, "if he were approaching to years of discretion, permission to do an act, while you inculcate upon him principles which forbid it, for the sake of teaching him to be governed by principles, rather than by any direct enactment. In such case you would expect him to obey the principle, and not avail himself of the permission." Now we fearlessly ask every reader whose moral sense has not been perverted by false logic, if such a proceeding would not be infinitely unworthy of the Father of mercies? According to Dr. Wayland's view, he beholds his children living and dying in the practice of an abominable sin, and looks on without the slightest note of admonition or warning. Nay, he gives them permission to continue in the practice of this frightful enormity, to which they are already bound by the triple tie of habit, interest, and feeling! Though he gives them line upon line, and precept upon precept, in order to detach them from other sins, he yet gives them permission to live and die in this awful sin! And why? To teach them, forsooth, not to follow his permission, but to be

guided by his principles! Even the guilty Eli
remonstrated with his sons. Yet if, instead of
doing this, he had given them permission to
practise the very sins they were bent upon, he
might have been, for all that, as pure and
faithful as the Father of mercies himself is
represented to be in the writings of Dr. Wayland. Such are the miserable straits, and such
the impious sophisms, to which even divines
are reduced, when, on the supposition that
slavery is a sin, they undertake to vindicate or
defend the word which they themselves are
ordained to preach!

Another reason, scarcely less remarkable than
the one already noticed, is assigned for the
omission of all precepts against slavery. "It
was no part of the scheme of the gospel revelation," we are told by Dr. Wayland, (who
quotes from Archbishop Whately,) "to lay
down any thing approaching to a complete system of *moral precepts*—to enumerate every thing
that is *enjoined* or *forbidden* by our religion."
If this method of teaching had been adopted,
"the New Testament would," says Dr. Wayland, "have formed a library in itself, more
voluminous than the laws of the realm of Great
Britain." Now, all this is very true; and hence

the necessity of leaving many points of duty to the enlightened conscience, and to the application of the more general precepts of the gospel. But how has it happened that slavery is passed over in silence? Because, we are told, "every thing" could not be noticed. If, indeed, slavery be so great a sin, would it not have been easier for the divine teacher to say, Let it be abolished, than to lay down so many minute precepts for its regulation? Would this have tended to swell the gospel into a vast library, or to abridge its teachings? Surely, when Dr. Wayland sets up such a plea, he must have forgotten that the New Testament, though it cannot notice "every thing," contains a multitude of rules to regulate the conduct of the master and the slave. Otherwise he could scarcely have imagined that it was from an aversion to minuteness, or from an impossibility to forbid every evil, that the sin of slavery is passed over in silence.

He must also have forgotten another thing. He must have forgotten the colors in which he had painted the evils of slavery. If we may rely upon these, then slavery is no trifling offence. It is, on the contrary, a stupendous sin, overspreading the earth, and crushing the

L   14*

faculties—both intellectual and moral—of millions of human beings beneath its odious and terrific influence. Now, if this be so, then would it have been too much to expect that at least one little word might have been directed against so great, so tremendous an evil? The method of the gospel may be comprehensive, if you please; it may teach by great principles rather than by minute precepts. Still, it is certain that St. Paul could give directions about his cloak; and he could spend many words in private salutations. In regard to the great social evil of the age, however, and beneath which a large majority of even the civilized world were crushed to the earth, he said nothing, lest he should become too minute,—lest his epistles should swell into too large a volume! Such is one of Dr. Wayland's defences of the gospel. We shall offer no remark; we shall let it speak for itself.

A third reason for the silence in question is the alleged ease with which precepts may be evaded. "A simple precept or prohibition," says Dr. Wayland, "is, of all things, the easiest to be evaded. Lord Eldon used to say, that 'no man in England could construct an act of Parliament through which he could not drive a coach-and-four.' We find this to have been illustrated by the case of the Jews in the time of our Saviour. The Pharisees, who prided themselves on their strict obedience to the *letter*, violated the *spirit* of every precept of the Mosaic code."

Now, in reply to this most extraordinary passage, we have several remarks to offer. In the first place, perhaps every one is not so good a driver as Lord Eldon. It is certain, that acts of Parliament have been passed, through which the most slippery of rogues have not been able to make their escape. They have been caught, tried, and condemned for their offences, in spite of all their ingenuity and evasion.

Secondly, a "principle" is just as easily evaded as a "precept;" and, in most cases, it is far more so. The great principle of the New Testament, which our author deems so applicable to the subject of slavery, is this: "Thou shalt love thy neighbor as thyself." Now, if this be the great principle intended to enlighten us respecting the sin of slavery, we confess it has been most completely evaded by every slave State in the Union. We have, indeed, so entirely deceived ourselves in regard to its true import, that it seems to us to have not the most remote application to such a subject. If any one will give our remarks on this great "principle" a candid examination, we think he will admit that we have deceived ourselves on very plausible, if not on unanswerable, grounds. If slavery be a sin,—*always and everywhere* a monstrous iniquity,—then we should have been far more thoroughly enlightened with respect to its true nature, and found evasion far more difficult, if the New Testament had explicitly declared it to be such, and commanded all masters everywhere to emancipate their slaves. We could have driven a coach-and-four neither through, nor around, any such express prohibition. It is indeed only in consequence of the default, or omission, of such precept or command, that the abolitionist appeals to what he calls the principles of the gospel. If he had only one such precept,—if he had only one such precise and pointed prohibition, he might then, and he *would*, most triumphantly defy evasion. He would say, There is *the word;* and none but the obstinate gainsayers, or unbelievers, would dare reply. But as it is, he is compelled to lose himself in vague generalities, and pretend to a certainty which nowhere exists, except in his own heated mind. This pretence, indeed, that an express precept, prohibitory of slavery, is not the most direct way to reveal its true nature, because a precept is so much more easily evaded than a principle, is merely one of the desperate expedients of a forlorn and hopeless cause. If the abolitionist would maintain that cause, or vindicate his principles, it will be found that he must retire, and hide himself from the light of revelation.

Thirdly, the above passage seems to present a very strange view of the Divine proceedings. According to that view, it appears that the Almighty tried the method of teaching by precept in the Old Testament, and the experiment failed. For precepts may be so easily evaded, that every one in the Mosaic code was violated by the Pharisees. Hence, the method of teaching by precept was laid aside in the New Testament, and the better method of teaching by principle was adopted. Such is the conclusion to which we must come, if we adopt the reasoning of Dr. Wayland. But we cannot adopt his reasoning; since we should then have to believe that the experiment made in the Old Testament proved a failure, and that its Divine Author, having grown wiser by experience, improved upon his former method.

The truth is, that the method of the one Testament is the same as that of the other. In both, the method of teaching by precept is adopted; by precepts of greater and of lesser generality. Dr. Wayland's principle is merely a general or comprehensive precept; and his precept is merely a specific or limited principle. The distinction he makes between them, and the use he makes of this distinction, only reflect discredit upon the wisdom and consistency of the Divine Author of revelation.

A third account which Dr. Wayland gives of the silence of the New Testament respecting the sin of slavery, is as follows: "If this form of wrong had been singled out from all the others, and had alone been treated preceptively, the whole system would have been vitiated. We should have been authorized to inquire why were not similar precepts in other cases delivered? and if they were not delivered, we should have been at liberty to conclude that they were intentionally omitted, and that the acts which they would have forbidden are innocent." Very well. But idolatry, polygamy, divorce, is each and every one singled out, and forbidden by precept, in the New Testament. Slavery alone is passed over in silence. Hence, according to the principle of Dr. Wayland himself, we are at liberty to conclude that a precept forbidding slavery was "intentionally omitted," and that slavery itself "is innocent."

Each one of these reasons is not only exceedingly weak in itself, but it is inconsistent with the others. For if a precept forbidding slavery were purposely omitted, in order to teach mankind to be governed by principle and to disregard permissions, then the omission could not have arisen from a love of brevity. Were it not, indeed, just as easy to give a precept forbidding, as to give one permitting, the existence of slavery? Again, if a great and world-devouring sin, such as the abolitionists hold slavery to be, has been left unnoticed, lest its condemnation should impliedly sanction other sins, then is it not worse than puerile to suppose that the omission was made for the sake of brevity, or to teach mankind that the permissions of the Most High may in certain cases be treated with contempt, may be set at naught, and despised as utterly inconsistent, as diametrically opposed to the principles and purity of his law?

If the abolitionist is so completely lost in his attempts to meet the argument from the silence of Scripture, he finds it still more difficult to cope with that from its express precepts and injunctions. *Servants, obey your masters*, is one of the most explicit precepts of the New Testament. This precept just as certainly exists therein as does the great principle of love itself. "The obedience thus enjoined is placed," says Dr. Wayland, "not on the ground of duty to man, but on the ground of duty to God." We accept the interpretation. It cannot for one moment disturb the line of our argument. It is merely the shadow of an attempt at an evasion. All the obligations of the New Testament are, indeed, placed on the same high ground. The obligation of the slave to obey his master could be placed upon no higher, no more sacred, no more impregnable, ground.

Rights and obligations are correlative. That is, every right implies a corresponding obligation, and every obligation implies a corresponding right. Hence, as the slave is under an obligation to obey the master, so the master has a right to his obedience. Nor is this obligation weakened, or this right disturbed, by the fact that the first is imposed by the word of God, and rests on the immutable ground of duty to him. If, by the divine law, the obedience of the slave is due to the master, then, by the same law, the master has a right to his obedience.

Most assuredly, the master is neither "a robber," nor "a murderer," nor "a manstealer," merely because he claims of the slave that which God himself commands the slave to render. All these epithets may be, as they have been, hurled at us by the abolitionist. His anathemas may thunder. But it is some consolation to reflect, that, as he was not consulted in the construction of the moral code of the universe, so, it is to be hoped, he will not be called upon to take part in its execution.

The most enlightened abolitionists are sadly puzzled by the precept in question; and, from the manner in which they sometimes speak of it, we have reason to fear it holds no very high place in their respect. Thus, says the Hon. Charles Sumner, "Seeking to be brief, I shall not undertake to reconcile texts of the Old Testament, which, whatever may be their import, are all absorbed in the New; nor shall I stop to consider the precise interpretation of the oft-quoted phrase, *Servants, obey your masters;* nor seek to weigh any such imperfect injunction in the scales against those grand commandments on which hang all the law and the prophets."* Now this is a very significant passage. The orator, its learned author, will not stop to consider the texts of the Old Testament bearing on the subject of slavery, because they are all merged in the New! Nor will he stop to consider any "such *imperfect injunction*" as those contained in the New, because they are all swallowed up and lost in the grand commandment, "Thou shalt love thy neighbor as thyself!"

If he had bestowed a little more attention on this grand commandment itself, he might have seen, as we have shown, that it in no wise conflicts with the precept which enjoins servants to obey their masters. He might have seen that it is not at all necessary to "weigh" the one of those precepts "in the scales against" the other, or to brand either of them as imperfect. For he might have seen a perfect harmony between them. It is no matter of surprise, however, that an abolitionist should find imperfections in the moral code of the New Testament.

It is certainly no wonder that Mr. Sumner

* Speech in the Metropolitan Theatre, 1855.

should have seen imperfections therein. For he has, in direct opposition to the plainest terms of the gospel, discovered that it is the first duty of the slave to fly from his master. In his speech delivered in the Senate of the United States, we find among various other quotations, a verse from Sarah W. Morton, in which she exhorts the slave to fly from bondage. Having produced this quotation "as part of the testimony of the times," and pronounced it "a truthful homage to the inalienable rights" of the slave, Mr. Sumner was in no mood to appreciate the divine precept, "Servants, obey your masters." Having declared fugitive slaves to be "the heroes of the age," he had not, as we may suppose, any very decided taste for the commonplace Scriptural duties of submission and obedience. Nay, he spurns at and rejects such duties as utterly inconsistent with the "inalienable rights of man." He appeals from the oracles of eternal truth to "the testimony of the times." He appeals from Christ and his apostles to Sarah W. Morton. And yet, although he thus takes ground directly against the plainest precepts of the gospel, and even ventures to brand some of them as "imperfect," he has the hardihood to rebuke those who find therein, not what it really contains, but only a reflection of themselves!

The precept in question is not an isolated injunction of the New Testament. It does not stand alone. It is surrounded by other injunctions, equally authoritative, equally explicit, equally unequivocal. Thus, in Eph. vi. 5: "Servants, be obedient to them that are your masters according to the flesh." Precisely the same doctrine was preached to the Colossians: (iii. 22:) "Servants, obey in all things your masters according to the flesh; not with eye-service, as men-pleasers, but in singleness of heart, fearing God." Again, in St. Paul's Epistle to Timothy, he writes: "Let as many servants as are under the yoke count their own masters worthy of all honor, that the name of God and his doctrine be not blasphemed." Likewise, in Tit. ii. 9, 10, we read: "Exhort servants to be obedient to their own masters, and to please them well in all things; not answering again; not purloining, but showing all good fidelity, that they may adorn the doctrine of God our Saviour in all things." And in 1 Pet. ii. 18, it is written: "Servants, be subject to your masters with all fear; not only to the good and gentle, but also to the froward." Yet, in the face of these passages, Mr. Sumner declares that it is the duty of slaves to fly from bondage, and thereby place themselves among " the heroes of the age." He does not attempt to interpret or explain these precepts; he merely sets them aside, or passes them by with silent contempt, as " imperfect." Indeed, if his doctrines be true, they are not only imperfect—they are radically wrong and infamously vicious. Thus, the issue which Mr. Sumner has made up is not with the slaveholders of the South; it is with the word of God itself. The contradiction is direct, plain, palpable, and without even the decency of a pretended disguise. We shall leave Mr. Sumner to settle this issue and controversy with the Divine Author of revelation.

In the mean time, we shall barely remind the reader of what that Divine Author has said in regard to those who counsel and advise slaves to disobey their masters, or fly from bondage. " They that have believing masters," says the great Apostle to the Gentiles, " let them not despise them because they are brethren; but rather do them service, because they are faithful and beloved, partakers of the benefit.

15*

These things teach and exhort. If any man teach otherwise, and consent not to wholesome words, even the words of our Lord Jesus Christ, and to the doctrine which is according to godliness, *he is proud, knowing nothing.*" Mr. Sumner congratulates himself that he has stripped "from slavery the apology of Christianity." Let servants "count their own masters worthy of all honor," and "do them service," says St. Paul. "Let servants disobey their masters," says Mr. Sumner, "and cease to do them service." "These things teach and exhort," says St. Paul. "These things denounce and abhor," says Mr. Sumner. "If any man teach otherwise," says St. Paul, "he is proud, knowing nothing." "I teach otherwise," says Mr. Sumner. And is it by such conflict that he strips from slavery the sanction of Christianity? If the sheer *ipse dixit* of Mr. Sumner be sufficient to annihilate the authority of the New Testament, which he professes to revere as divine, then, indeed, has he stripped the sanction of Christianity from the relation of master and slave. Otherwise, he has not even stripped from his own doctrines the burning words of her condemnation.

Dr. Wayland avoids a direct conflict with the

teachings of the gospel. He is less bold, and more circumspect, than the Senator from Massachusetts. He has honestly and fairly quoted most of the texts bearing on the subject of slavery. He shows them no disrespect. He pronounces none of them imperfect. But with this array of texts before him he proceeds to say: "Now, I do not see that the scope of these passages can be misunderstood." Nor can we. It would seem, indeed, impossible for the ingenuity of man to misunderstand the words, quoted by Dr. Wayland himself, "Servants, *obey* in all things your masters according to the flesh." Dr. Wayland does not misunderstand them. For he has said, in his Moral Science: "The *duty of slaves* is explicitly made known in the Bible. They are bound to obedience, fidelity, submission, and respect to their masters, not only to the good and kind, but also to the unkind and froward." But when he comes to reason about these words, which he finds it so impossible for any one to misunderstand, he is not without a very ingenious method to evade their plain import and to escape from their influence. Let the reader hear, and determine for himself.

"I do not see," says Dr. Wayland, "that the

scope of these passages can be misunderstood. They teach patience, meekness, fidelity, and charity—duties which are obligatory on Christians toward all men, and, of course, toward masters. These duties are obligatory on us toward enemies, because an enemy, like every other man, is a moral creature of God." True. But is this all? Patience, meekness, fidelity, charity—duties due to all men! But what has become of the word *obedience?* This occupies a prominent—nay, the most prominent—place in the teachings of St. Paul. It occupies no place at all in the reasonings of Dr. Wayland. It is simply dropped out by him, or overlooked; and this was well done, for this word *obedience* is an exceedingly inconvenient one for the abolitionist. If Dr. Wayland had retained it in his argument, he could not have added, "duties which are obligatory on Christians toward all men, and, of course, toward masters." Christians are not bound to obey all men. But slaves are bound to obey "their own masters." It is precisely upon this injunction to obedience that the whole argument turns. And it is precisely this injunction to obedience which Dr. Wayland leaves out in his argument. He does not, and he cannot, misunderstand the word.

But he can just drop it out, and, in consequence, proceed to argue as if nothing more were required of slaves than is required of all Christian men!

The only portion of Scripture which Mr. Sumner condescends to notice is the Epistle of St. Paul to Philemon. He introduces the discussion of this epistle with the remark that, "In the support of slavery, it is the habit to pervert texts and to invent authority. Even St. Paul is vouched for a wrong which his Christian life rebukes."* Now we intend to examine who it is that really perverts texts of Scripture, and invents authority. We intend to show, as in the clear light of noonday, that it is the conduct of Mr. Sumner and other abolitionists, and not that of the slaveholder, which is rebuked by the life and writings of the great apostle.

The epistle in question was written to a slaveholder, who, if the doctrine of Mr. Sumner be true, lived in the habitual practice of "a wrong so transcendent, so loathsome, so direful," that it "must be encountered *wherever it can be reached*, and the battle must be continued, without truce or compromise, until the field is en-

---

* Speech at the Metropolitan Theatre, 1855.

M

tirely won." Is there any thing like this in
the Epistle to Philemon? Is there any thing
like it in any of the epistles of St. Paul? Is
there anywhere in his writings the slightest
hint that slavery is a sin at all, or that the act
of holding slaves is in the least degree inconsistent with the most exalted Christian purity
of life? We may safely answer these questions
in the negative. The very epistle before us is
from "Paul, a prisoner of Jesus Christ, and
Timothy our brother, unto Philemon, *our dearly-
beloved, and fellow-laborer*." The inspired writer
then proceeds in these words: "I thank my
God, making mention of thee always in my
prayers. Hearing of thy love and faith, which
thou hast toward the Lord Jesus, and toward
all saints; that the communication of thy faith
may become effectual by the acknowledging
of every good thing which is in you in Christ
Jesus. For we have great joy and consolation
in thy love, because the bowels of the saints are
refreshed by thee, brother."

Now if, instead of leaving out this portion
of the epistle, Mr. Sumner had pronounced it
in the hearing of his audience, the suspicion
might have arisen in some of their minds that
the slaveholder may not, after all, be so vile a

wretch. It might even have occurred to some, perhaps, that the Christian character of Philemon, the slaveholder, might possibly have been as good as that of those by whom all slaveholders are excommunicated and consigned to perdition. It might have been supposed that a Christian man may possibly hold slaves without being as bad as robbers, or cut-throats, or murderers. We do not say that Mr. Sumner shrunk from the reading of this portion of the epistle in the hearing of his audience, lest it should seem to rebuke the violence and the uncharitableness of his own sentiments, as well as those of his brother abolitionists at the North. We do say, however, that Mr. Sumner had no sort of use for this passage. It could in no way favor the impression his oration was designed to make. It breathes, indeed, a spirit of goodwill toward the Christian master as different from that which pervades the speeches of the honorable Senator, as the pure charity of heaven is from the dire malignity of earth.

"It might be shown," says Mr. Sumner, "that the present epistle, when truly interpreted, is a protest against slavery, and a voice for freedom." If, instead of merely asserting that this "might be done," the accomplished orator had actually done it, he would have achieved far more for the cause of abolitionism than has been effected by all the splendors of his showy rhetoric. He has, indeed, as we shall presently see, made some attempt to show that the Epistle to Philemon is an emancipation document! When we come to examine this most extraordinary attempt, we shall perceive that Mr. Sumner's power "to pervert texts and to invent authority," has not been wholly held in reserve for what "might be done." If his view of this portion of Scripture be not very profound, it certainly makes up in originality what it lacks in depth. If it should fail to instruct, it will at least amuse the reader. It shall be noticed in due time.

The next point that claims our attention is the intimation that St. Paul's "real judgment of slavery" may be inferred "from his condemnation, on another occasion, of 'manstealers,' or, according to the original text, slave-traders, in company with murderers of fathers and murderers of mothers." Were we disposed to enter into the exegesis of the passage thus referred to, we might easily show that Mr. Sumner is grossly at fault in his Greek. We might show that something far more enormous than even trading in slaves is aimed at by the condemna-

tion of the apostle. But we have not undertaken to defend "manstealers," nor "slave-
traders," in any form or shape. Hence, we
shall dismiss this point with the opinion of
Macknight, who thinks the persons thus condemned in company with murderers of fathers
and mothers, are "they who make war for the
inhuman purpose of selling the vanquished as
slaves, as is the practice of the African princes."
To take any free man, whether white or black,
by force, and sell him into bondage, is man-
stealing. To make war for such a purpose,
were, we admit, wholesale murder and man-
stealing combined. This view of the passage
in question agrees with that of the great abolitionist, Mr. Barnes, who holds that "the *essential*
idea of the term" in question, "is *that of convert-
ing a free man into a slave*" .... the "changing
of a freeman into a slave, especially by traffic,
subjection, &c." Now, as we of the South,
against whom Mr. Sumner is pleased to inveigh,
propose to make no such changes of freemen
into slaves, much less to wage war for any such
purpose, we may dismiss his gross perversion
of the text in question. He may apply the
condemnation of the apostle to us now, if it so
please the benignity of his Christian charity,

16

but it will not, we assure him, enter into our consciences, until we shall not only become "slave-traders," but also, with a view to the gain of such odious traffic, make war upon freemen.

We have undertaken to defend, as we have said, neither "slave-traders," nor "mansteaters." We leave them both to the tender mercies of Mr. Sumner. But we have undertaken to defend slavery, that is, *the* slavery of the South, and to vindicate the character of Southern masters against the aspersions of their calumniators. And in this vindication we shrink not from St. Paul's "real judgment of slavery." Nay, we desire, above all things, to have his real judgment. His judgment, we mean, not of mansteaters or of murderers, but of slavery and slaveholders. We have just seen "his real judgment" respecting the character of one slaveholder. We have seen it in the very epistle Mr. Sumner is discussing. Why, then, does he fly from St. Paul's opinion of the slaveholder to what he has said of the manstealer and the murderer? We would gather an author's opinion of slavery from what he has said of slavery itself, or of the slaveholder. But this does not seem to suit Mr. Sumner's purpose quite so well.

Entirely disregarding the apostle's opinion of the slaveholder contained in the passage right before him, as well as elsewhere, Mr. Sumner infers his "real judgment of slavery" from what he has said of mansteelers and murderers! He might just as well have inferred St. Paul's opinion of Philemon from what he has, "on another occasion," said of Judas Iscariot.

Mr. Sumner contents himself with "calling attention to two things, apparent on the face" of the epistle itself; and which, in his opinion, are "in themselves an all-sufficient response." The first of these things is, says he: "While it appears that Onesimus had been in some way the servant of Philemon, it does not appear that he had ever been held as a slave, much less as a chattel." It does not appear that Onesimus was the slave of Philemon, is the position of the celebrated senatorial abolitionist. We cannot argue this position with him, however, since he has not deigned to give any reasons for it, but chosen to let it rest upon his assertion merely. We shall, therefore, have to argue the point with Mr. Albert Barnes, and other abolitionists, who have been pleased to attempt to bolster up so novel, so original, and so bold an interpretation of Scripture with exegetical reasons and arguments.

In looking into these reasons and arguments,—if reasons and arguments they may be called,—we are at a loss to conceive on what principle their authors have proceeded. The most plausible conjecture we can make is, that it was deemed sufficient to show that it is possible, by a bold stroke of interpretation, to call in question the fact that Onesimus was the slave of Philemon; since, if this may only be questioned by the learned, then the unlearned need not trouble themselves with the Scripture, but simply proceed with the work of abolitionism. Then may they cry, "Who shall decide when doctors disagree?"* and give all such disputings to the wind. Such seems to us to have been the principle on which the assertion of Mr. Sumner and Mr. Barnes has proceeded; evincing, as it does, an utter, total, and reckless disregard of the plainest teachings of inspiration. But let the candid reader hear, and then determine for himself.

---

* Fools may hope to escape responsibility by such a cry. But if there be any truth in moral science, then every man should examine and decide, or else forbear to act.

The Greek word δοῦλος, applied to Onesimus, means, according to Mr. Barnes, either a slave, or a hired servant, or an apprentice. It is not denied that it means a *slave*. "The word," says Mr. Barnes himself, "is that which is commonly applied to a slave." Indeed, to assert that the Greek word δοῦλος does not mean *slave*, were only a little less glaringly absurd than to affirm that no such meaning belongs to the English term *slave* itself. If it were necessary, this point might be most fully, clearly, and conclusively established; but since it is not denied, no such work of supererogation is required at our hands.

But it is insisted, that the word in question has a more extensive signification than the English term *slave*. "Thus," says Mr. Barnes, "it is so extensive in its signification as to be applicable to any species of servitude, whether voluntary or involuntary." Again: "All that is necessarily implied by it is, that he was, in some way, the servant of Philemon — whether *hired or bought cannot be shown.*" Once more, he says: "The word denotes *servant* of any kind, and it should never be assumed that those to whom it was applied were slaves." Thus, according to Mr. Barnes, the word in question denotes a slave, or a hired servant, or, as he has elsewhere said, an apprentice. It denotes "servant of *any* kind," whether "voluntary or involuntary."

Such is the positive assertion of Mr. Barnes. But where is the proof? Where is the authority on which it rests? Surely, if this word is applied to hired servants, either in the Greek classics or in the New Testament, Mr. Barnes, or Mr. Sumner, or some other learned abolitionist, should refer us to the passage where it is so used. We have Mr. Barnes' assertion, again and again repeated, in his very elaborate Notes on the Epistle to Philemon; but not the shadow of an authority for any such use of the word. But stop: in making this assertion, he refers us to his "Notes on Eph. vi. 5, and 1 Tim. vi." Perhaps we may find his authority by the help of one of these references. We turn, then, to Eph. vi. 5; and we find the following note: "Servants. *Oἱ δοῦλοι.* The word here used denotes one who is bound to render service to another, whether that service be free or voluntary, and may denote, therefore, either a slave, or one who binds himself to render service to another. *It is often used in these senses in the New Testa-*

ment, just as it is elsewhere."* Why, then, if
it is so often used to denote a hired servant, or
an apprentice, or a voluntary servant of any
kind, in the New Testament, is not at least one
such instance of its use produced by Mr.
Barnes? He must have been aware that one
such authority from the New Testament were
worth more than his bare assertion, though it
were a hundred times repeated. Yet no such
authority is adduced or referred to; he merely
supports his assertion in the one place by his
assertion in the other!

Let us look, in the next place, to his other
reference, which is to 1 Tim. vi. 1. Here,
again, we find not the shadow of an authority that the word in question is applicable to
"hired servants," or "apprentices." We simply meet the oft-repeated assertion of the
author, that it is applicable to *any* species of
servitude. He refers from assertion to assertion, and nowhere gives a single authority to
the point in question. If we may believe him,
such authorities are abundant, even in the
New Testament; yet he leaves the whole matter to rest upon his own naked assertion!

---

* The Italics are ours.

Yea, as Greek scholars, he would have us to believe that δοῦλος may mean a "hired servant," just as well as a slave; and he would have us to believe this, too, not upon the usage of Greek writers, but upon his mere assertion! We look for other evidence; and we intend to pin him down to proof, ere we follow him in questions of such momentous import as the one we have in hand.

Why is it, then, we ask the candid reader, if the term in question mean "a hired servant," as well as a slave, that no such application of the word is given? If such applications be as abundant as our author asserts they are, why not refer us to a single instance, that our utter ignorance may be at least relieved by one little ray of light? Why refer us from assertion to assertion, if authorities may be so plentifully had? We cannot conceive, unless the object be to deceive the unwary, or those who may be willingly deceived. An assertion merely, bolstered up with a "See note," here or there, may be enough for such; but if, after all, there be nothing but assertion on assertion piled, we shall not let it pass for proof. Especially, if such assertion be at war with truth, we shall track its author, and, if possible, efface his footprints from the immaculate word of God.

If the term δοῦλος signifies "a hired servant," or "an apprentice," it is certainly a most extraordinary circumstance that the best lexicographers of the Greek language have not made the discovery. This were the more wonderful, if, as Mr. Barnes asserts, the word "is often used in these senses" by Greek writers. We have several Greek lexicons before us, and in not one of them is there any such meaning given to the word. Thus, in Donnegan, for example, we find: "δοῦλος, a slave, a servant, as opposed to δεσποτης, a master." But we do not find from him that it is ever applied to hired servants or apprentices. In like manner, Liddell and Scott have "δοῦλος, a *slave*, *bondman*, strictly one born so, opposed to ανδραποδον." But they do not lay down "a hired servant," or "an apprentice," as one of its significations. If such, indeed, be found among the meanings of the word, these celebrated lexicographers were as ignorant of the fact as ourselves. Stephens also, as any one may see by referring to his "Thesaurus, Ling. Græc., Tom I. art. Δοῦλος," was equally ignorant of any such use of the term in question. Is it not a pity, then, that, since such knowledge rested with Mr. Barnes, and since, according to his own statement, proofs of its accuracy were so abundant, he should have withheld all the evidence in his possession, and left so important a point to stand or fall with his bare assertion? Even if the rights of mankind had not been in question, the interests of Greek literature were, one would think, sufficient to have induced him to enlighten our best lexicographers with respect to the use of the word under consideration. Such an achievement would, we can assure him, have detracted nothing from his reputation for scholarship.

But how stands the word in the New Testament? It is certain that, however "often it may be applied" to hired servants in the New Testament, Mr. Barnes has not condescended to adduce a single application of the kind. This is not all. Those who have examined every text of the New Testament in which the word δοῦλος occurs, and compiled lexicons especially for the elucidation of the sacred volume, have found no such instance of its application.

Thus, Schleusner, in his Lexicon of the New Testament, tells us that it means slave as opposed to ελευθερος, *freeman*. His own words are: "*Δοῦλος, ου, ὁ*, (1) proprie: *servus, minister, homo*

non liber nec sui juris, et opponitur τῷ ελευθερος.
Matt. viii. 9; xiii. 27, 28; 1 Cor. vii. 21, 22; xii.
13; εἴτε δοῦλοι, εἴτε ἐλεύθεροι. Tit. ii. 9."

We next appeal to Robinson's Lexicon of the
New Testament. We there find these words:
"δοῦλος, ου, ὁ, *a bondman, slave, servant, pr. by
birth;* diff. from ανδραποδον, 'one enslaved in
war,' comp. Xen. An., iv. 1, 12," &c. Now if, as
Mr. Barnes asserts, the word in question is so
often applied to hired servants in the New Testament, is it not passing strange that neither
Schleusner nor Robinson should have discovered any such application of it? So far, indeed, is Dr. Robinson from having made any
such discovery, that he expressly declares that
the δοῦλος "WAS NEVER A HIRED SERVANT; *the
latter being called* μισθιος, μισθωτος." "In a family," continues the same high authority, "the
δοῦλος was *bound to serve, a slave,* and was the
property of his master, 'a living possession,' as
Aristotle calls him."

"The Greek δοῦλος," says Dr. Smith, in his
Dictionary of Antiquities, "like the Latin *servus,*
corresponds to the usual meaning of our word
slave. . . . . Aristotle (Polit. i. 3.) says that a complete household is that which consists of slaves and
freemen; (οἰκία δὲ τέλειος εκ δουλων καὶ ελευθερων,)

and he defines a slave to be a living working-tool
and possession. (῾Ο δοῦλος ἔμψυχον ὄργανον, Ethic.
Nicim. viii. 13; ὁ δοῦλος κτῆμα τι ἐμψυχον, Pol. i.
4.) Thus Aristotle himself defines the δοῦλος
to be, not a "servant of any kind," but a slave;
and we presume that he understood the force
of this Greek word at least as well as Mr.
Barnes or Mr. Sumner. And Dr. Robinson,
as we have just seen, declares that it never
means a hired servant.

Indeed, all this is so well understood by Greek
scholars, that Dr. Macknight does not hesitate
to render the term δοῦλος, applied to Onesimus in
the Epistle to Philemon, by the English word
slave. He has not even added a footnote, as
is customary with him when he deems any
other translation of a word than that given by
himself at all worthy of notice. In like manner, Moses Stuart just proceeds to call Onesimus
"the slave of Philemon," as if there could be
no ground for doubt on so plain a point. Such
is the testimony of these two great Biblical
critics, who devoted their lives in great measure
to the study of the language, literature, and
interpretation of the Epistles of the New Testament.

Now, it should be observed, that not one of

the authorities quoted by us had any motive "to pervert texts," or "to invent authorities," "in support of slavery." Neither Donnegan, nor Liddell and Scott, nor Stephens, nor Schleusner, nor Robinson, nor Smith, nor Macknight, nor Stuart, could possibly have had any such motive. If they were not all perfectly unbiassed witnesses, it is certain they had no bias in favor of slavery. It is, indeed, the abolitionist, and not the slaveholder, who, in this case, "has perverted texts;" and if he has not "invented authorities," it is because his attempts to do so have proved abortive.

Beside the clear and unequivocal import of the word applied to Onesimus, it is evident, from other considerations, that he was the slave of Philemon. To dwell upon all of these would, we fear, be more tedious than profitable to the reader. Hence we shall confine our attention to a single circumstance, which will, we think, be sufficient for any candid or impartial inquirer after truth. Among the arguments used by St. Paul to induce Philemon to receive his fugitive slave kindly, we find this: "For perhaps he therefore departed *for a season*, that thou shouldest receive him *forever*." This verse is thus paraphrased by Macknight: "To mitigate thy resentment, consider, that *perhaps also for this reason he was separated* from thee *for a little while,* (so προς ὡραν signified, 1 Thess. ii. 17, note 2,) *that thou mightest have him* thy slave *for life.*" Dr. Macknight also adds, in a footnote: "By telling Philemon that he would now have Onesimus forever, the apostle intimates to him his firm persuasion that Onesimus would never any more run away from him." Such seems to be the plain, obvious import of the apostle's argument. No one, it is believed, who had no set purpose to subserve, or no foregone conclusion to support, would view this argument in any other light. Perhaps he was separated for a while as a slave, that "thou mightest have him forever," or for life. How have him? Surely, one would think, as a slave, or in the same capacity from which he was separated for a while. The argument requires this; the opposition of the words, and the force of the passage, imperatively require it. But yet, if we may believe Mr. Barnes, the meaning of St. Paul is, that perhaps Onesimus was separated for a while *as a servant,* that Philemon might never receive him again as a servant, but forever as a Christian brother! Lest we should be suspected of misrepresentation, we shall give his own words. "The meaning is," says he, "that it was possible that this was permitted in the providence of God, *in order* that Onesimus might be brought under the influence of the gospel, and be far more serviceable to Philemon as a Christian than he could have been in his former relation to him."

In the twelfth verse of the epistle, St. Paul says: "Whom I have sent again," or, as Macknight more accurately renders the words, "Him I have sent back," (ὃν ανεπεμψα.) Here we see the great apostle *actually sending back a fugitive slave to his master.* This act of St. Paul is not, and cannot be, denied. The words are too plain for denial. Onesimus *"I have sent back."* Surely it cannot be otherwise than a most unpleasant spectacle to abolitionist eyes thus to see Paul, the aged,—perhaps the most venerable and glorious hero whose life is upon record,—assume such an attitude toward the institution of slavery. Had he dealt with slavery as he always dealt with every thing which he regarded as sin; had he assumed toward it an attitude of stern and uncompromising hostility, and had his words been thunderbolts of denunciation, then indeed would he have been a hero after the very hearts of the abolitionists. But, as it is, they have to *apologize* for the great apostle, and try, as best they may, to deliver him from his *very equivocal position!* But if they are true apostles, and not false, then, we fear, the best apology for his conduct is that he had never read the Declaration of Independence, nor breathed the air of Boston.

This point, however, we shall not decide. We shall examine their apologies, and let the candid reader decide for himself. St. Paul, it is not denied, sent back Onesimus. But, says Mr. Barnes, he did not *compel* or *urge* him to go. He did not send him back against his will. Onesimus, no doubt, desired to return, and St. Paul was moved to send him by his own request. Now, in the first place, this apology is built on sheer assumption. There is not the slightest evidence that Onesimus requested St. Paul to send him back to his master. "There may have been many reasons," says Mr. Barnes, "why Onesimus desired to return to Colosse, and no one can prove that he did not express that desire to St. Paul, and that his 'sending' him was not in consequence of such request." True; even if Onesimus had felt no such desire, and had expressed no such desire to St. Paul, it would have been impossible, in the very nature of things, for any one to prove such negatives, unless he had been expressly informed on the subject by the writer of the epistle. But is it not truly wonderful, that any one should, without the least particle or shadow of evidence, be pleased to imagine a series of propositions, and then call upon the opposite party to disprove them? Is not such proceeding the very stuff that dreams are made of?

No doubt there may have been reasons why Onesimus should desire to return to his master. There were certainly reasons, and reasons of tremendous force, too, why he should have desired no such thing. The fact that Philemon, whom he had offended by running away, had, according to law, the power of life and death over him, is one of the reasons why he should have dreaded to return. Hence, unless required by the apostle to return, he *may* have desired no such thing, and no one can prove that an expression of such desire on his part was the ground of the apostle's action. It is certain, that he who affirms should prove.

In the second place, if St. Paul were an abolitionist at heart, he should have avoided the appearance of so great an evil. He should not, for a moment, have permitted himself to stand before the world in the simple and unexplained attitude of one who had sent back a fugitive slave to his master. No honest abolitionist would permit himself to appear in such a light. He would scorn to occupy such a position. Hence, we repeat, if St. Paul were an abolitionist at heart, he should have let it be known that, in sending Onesimus back, he was moved, not originally by the principles of his own heart, but by the desire and request of the fugitive himself. By such a course, he would have delivered himself from a false position, and spared his friends among the abolitionists the necessity of making awkward apologies for his conduct.

Thirdly, the positions of Mr. Barnes are not merely sheer assumptions; they are perfectly gratuitous. For it is easy to explain the determination of St. Paul to send Onesimus back, without having recourse to the supposition that Onesimus desired him to do so. Such determination was, indeed, the natural and necessary result of the well-known principles of the great apostle. He had repeatedly, and most emphatically, inculcated the principle, that it is the duty of slaves to "obey their masters," and to "count them worthy of all honor." This duty Onesimus had clearly violated in running away from his master. If St. Paul, then, had not taught Onesimus a different doctrine from that which he had taught the churches, he must have felt that he had done wrong in absconding from Philemon, and desired to repair the wrong by returning to him. "It is," says Mr. Barnes, "by no means necessary to suppose that Paul felt that Onesimus was under *obligation* to return." But we must suppose this, unless we suppose that Paul felt that Onesimus was under no obligation to obey the precepts which he himself had delivered for the guidance and direction of all Christian servants.

We shall now briefly notice a few other of Mr. Barnes' arguments, and then dismiss this branch of the subject. "If St. Paul sent back Onesimus," says he, "this was, doubtless, at his own request; for there is not the slightest evidence that he *compelled* him, or even urged him, to go." We might just as well conclude that St. Paul first required Onesimus to return, because there is not the slightest evidence that Onesimus made any such request.

"Paul," says Mr. Barnes, "had no power to

send Onesimus back to his master unless he chose
to go." This is very true. But still Onesimus
may have chosen to go, just because St. Paul,
his greatest benefactor and friend, had told him
it was his duty to do so. He may have chosen
to go, just because the apostle had told him it
is the duty of servants not to run away from
their masters, but to obey them, and count
them worthy of all honor. It is also true, that
"there is not the slightest evidence that he
compelled him, or even *urged* him, to go." It
is, on the other hand, equally true, that there
is not the slightest evidence that any thing
more than a bare expression of the apostle's
opinion, or a reiteration of his well-known
sentiments, was necessary to induce him to
return.

"The language is just as would have been
used," says our author, "on the supposition,
either that he requested him to go and bear a
letter to Colosse, or that Onesimus desired to
go, and that Paul sent him agreeably to his request. Compare Phil. ii. 25: 'Yet I suppose it
necessary *to send* Epaphroditus, my brother, and
companion in labor,' &c.; Col. iv. 7, 8: 'All
my estate shall Tychicus declare unto you,
who is a beloved brother, and a faithful mi-

nister and fellow-servant in the Lord: whom I have *sent* unto you for the same purpose, that he might know your estate.' But Epaphroditus and Tychicus were not sent against their own will,—nor is there any more reason to think that Onesimus was." Now there is not the least evidence that either Epaphroditus or Tychicus *requested* the apostle to *send* them as he did; and, so far as appears from his statements, the whole thing originated with himself. It is simply said that he *sent* them. It is true, they were "not sent against their own will," for they were ready and willing to obey his directions. We have good reason, as we have seen, to believe that precisely the same thing was true in regard to the sending of Onesimus.

But there is another case of *sending* which Mr. Barnes has overlooked. It is recorded in the same chapter of the same epistle which speaks of the sending of Epaphroditus. We shall adduce it, for it is a case directly in point. "But ye know the proof of him, (*i. e.* of Timothy,) that, as a son with the father, he hath served with me in the gospel. Him, therefore, I hope to *send* presently, so soon as I shall see how it will go with me." Now, here the apostle proposes to send Timothy, not so soon as Timothy should request to be sent, but so soon as he should see how it would go with himself as a prisoner at Rome. "As a son with the father," so Timothy, after his conversion, served with the great apostle, and, not against his own will, but most cheerfully, obeyed his directions. And in precisely the same ineffably endearing relation did Onesimus stand to the apostle. As a recent convert,—as a sincere and humble Christian,—he naturally looked to his great inspired teacher for advice, and was, no doubt, with more than filial affection, ready to obey.

Hence, we insist that Paul was responsible for the return of Onesimus to his master. He might have prevented his return, had he so desired; for he tells us so himself, (ver. 13.) But he chose to send him back. And why? Because Onesimus requested? The apostle says not so. "I would have retained him with me," says he to Philemon, "that in thy stead he might have ministered unto me in the bonds of the gospel. BUT WITHOUT THY MIND WOULD I DO NOTHING." Nay, whatever may have been his own desires, or those of Onesimus, he would do nothing without the mind of Philemon. Such is the reason which the apostle assigns for his own conduct, for his own determination not to retain the fugitive slave.

"What the apostle wrote to Philemon on this occasion is," says Dr. Macknight, "highly worthy of notice; namely, that although he had great need of an affectionate, honest servant to minister to him in his bonds, such as Onesimus was, who had expressed a great inclination to stay with him; and although, if Onesimus had remained with him, he would only have discharged the duty which Philemon himself owed to his spiritual father, yet the apostle would by no means detain Onesimus without Philemon's leave, because it belonged to him to dispose of his own slave in the way he thought proper. Such was the apostle's regard to justice, and to the rights of mankind!"

According to Mr. Barnes, however, the apostle was governed in this transaction, not by a regard to principle or the rights of mankind, but by a regard for the feelings of the master! Just listen, for one moment, to his marvellous discourse: "It is probable," says he, "that *if* Onesimus had proposed to return, it would have been easy for Paul to have retained him with him. He might have represented his own want of a friend. He might have appealed to his

gratitude on account of his efforts for his conversion. He might have shown him that he
was under no moral obligation to go back. He
might have refused to give him this letter, and
might have so represented to him the dangers
of the way, and the probability of a harsh reception, as effectually to have dissuaded him
from such a purpose. But, in that case, it is
clear that this might have caused hard feeling
in the bosom of Philemon, and rather than do
that, he preferred to let him return to his master,
and to plead for him that he might have a kind
reception. It is, therefore, by no means necessary to suppose that Paul felt that Onesimus
was under *obligation* to return, or that he was
disposed to *compel* him, or that Onesimus was
not inclined to return voluntarily; but all the
circumstances of the case are met by the supposition that, if Paul had retained him, Philemon might conceive that he had injured
him."

Alas! that so much truth should have been
suppressed; and that, too, by the most glorious
champion of truth the world has ever seen.
He tells not his "son Onesimus" that he is
under no moral obligation to return to his
master. On the contrary, he leaves him igno-

rant of his rights—of his inherent, sacred, and eternal rights. He sees him blindly put off "the hero," and put on "the brute" again. And why? Because, forsooth, if he should only speak, *he might cause hard feeling in the bosom of his master!* Should he retain Onesimus, his son, he would not injure Philemon at all. But then Philemon "might *conceive*" that he had injured him. Ah! when will abolitionist again suppress such mighty truth, lest he disturb some *fancied* right, or absurd feeling ruffle? When the volcano of his mind suppress and keep its furious fires in, lest he consume some petty despot's despicable sway; or else, at least, touch his tender sensibilities with momentary pain? "*Fiat justitia, ruat cœlum,*" is a favorite maxim with other abolitionists. But St. Paul, it seems, could not assume quite so lofty a tone. He could not say, "Let justice be done, though the heavens should fall." He could not even say, "Let justice be done," though the feelings of Philemon should be hurt.

It is evident, we think, that St. Paul needs to be defended against Mr. Barnes' defences of him, and vindicated against his apologies. If, indeed, he were so pitiful a pleader of "the innocent cause" as Mr. Barnes would have us to believe he is, then, we ask if those abolitionists are not in the right who despise both the apostle and his doctrine? No other abolitionist, it is certain, will ever imitate his example, as that example is represented by Mr. Barnes. No other abolitionist will ever suppress the great truths—as he conceives them to be—with which his soul is on fire, and which, in his view, lie at the foundation of human happiness, lest he should "cause hard feelings" in the bosom of a slaveholder.

It may be said, perhaps, that the remarks and apology of Mr. Barnes do not proceed on the supposition that Onesimus was a slave. If so, the answer is at hand. For surely Mr. Barnes cannot think it would have been dishonorable in the apostle to advise, or even to urge, "a hired servant," or "an apprentice," to return and fulfil his contract. It is evident that, although Mr. Barnes would have the reader to believe that Onesimus was merely a hired servant or an apprentice, he soon forgets his own interpretation, and proceeds to reason just as if he himself regarded him as a slave. This, if possible, will soon appear still more evident.

The apostle did not, according to Mr. Barnes, wholly conceal his abolition sentiments. He made them known to Philemon. Yes, we are gravely told, the letter which Onesimus carried in his pocket, as he wended his way back from Rome to Colosse, was and is an emancipation document! This great discovery is, we believe, due to the abolitionists of the present day. It was first made by Mr. Barnes, or Dr. Channing, or some other learned emancipationist, and after them by Mr. Sumner. Indeed, the discovery that it appears from the face of the epistle itself that it is an emancipation document, is the second of the two "conclusive things" which, in Mr. Sumner's opinion, constitute "an all-sufficient response" to anti-abolitionists.

Now supposing St. Paul to have been an abolitionist, such a disclosure of his views would, we admit, afford some little relief to our minds. For it would show that, although he did not provoke opposition by proclaiming the truth to the churches and to the world, he could at least run the risk of hurting the feelings of a slaveholder. But let us look into this great discovery, and see if the apostle has, in reality, whispered any such words of emancipation in the ear of Philemon.

In his note to the sixteenth verse of the epistle, Mr. Barnes says: "Not now as a servant. The adverb rendered 'not now,' (οὐκέτι,) means *no more, no further, no longer.*" So let it be. We doubt not that such is its meaning. Hence, we need not examine Mr. Barnes' numerous authorities, to show that such is the force of the adverb in question. He has, we admit, most abundantly established his point that οὐκέτι means *no longer.* But then this is a point which no anti-abolitionist has the least occasion to deny. We find precisely the same rendition in Macknight, and we are perfectly willing to abide by his translation. If Mr. Barnes had spared himself the trouble of producing these authorities, and adduced only one to show that δοῦλος means *a hired servant,* or *an apprentice,* his labor would have been bestowed where it is needed.

As the passage stands, then, St. Paul exhorts Philemon to receive Onesimus, "no longer as a servant." Now this, we admit, is perfectly correct *as far as it goes.* "It (*i. e.* this adverb) implies," says Mr. Barnes, "that he had been in this condition, *but was not to be now.*" He was *no longer* to be a servant! Over this view of the passage, Mr. Sumner goes into quite a

paroxysm of triumphant joy.' "Secondly," says
he, "in charging Onesimus with this epistle to
Philemon, the apostle announces him as 'not
now a servant, but above a servant,—a brother
beloved;' and he enjoins upon his correspond-
ent the hospitality due only to a freeman, say-
ing expressly, 'If thou count me, therefore, as
a partner, *receive him as myself;*' ay, sir, not as
slave, not even as servant, but as a brother
beloved, even as the apostle himself. Thus
with apostolic pen wrote Paul to his disciple
Philemon. Beyond all doubt, in these words
of gentleness, benediction, and EMANCIPATION,*
dropping with celestial, soul-awakening power,
there can be no justification for a conspiracy,
which, beginning with the treachery of Iscariot,
and the temptation of pieces of silver, seeks
by fraud, brutality, and violence, through officers of the law armed to the teeth like pirates,
and amid soldiers who degrade their uniform,
to hurl a fellow-man back into the lash-resound-
ing den of American slavery; and if any one
can thus pervert this beneficent example, allow
me to say that he gives too much occasion to
doubt his intelligence or his sincerity."

---

* The emphasis is ours.

Now in regard to the spirit of this passage we have at present nothing to say. The sudden transition from the apostle's "words of blessing and benediction," to Mr. Sumner's words of railing and vituperation, we shall pass by unnoticed. Upon these the reader may make his own comments. It is our object simply to comment on the words of the great apostle. And, in the first place, we venture to suggest that there are several very serious difficulties in the way of Mr. Barnes' and Mr. Sumner's interpretation of the passage in question.

Let us, for the sake of argument, concede to these gentlemen that Onesimus was merely the hired servant, or apprentice, of Philemon. What then follows? If they are not in error, it clearly and unequivocally follows that St. Paul's "words of emancipation" were intended, not for slaves merely, but for hired servants and apprentices! For servants of any and every description! Mr. Sumner expressly tells us that he was to return, "not as a slave, *not even as a servant*, but as a brother beloved." Now such a scheme of emancipation would, it seems to us, suit the people of Boston as little as it would those of Richmond. It would abolish every kind of "servitude, whether voluntary or involuntary," and release all hired servants, as well as apprentices, from the obligation of their contracts. Such is one of the difficulties in their way. It may not detract from the "sincerity," it certainly reflects no credit on the "intelligence," of Mr. Sumner, to be guilty of such an oversight.

There is another very grave difficulty in the way of these gentlemen. St. Paul writes that the servant Onesimus, who had been unprofitable to Philemon in times past, would now be profitable to him. But how profitable? As a servant? No! he was no longer to serve him at all. His "emancipation" was announced! He was to be received, not as a slave, not even as a servant, but *only* as a brother beloved! Philemon was, indeed, to extend to him the hospitalities due to a freeman, even such as were due to the apostle himself? Now, for aught we know, it may have been very agreeable to the feelings of Philemon, to have his former servant thus unceremoniously "emancipated," and quartered upon him as "a gentleman of elegant leisure;" but how this could have been so *profitable* to him is more than we can conceive.

It must be admitted, we think, that in a worldly

point of view, all the profits would have been on the side of Onesimus. "But," says Mr. Barnes, "he would now be more profitable as a Christian brother." It is true, Onesimus had not been very profitable as a Christian brother before he ran away, for he had not been a Christian brother at all. But if he were sent back by the apostle, because he would be profitable merely as a Christian brother, we cannot see why any other Christian brother would not have answered the purpose just as well as Onesimus. If such, indeed, were the apostle's object, he might have conferred a still greater benefit upon Philemon by sending several Christian brethren to live with him, and to feast upon his good things.

Thirdly, the supposition that St. Paul thus announced the emancipation of Onesimus, is as inconsistent with the whole scope and design of the passage, as it is with the character of the apostle. If he would do nothing without the consent of Philemon, not even retain his servant to minister to himself while in prison, much less would he declare him emancipated, and introduce him to his former master as a freeman. We submit to the candid reader, we submit to every one who has the least perception of the character and spirit of the apostle, if such an interpretation of his words be not simply ridiculous.

It is certain that such an interpretation is peculiar to abolitionists. "Men," says Mr. Sumner, "are prone to find in uncertain, disconnected texts, a confirmation of their own personal prejudices or prepossessions. And I,"—he continues, "who am no divine, but only a simple layman—make bold to say, that whosoever finds in the gospel any sanction of slavery, finds there merely a reflection of himself." He must have been a very simple layman indeed, if he did not perceive how very easily his words might have been retorted. We venture to affirm that no one, except an abolitionist, has ever found the slightest tincture of abolitionism in the writings of the great apostle to the Gentiles.

The plain truth is, that Philemon is exhorted to receive Onesimus "no longer as a slave ONLY, but above a slave,—a brother beloved." Such is the translation of Macknight, and such, too, is the concurrent voice of every commentator to whom we have access. Pool, Clarke, Scott, Benson, Doddridge—all unite in the interpretation that Onesimus was, in the heaven-inspired and soul-subduing words of the loving apostle, commended to his master, not as a slave *merely*, but also as a Christian brother. The great fact—the "words of emancipation," which Mr. Sumner sees so clearly on "the face of the epistle,"—they cannot see at all. Neither sign nor shadow of any such thing can they perceive. It is a sheer reflection of the abolitionist himself. Thus, the Old Testament is not only merged in the New, but the New itself is merged in Mr. Charles Sumner, of Massachusetts.

We shall notice one passage more of Scripture. The seventh chapter of the Epistle to the Corinthians begins thus: "Now concerning the things whereof ye wrote unto me;" and it proceeds to notice, among other things, the relation of master and slave. This passage was designed to correct the disorders among the Christian slaves at Corinth, who, agreeably to the doctrine of the false teacher, *claimed their liberty, on pretence that, as brethren in Christ, they were on an equality with their Christian masters.*" Here, then, St. Paul met abolitionism face to face. And how did he proceed? Did he favor the false teacher? Did he recognise the claim of the discontented Christian slaves? Did he even once hint that they were entitled to their freedom, on the ground that all men are equal, or on any other ground whatever? His own words will furnish the best answer to these questions.

"Let every man," says he, "abide in the same calling wherein he was called. Art thou called, being a servant? *care not for it.*" Thus, were Christian slaves exhorted to continue in that condition of life in which they were when converted to Christianity. This will not be denied. It is too plain for controversy. It is even admitted by Mr. Barnes himself. In the devout contemplation of this passage Chrysostom exclaims: "Hast thou been called, being a slave? Care not for it. Continue to be a slave. Hast thou been called, being in uncircumcision? Remain uncircumcised. Being circumcised, didst thou become a believer? Continue circumcised. For these are no hindrances to piety. Thou art called, being a slave; another, with an unbelieving wife; another, being circumcised. Astonishing! Where has he put slavery? As circumcision profits not, and uncircumcision does no harm, so neither doth slavery nor yet liberty."

"The great argument" against slavery is, according to Dr. Channing and other abolitionists drawn from the immortality of the soul. "Into every human being," says he, "God has breathed an immortal spirit, more precious than the whole outward creation. No earthly nor celestial language can exaggerate the worth of a human being." The powers of this immortal spirit, he concludes, "reduce to insignificance all outward distinctions." Yea, according to St. Paul himself, they reduce to utter insignificance all outward distinctions, and especially the distinction between liberty and slavery. "Art thou called," says he, "being a slave? care not for it." Art thou, indeed, the Lord's freeman, and *as such* destined to reign on a throne of glory forever? Oh, then, care not for the paltry distinctions of the passing world!

Now, whom shall the Christian teacher take for his model?—St. Paul, or Dr. Channing? Shall he seek to make men contented with the condition in which God has placed them, or shall he stir up discontent, and inflame the restless passions of men? Shall he himself, like the great apostle, be content to preach the doctrines of eternal life to a perishing world; or shall he make politics his calling, and inveigh against the domestic relations of society? Shall he exhort men not to continue in the condition of life in which God has placed them, but to take his providence out of his hands, and, *in direct opposition to his word*, assert their rights? In one word, shall he preach the gospel of Christ and his apostles, or shall he preach the gospel of the abolitionist?

"Art thou called, being a servant? care not for it; but if thou mayest be made free, use it rather." The Greek runs thus: ἀλλ' εἰ καὶ δύνασαι ἐλεύθερος γενέσθαι, μᾶλλον χρῆσαι,—literally, "but even if thou canst become free, rather make use of." Make use of what? The Greek verb is left without a case. How, then, shall this be supplied? To what does the ambiguous *it* of our translation refer? "One and all of the native Greek commentators in the early ages," says Stuart, "and many expositors in modern times, say that the word to be supplied is δουλείᾳ, i. e. *slavery, bondage*. The reason which they give for it is, that this is the only construction which can support the proposition the apostle is laboring to establish, viz.: 'Let every man abide in *statu quo*.' Even De Wette, (who, for his high liberty notions, was banished from Germany,) in his commentary on this passage, seems plainly to accede to the force of this reason-

19

ing; and with him many others have agreed.
No man can look at the simple continuity of
logic in the passage without feeling that there
is force in the appeal." Yet the fact should
not be concealed, that Stuart himself is "not
satisfied with this exegesis of the passage;"
which, acccording to his own statement, was
the universal interpretation from "the early
ages" down to the sixteenth century. This
change, says he, "seems to have been the
spontaneous prompting of the spirit of
liberty, that beat high" in the bosom of its
author.

Now have we not some reason to distrust an
interpretation which comes not exactly from
Heaven, but from a spirit beating high in the
human breast? *That* is certainly not an unerring spirit. We have already seen what it
can do with the Scriptures. But whether it
has erred in this instance, or not, it is certain
that it should never be permitted to beat so
very high in any human breast as to annul the
teachings of the apostle, or to make him contradict himself. This has been too often done.
We too frequently hear those who admit that
St. Paul exhorts "slaves to continue in slavery,"
still contend that "if they may be made free,"

they should move heaven and earth to attain so desirable an object. They "should continue in that state," and yet exert all their power to escape therefrom!

Conybeare and Howson, who are acknowledged to be among the best commentators on the Epistles of St. Paul, have restored "the continuity of his logic." They translate his words thus: "Nay, though thou have power to gain thy freedom, seek rather to remain content." This translation certainly possesses the advantage that it makes the doctrine of St. Paul perfectly consistent with itself.

But let us return to the point in regard to which there is no controversy. It is on all sides agreed, that St. Paul no less than three times exhorts every man to continue in the condition in which Providence has placed him. "And this rule," says he, "ordain I in all the churches." Yet—would any man believe it possible?—the very quintessence of abolitionism itself has been extracted from this passage of his writings! Let us consider for a moment the wonderful alchemy by which this has been effected.

We find in this passage the words: "Be not ye the servants of men." These words are

taken from the connection in which they stand,
dissevered from the words which precede and
follow them, and then made to teach that
slaves should not submit to the authority of their
masters, should not continue in their present
condition. It is certain that no one but an
abolitionist, who has lost all respect for revelation except when it happens to square with his
own notions, could thus make the apostle so
directly and so flatly contradict himself and
all his teaching. Different interpretations have
been given to the words just quoted; but until
abolitionism set its cloven foot upon the Bible,
such violence had not been done to its sacred
pages.

Conybeare and Howson suppose that the
words in question are intended to caution the
Corinthians against "their servile adherence to
party leaders." Bloomfield, in like manner,
says: "The best commentators are agreed,"
that they are "to be taken figuratively, in the
sense, 'do not be blindly followers of men, con-
forming to their opinions,' &c." It is certain
that Rosenmüller, Grotius, and we know not
how many more, have all concurred in this
interpretation. But be the meaning what it
may, *it is not* an exhortation to slaves to burst

their bonds in sunder, unless the apostle has, in one and the same breath, taught diametrically opposite doctrines.

Yet, in direct opposition to the plain words of the apostle, and to the concurrent voice of commentators and critics, is he made to teach that slaves should throw off the authority of their masters! Lest such a thing should be deemed impossible, we quote the words of the author by whom this outrage has been perpetrated. "The command of the 23d verse," says he, "'be not ye the servants of men,' is equally plain. There are no such commands uttered in regard to the relations of husband and wife, parent and child, as are here given in regard to slavery. *No one is thus urged to dissolve the marriage relation. No such commands are given to relieve children from obedience to their parents*," &c.* Nor is any such command, we repeat, given to relieve slaves from obedience to their masters, or to dissolve the relation between them.

If such violence to Scripture had been done by an obscure scribbler, or by an infidel quoting the word of God merely for a purpose, it

---

* Elliott on Slavery, Vol. I., p. 295.

19*

would not have been matter of such profound astonishment. But is it not unspeakably shocking that a Christian man, nay, that a Christian minister and doctor of divinity, should thus set at naught the clearest, the most unequivocal, and the most universally received teachings of the gospel? If he had merely accused the Christian men of the South, as he has so often done in his two stupid volumes on slavery, of the crimes of "swindling," of "theft," of "robbing," and of "manstealing," we could have borne with him well; and, as we have hitherto done, continued to pass by his labors with silent contempt. But we have deemed it important to show in what manner, and to what extent, the spirit of abolitionism can wrest the pure word of God to its antichristian purpose.

We shall conclude the argument from Scripture with the following just and impressive testimony of the Princeton Review: "The mass of the pious and thinking people in this country are neither abolitionists nor the advocates of slavery. They stand where they ever have stood—on the broad Scriptural foundation; maintaining the obligation of all men, in their several places and relations, to act on the law of love, and to promote the spiritual and temporal welfare of others by every means in their power. They stand aloof from the abolitionists for various reasons. In the first place, they disapprove of their principles. The leading characteristic doctrine of this sect is that slaveholding is in all cases a sin, and should, therefore, under all circumstances, be immediately abandoned. *As nothing can be plainer than that slaveholders were admitted to the Christian church by the inspired apostles, the advocates of this doctrine are brought into direct collision with the Scriptures. This leads to one of the most dangerous evils connected with the whole system, viz., a disregard of the authority of the word of God, a setting up a different and higher standard of truth and duty, and a proud and confident wresting of Scripture to suit their own purposes.* THE HISTORY OF INTERPRETATION FURNISHES NO EXAMPLES OF MORE WILFUL AND VIOLENT PERVERSIONS OF THE SACRED TEXT THAN ARE TO BE FOUND IN THE WRITINGS OF THE ABOLITIONISTS. THEY SEEM TO CONSIDER THEMSELVES ABOVE THE SCRIPTURES; AND WHEN THEY PUT THEMSELVES ABOVE THE LAW OF GOD, IT IS NOT WONDERFUL THAT THEY SHOULD DISREGARD THE LAWS OF MEN. Significant manifestations of the result of this disposition to

consider their own light a surer guide than
the word of God, are visible in the anarchical
opinions about human governments, civil and
ecclesiastical, and on the rights of women,
which have found appropriate advocates in the
abolition publications. Let these principles be
carried out, and there is an end to all social
subordination, to all security for life and property, to all guarantee for public or domestic
virtue. If our women are to be emancipated
from subjection to the law which God has imposed upon them, if they are to quit the retire-
ment of domestic life, where they preside in
stillness over the character and destiny of society; if they are to come forth in the liberty
of men, to be our agents, our public lecturers,
our committee-men, our rulers; if, in studied
insult to the authority of God, we are to renounce in the marriage contract all claim to
obedience, we shall soon have a country over
which the genius of Mary Wolstonecraft would
delight to preside, but from which all order
and all virtue would speedily be banished.
There is no form of human excellence before
which we bow with profounder deference than
that which appears in a delicate woman,
adorned with the inward graces and devoted

to the peculiar duties of her sex; and there is no deformity of human character from which we turn with deeper loathing than from a woman forgetful of her nature, and clamorous for the vocation and rights of men. It would not be fair to object to the abolitionists the disgusting and disorganizing opinions of even some of their leading advocates and publications, did they not continue to patronize those publications, and were not these opinions the legitimate consequences of their own principles. Their women do but apply their own method of dealing with Scripture to another case. This no inconsiderable portion of the party have candor enough to acknowledge, and are therefore prepared to abide the result."

CHAPTER IV.

THE ARGUMENT FROM THE PUBLIC GOOD.

WE have not shunned the abstractions of the abolitionist. We have, on the contrary, examined all his arguments, even the most abstract, and endeavored to show that they either rest on false assumptions, or consist in false deductions. While engaged in this analysis of his errors, we have more than once had occasion to remind him that the great practical problem of slavery is to be determined, if determined at all, not by an appeal to abstractions, but simply by a consideration of the public good. It is under this point of view, or with reference to the highest good of the governed, that we now proceed to consider the institution of slavery.

The way is open and clear for this view of the subject. For we have seen, we trust, that slavery is condemned neither by any principle of natural justice, nor by any precept of divine revelation. On the other hand, if we mistake not, it has been most clearly shown that the doctrines and practices of the abolitionist are at war with the most explicit words of God, as well as with the most unquestionable principles of political ethics. Hence, without the least disrespect to the eternal principles of right, we may now proceed to subject his doctrines to the only remaining test of political truth, namely, *to the test of experience.* Having examined the internal qualities of the tree and found them bad, we may now proceed to inquire if "its fruits" be not poison. And if the sober lessons of history, if the infallible records of experience, be found in perfect harmony with the conclusions of reason and of revelation, then shall we not be triply justified in pronouncing abolitionism a social and a moral curse?

§ I. *The Question.*

Here, at the outset, we may throw aside a mass of useless verbiage, with which our inquiry is usually encumbered. We are eternally told that Kentucky has fallen behind Ohio, and Virginia behind Pennsylvania, because their energies have been crippled, and their prosperity over-clouded, by the institution of slavery. Now, it is of no importance to our argument that we should either deny the fact,

or the explanation which is given of it by abolitionists. If the question were, whether slavery
should be introduced among us, or into any
non-slaveholding State, then such facts and ex-
planations would be worthy of our notice.
Then such an appeal to experience would be
relevant to the point in dispute. But such is
not the question. We are not called upon to
decide whether slavery shall be established in
our midst or not. This question has been decided for us. Slavery—as everybody knows—
was forced upon the colonies by the arbitrary
and despotic rule of Great Britain, and that, too,
against the earnest remonstrances of our ancestors. The thing has been done. The past is
beyond our control. It is fixed and unalterable.
The only inquiry which remains for us now is,
whether the slavery which was thus forced upon
our ancestors shall be continued, or whether it
shall be abolished? The question is not what
Virginia, or Kentucky, or any other slave State,
might have been, but what they would be in
case slavery were abolished. If abolitionists
would speak to the point, then let them show
us some country in which slavery has been abolished, and we will abide by the experiment.
Fortunately for us, we need not look far for

such an experiment;—an experiment which has been made, not upon mere chattels or brutes, but upon the social and moral well-being of more than a million of human beings. We refer, of course, to the emancipation of the slaves in the British Colonies. This work, as every one knows, was the great vaunted achievement of British abolitionists. Here, then, we may see their philosophy—if philosophy it may be called—"teaching by example." Here we may see and taste the fruits of abolitionism, ere we conclude to grow them upon our own soil.

§ II. *Emancipation in the British Colonies.*

It is scarcely in the power of human language to describe the enthusiastic delight with which the abolitionists, both in England and in America, were inspired by the spectacle of West India Emancipation. We might easily adduce a hundred illustrations of the almost frantic joy with which it intoxicated their brains. We shall, however, for the sake of brevity, confine our attention to a single example,—which will, at the same time, serve to show, not only how wild the abolitionist himself was, but also how indignant he became that others were not equally disposed to part

with their sober senses. "The prevalent state
of feeling," said Dr. Channing in 1840, "in the
free States in regard to slavery is indifference—
an indifference strengthened by the notion of
great difficulties attending the subject. The fact
is painful, but the truth should be spoken. The
majority of the people, even yet, care little
about the matter. A painful proof of this in-
sensibility was furnished about a year and a
half ago, when the English West Indies were
emancipated. An event surpassing this in
moral grandeur is not recorded in history. In
one day, probably seven hundred thousand of
human beings were rescued from bondage to
full, unqualified freedom. The consciousness
of wrongs, in so many breasts, was exchanged
into rapturous, grateful joy. What shouts of
thanksgiving broke forth from those liberated
crowds! What new sanctity and strength were
added to the domestic ties! What new hopes
opened on future generations! The crowning
glory of this day was the fact that the work of
emancipation was wholly due to the principles
of Christianity. The West Indies were freed,
not by force, or human policy, but by the reverence of a great people for justice and humanity. The men who began and carried on this

cause were Christian philanthropists; and they prevailed by spreading their own spirit through a nation. In this respect, the emancipation of the West Indies was a grander work than the redemption of the Israelites from bondage. This was accomplished by force, by outward miracles, by the violence of the elements. That was achieved by love, by moral power, by God, working, not in the stormy seas, but in the depths of the human heart. And how was this day of emancipation—one of the most blessed days that ever dawned upon the earth—received in this country? While in distant England a thrill of gratitude and joy pervaded thousands and millions, we, the neighbors of the West Indies, and who boast of our love of liberty, saw the sun of that day rise and set with hardly a thought of the scenes on which it was pouring its joyful light. The greater part of our newspapers did not refer to the event. The great majority of the people had forgotten it. Such was the testimony we gave to our concern for the poor slave; and is it from discussions of slavery among such a people that the country is to be overturned?"

Such were the glowing expectations of the abolitionists. It now remains to be seen whether they were true prophets, or merely "blind leaders of the blind." Be that as it may, for the present we cannot agree with Dr. Channing, that the good people of the free States were insincere in boasting of their "love of liberty," because they did not go into raptures over so fearful an experiment before they had some little time to see how it would work. They did, no doubt, most truly and profoundly love liberty. But then they had some reason to suspect, perhaps, that liberty may be one thing, and abolitionism quite another. Liberty, they knew, was a thing of light and love; but as for abolitionism, it was, for all they knew, a demon of destruction. Hence they would wait, and see. We do well to rejoice at once, exclaims Dr. Channing. If a man-child is born into the world, says he, do we wait to read his future life ere we rejoice at his birth? Ah, no! But then, perhaps, this offspring of abolitionism is no man-child at all. It may, for aught we know, be an abortion of night and darkness merely. Hence, we shall wait, and mark his future course, ere we rend the air with shouts that he is born at last.

This man-child, or this monster, is now seventeen years and four months old. His character is developed, and fixed for life. We may now read his history, written by impartial men, and determine for ourselves, whether it justifies the bright and boundless hopes of the abolitionists, or the "cold indifference," nay, the suspicions and the fears, of the good people of the free States.

We shall begin with Jamaica, which is by far the largest and most valuable of the British West Indies. The very first year after the complete emancipation of the slaves of this island, its prosperity began to manifest symptoms of decay. As long as it was possible, however, to find or invent an explanation of these fearful signs, the abolitionists remained absolutely blind to the real course of events. In 1839, the first year of complete emancipation, it appeared that the crop of sugar exported from the island had fallen off no less than eight thousand four hundred and sixty-six hogsheads. But, then, it was discovered that the hogsheads had been larger this year than the preceding! It is true, there was not exactly any proof that larger hogsheads had been used all over the island, but it was rumored; and the rumor was, of course, eagerly swallowed by the abolitionists.

20*

And besides, it was quite certain that the free negroes had eaten more sugar than while they were slaves, which helped mightily to account for the great diminution in the exports of the article. No one could deny this. It is certain, that if the free negroes only devoured sugar as eagerly as such floating conjectures were gulped down by the abolitionists, the whole phenomenon needed no other cause for its perfect explanation. It never once occurred, however, to these reasoners to imagine that the decrease in the amount of rum exported from another island *might* be owing to the circumstance that the free blacks had swallowed a little more of that article as well as of sugar. On the contrary, this fact was held up as a most conclusive and triumphant proof that the free negroes had not only become temperate themselves, but also so virtuous that they scorned to produce such an article to poison their fellow-men. The English abolitionists who rejoiced at such a reflection were, it must be confessed, standing on rather delicate ground. For if such an inference proved any thing, it proved that the blacks of the island in question had, at one single bound, passed from the depths of degradation to an exaltation of virtue

far above their emancipators, the English people
themselves; since these, as every reader of history knows, not only enforced the culture of
opium in India, but also absolutely compelled
the poor Chinese to receive it at the mouth of
the cannon!

It also appears that, for 1839, the amount of
coffee exported had fallen off 38,554 cwt., or
about one third of the whole amount of the
preceding year. "The coffee is a very uncertain crop," said a noted English emancipationist, in view of this startling fact, "and the
deficiency, on the comparison of these two years,
is not greater, I believe, than has often occurred
before." This is true, for a drought or a hurricane had before created quite as great a
deficiency. But while the fact is true, it only
proves that the first year of emancipation was
no worse on the coffee crop than a drought or
a hurricane.

"We should also remember," says this zeal-
ous abolitionist, "that, both in sugar and coffee,
the profit to the planter may be increased by
the saving of expense, even where the produce
is diminished." Such a thing, we admit, is
possible; it *may* be true. But *in point of fact,*

as we shall soon see, the expense was increased, while the crop was diminished.

But after every possible explanation, even Dr. Channing and Mr. Gurney were bound to admit "that some decrease has taken place in both the articles, in connection with the change of system." They also admitted that "so far as this decrease of produce is connected with the change of system, *it is obviously to be traced to a corresponding decrease in the quantity of labor.*"

May we not suppose, then, that here the ingenuity of man is at an end, and the truth begins to be allowed to make its appearance? By no means. For here "comes the critical question,"—says Mr. Gurney, "the real turning point. To what is this decrease in the quantity of labor owing? I answer deliberately but without reserve, '*Mainly* to causes which class under slavery and not under freedom.' It is, for the most part, the result of those impolitic attempts to force the labor of freemen which have disgusted the peasantry, and have led to the desertion of many of the estates."

Now suppose this were the case, is it not the business, is it not the duty, of the legislator to consider the passions, the prejudices, and

the habits of those for whom he legislates?
Indeed, if he overlook these, is he not a reckless experimenter rather than a wise statesman?
If he legislates, not for man as he *is*, but for
man as he *ought to be*, is he not a political
dreamer rather than a sound philosopher?

The abolitionist not only closed his eyes on
every appearance of decline in the prosperity
of the West Indies, he also seized with avidity
every indication of the successful operation of
his scheme, and magnified it both to himself
and to the world. He made haste, in particular, to paint in the most glowing colors the
rising prosperity of Jamaica.* His narrative
was hailed with eager delight by abolitionists
in all parts of the civilized world. It is a pity,
we admit, to spoil so fine a story, or to put a
damper on so much enthusiasm. But the truth,
especially in a case like the present, should be
told. While, then, to the enchanted imagination of the abolitionist, the wonderful industry
of the freed negroes and the exuberant bounty
of nature were concurring to bring about a
paradise in the island of Jamaica, the dark
stream of emancipation was, in reality, under-

---

* Life of Joseph John Gurney, vol. ii. p. 214.

mining its prosperity and glory. We shall now proceed to adduce the evidence of this melancholy fact, which has in a few short years become so abundant and so overwhelming, that even the most blind and obstinate must feel its force.

After describing the immense sources of wealth to be found in Jamaica, an intelligent eye-witness says: "Such are some of the natural resources of this dilapidated and poverty-stricken country. Capable as it is of producing almost every thing, and actually producing nothing which might not become a staple with a proper application of capital and skill, its inhabitants are miserably poor, and daily sinking deeper and deeper into the utter helplessness of abject want.

"'Magnas inter opes inops.'

"Shipping has deserted her ports; her magnificent plantations of sugar and coffee are running to weeds; her private dwellings are falling to decay; the comforts and luxuries which belong to industrial prosperity have been cut off, one by one, from her inhabitants; and the day, I think, is at hand when there will be none left to represent the wealth, intelligence, and hospitality for which the Jamaica planter was once distinguished."*

"It is impossible," says Mr. Carey, "to read Mr. Bigelow's volume, without arriving at the conclusion that the freedom granted to the negro has had little effect except that of enabling him to live at the expense of the planter so long as any thing remained. Sixteen years of freedom did not appear to its author to have 'advanced the dignity of labor or of the laboring classes one particle,' while it had ruined the proprietors of the land, and thus great damage had been done to the one class without benefit of any kind to the other."

From a statistical table, published in August, 1853, it appears, says one of our northern journals, that, since 1846, "the number of sugar estates on the island that have been totally abandoned amounts to one hundred and sixty-eight, and the number partially abandoned to sixty-three; the value of which two hundred and thirty-one estates was assessed, in 1841, at £1,655,140, or nearly eight millions and a half of dollars. Within the same period two hun-

---

* Bigelow's Notes on Jamaica in 1850, as quoted in Carey's "Slave Trade, Foreign and Domestic."

dred and twenty-three coffee-plantations have been totally, and twenty partially, abandoned, the assessed value of which was, in 1841, £500,000, or two millions and a half of dollars; and of cattle-pens, (grazing farms,) one hundred and twenty-two have been totally, and ten partially, abandoned, the value of which was a million and a half of dollars. The aggregate value of these six hundred and six estates, which have been thus ruined and abandoned in the island of Jamaica, within the last seven or eight years, amounted by the regular assessments, ten years since, to the sum of nearly two and a half millions of pounds sterling, or twelve and a half millions of dollars."*

In relation to Jamaica, another witness says: "The marks of decay abound. Neglected fields, crumbling houses, fragmentary fences, noiseless machinery—these are common sights, and soon become familiar to observation. I sometimes rode for miles in succession over fertile ground, which used to be cultivated, and which is now lying waste. So rapidly has cultivation retrograded, and the wild luxuriance of nature replaced the conveniences of art, that

---

* Quoted by Mr. Carey.

parties still inhabiting these desolated districts have sometimes, in the strong language of a speaker at Kingston, 'to seek about the bush to find the entrance into their houses.'

"The towns present a spectacle no less gloomy. A great part of Kingston was destroyed, some years ago, by an extensive conflagration: yet multitudes of the houses which escaped that visitation are standing empty, though the population is little, if at all, diminished. The explanation is obvious. Persons who have nothing, and can no longer keep up their domestic establishments, take refuge in the abodes of others, where some means of subsistence are still left; and in the absence of any discernible trade or occupation, the lives of crowded thousands appear to be preserved from day to day by a species of miracle. The most busy thoroughfares of former times have now almost the quietude of a Sabbath.

" 'The finest land in the world,' says Mr. Bigelow, 'may be had at any price, and almost for the asking.' Labor 'receives no compensation, and the product of labor does not seem to know how to find the way to market.' "*

---

* Carey's Slave Trade.

From the report made in 1849, and signed by various missionaries, the moral and religious state of the island appears no less gloomy than its scenes of poverty and distress. The following extract from that report we copy from Mr. Carey's "Slave Trade, Domestic and Foreign:"—

"Missionary efforts in Jamaica are beset at the present time with many and great discouragements. Societies at home have withdrawn or diminished the amount of assistance afforded by them to chapels and schools throughout this island. The prostrate condition of its agriculture and commerce disables its own population from doing as much as formerly for maintaining the worship of God and the tuition of the young, and induces numbers of negro laborers to retire from estates which have been thrown up, to seek the means of subsistence in the mountains, where they are removed in general from moral training and superintendence. The consequences of this state of matters are very disastrous. Not a few missionaries and teachers—often struggling with difficulties which they could not overcome—have returned to Europe, and others are preparing to follow them. Chapels and schools are abandoned, or they have passed into the hands of very incompetent instructors."

We cannot dwell upon each of the West India Islands. Some of these have not suffered so much as others; but while some, from well-known causes, have been partially exempt from the evils of emancipation, all have suffered to a fearful extent. This, as we shall now show, is most amply established by English authorities.

Mr. Bigelow, whose "Notes on Jamaica in 1850" we have noticed, is an American writer; a Northern man; and, it is said, by no means a friend to the institution of slavery. It is certain that Mr. Robert Baird, from whom we shall now quote, is not only a subject of Great Britain, but also a most enthusiastic advocate of "the glorious Act of British Emancipation." But although he admires that act, yet, on visiting the West Indies for his health, he could not fail to be struck with the appalling scenes of distress there exhibited. In describing these, his object is not to reflect shame on the misguided philanthropy of Great Britain; but only to urge the adoption of other measures, in order to rescue the West Indies from the utter ruin and desolation which must otherwise soon overtake them. We might easily adduce many impressive extracts from his work; but, for the sake of brevity, we shall confine our attention to one or two passages.

"Hope," says Mr. Baird, "delights to brighten the prospects of the future; and thus it is that the British West Indian planter goes on from year to year, struggling against his downward progress, and still hoping that something may yet turn up to retrieve his ruined fortunes. But all do not struggle on. Many have given in, and many more can and will confirm the statement of a venerable friend of my own —a gentleman high in office in one of the islands above-mentioned—who, when showing me his own estate and sugar-works, assured me, that for above a quarter of a century they had yielded him nearly £2000 per annum; and that now, despite all his efforts and improvements, (which were many,) he could scarcely manage to make the cultivation pay itself. Instances of this kind might be multiplied till the reader was tired, and even heart-sick, of such details. But what need of such? Is it not notorious? Has it not been proved by the numerous failures that have taken place of late years among our most

extensive West Indian merchants? Are not
the reports of almost all the governors of our
colonial possessions filled with statements to
the effect that great depreciation of property
has taken place in all and each of our West
Indian colonies, and that great has been the
distress consequent thereupon? These governors are, of course, all of them imbued, to some
extent, with the ministerial policy—at least it
is reasonable to assume that they are so. At
all events, whether they are so or not, their
position almost necessitates their doing their
utmost to carry out, with success, the ministerial views and general policy. To embody
the substance of the answer given by a talented
lieutenant-governor, in my own hearing, to an
address which set forth, somewhat strongly, the
ruined prospects and wasted fortunes of the
colonists under his government: 'It must, or
it ought to be, the object and the desire of
every governor or lieutenant-governor in the
British West Indian Islands, to disappoint and
stultify, if he can, the prognostications of coming ruin with which the addresses he receives
from time to time are continually charged?'
Yet what say these governors? Do not the
reports of one and all of them confirm the

above statement as to the deplorable state of distress to which the West Indian planters in the British Colonies are reduced?"*

Again, he says: "That the British West Indian colonists have been loudly complaining that they are ruined, is a fact so generally acknowledged, that the very loudness and frequency of the complaint has been made a reason for disregarding or undervaluing the grounds of it. That the West Indians are always grumbling is an observation often heard; and, no doubt, it is very true that they are so. But let any one who thinks that the extent and clamor of the complaint exceeds the magnitude of the distress which has called it forth, go to the West Indies and judge for himself. Let him see with his own eyes the neglected and abandoned estates,— the uncultivated fields, fast hurrying back into a state of nature, with all the speed of tropical luxuriance—the dismantled and silent machinery, the crumbling walls, and deserted mansions, which are familiar sights in most of the British West Indian colonies. Let him, then, transport himself to the Spanish islands of Porto

---

* "The West Indies and North America," by Robt. Baird, A.M., p. 145.

Rico and Cuba, and witness the life and activity which in these slave colonies prevail. Let him observe for himself the activity of the slavers—the improvements daily making in the cultivation of the fields and in the processes carried on at the Ingenios or sugar-mills—and *the general indescribable air of thriving and prosperity which surrounds the whole,*—and then let him come back to England and say, if he honestly can, that the British West Indian planters and proprietors are grumblers, who complain without adequate cause."*

Great Britain has shown no little solicitude to ascertain the real state of things in her West India colonies. For this purpose, she appointed, in 1842, a select committee, consisting of some of the most prominent members of Parliament, with Lord Stanley at their head. In 1848, another committee was appointed by her, with Lord George Bentinck as its chairman, to inquire into the condition of her Majesty's East and West India possessions and the Mauritius, and to consider whether any measures could be adopted for their relief. The report of both

---

* "The West Indies and North America," by Robt. Baird, A.M., p. 143.

committees show, beyond all doubt, that unexampled distress existed in the colonies. The report of 1848 declares: "That many estates in the British West India colonies have been already abandoned, that many more are in the course of abandonment, and that from this cause a very serious diminution is to be apprehended in the total amount of production. That the first effect of this diminution will be an increase in the price of sugar, and the ultimate effect a greater extension to the growth of sugar in slave countries, and a greater impetus to slavery and the slave-trade." From the same report, we also learn that the prosperity of the Mauritius, no less than that of the West India Islands, had suffered a fearful blight, in consequence of the "glorious act of emancipation."

A third commission was appointed, in 1850, to inquire into the condition and prospects of British Guiana. Lord Stanley, in his second letter to Mr. Gladstone, the Secretary of the British Colonies, has furnished us with the following extracts from the report of this committee:—

"Of Guiana generally they say—'It would be but a melancholy task to dwell upon the misery and ruin which so alarming a change must have occasioned to the proprietary body; but your commissioners feel themselves called upon to notice the effects which this wholesale abandonment of property has produced upon the colony at large. Where whole districts are fast relapsing into bush, and occasional patches of provisions around the huts of village settlers are all that remain to tell of once flourishing estates, it is not to be wondered at that the most ordinary marks of civilization are rapidly disappearing, and that in many districts of the colony all travelling communication by land will soon become utterly impracticable.'

" Of the Abary district:—' Your commission find that the line of road is nearly impassable, and that a long succession of formerly cultivated estates presents now a series of pestilent swamps, overrun with bush, and productive of malignant fevers.'

"Nor are matters," says Lord Stanley, "much better farther south.

" ' Proceeding still lower down, your commissioners find that the public roads and bridges are in such a condition that the few estates still remaining on the upper west bank of Mahaica Creek are completely cut off, save in the very dry season; and that with regard to the whole district, unless something be done very shortly, travelling by land will entirely cease. In such a state of things it cannot be wondered at that the herdsman has a formidable enemy to encounter in the jaguar and other beasts of prey, and that the keeping of cattle is attended with considerable loss from the depredations committed by these animals.'

"It may be worth noticing," continues Lord Stanley, "that this district—now overrun with wild beasts of the forest—was formerly the very garden of the colony. The estates touched one another along the whole line of the road, leaving no interval of uncleared land.

"The east coast, which is next mentioned by the commissioners, is better off. Properties, once of immense value, had there been bought at nominal prices; and the one railroad of Guiana passing through that tract, a comparatively industrious population—composed of former laborers on the line—enabled the planters still to work these to some profit. Even of this favored spot, however, they report that it 'feels most severely the want of continuous labor.'

"The commissioners next visit the east bank of the Demerara River, thus described:—

" 'Proceeding up the east bank of the river

Demerara, the generally prevailing features of ruin and distress are everywhere perceptible. Roads and bridges almost impassable are fearfully significant exponents of the condition of the plantations which they traverse; and Canal No. 3, once covered with plantains and coffee, presents now a scene of almost total desolation.'

"Crossing to the west side, they find prospects somewhat brighter: 'A few estates' are still 'keeping up a cultivation worthy of better times.' But this prosperous neighborhood is not extensive, and the next picture presented to our notice is less agreeable:—

" 'Ascending the river still higher, your commissioners learn that the district between Hobaboe Creek and "Stricken Heuvel" contained, in 1829, eight sugar and five coffee and plantain estates, and now there remain but three in sugar, and four partially cultivated with plantains, by petty settlers; while the roads, with one or two exceptions, are in a state of utter abandonment. Here, as on the opposite bank of the river, hordes of squatters have located themselves, who avoid all communication with Europeans, and have seemingly given themselves up altogether to the rude pleasures of a completely savage life.'

"The west coast of Demerara—the only part of the country which still remains unvisited—is described as showing *only* a diminution of fifty per cent. upon its produce of sugar; and with this fact the evidence concludes as to one of the three sections into which the colony is divided. Does Demerara stand alone in its misfortunes?

"Again hear the report:—'If the present state of the county of Demerara affords cause for deep apprehension, your commissioners find that Essequibo has retrograded to a still more alarming extent. In fact, unless a large and speedy supply of labor be obtained to cultivate the deserted fields of this once flourishing district, there is great reason to fear that it will relapse into total abandonment.'

"Describing another portion of the colony— they say of one district, 'Unless a fresh supply of labor be very soon obtained, there is every reason to fear that it will become completely abandoned.' Of a second, 'speedy immigration alone can save this island from total ruin.' 'The prostrate condition of this once beautiful part of the coast,' are the words which begin another paragraph, describing another tract of country. Of a fourth, 'the proprietors on this coast seem to be keeping up a hopeless struggle against approaching ruin.' Again, 'the once famous Arabian coast, so long the boast of the colony, presents now but a mournful picture of departed prosperity. Here were formerly situated some of the finest estates in the country, and a large resident body of proprietors lived in the district, and freely expended their incomes on the spot whence they derived them.' Once more, 'the lower part of the coast, after passing Devonshire Castle, to the river Pomeroon, presents a scene of almost total desolation.' Such is Essequibo!

"Berbice," says Lord Stanley, "has fared no better. Its rural population amounts to 18,000. Of these, 12,000 have withdrawn from the estates, and mostly from the neighborhood of the white man, to enjoy a savage freedom of ignorance and idleness, beyond the reach of example and sometimes of control. But on the condition of the negro I shall dwell more at length hereafter; at present it is the state of property with which I have to do. What are the districts which together form the county of Berbice? The Corentyne coast—the Canje Creek—east and west banks of the Berbice River—and the west coast, where, however, cotton was formerly the chief article produced. To each of these respectively the following passages, quoted in order, apply:—

"'The abandoned plantations on this coast,* which, if capital and labor could be procured, might easily be made very productive, are either wholly deserted, or else appropriated by hordes of squatters, who of course are unable to keep up at their own expense the public roads and bridges; and consequently all communication by land between the Corentyne and New Amsterdam is nearly at an end. The roads are impassable for horses or carriages, while for foot passengers they are extremely dangerous. The number of villages in this deserted region must be upward of 2500, and as the country abounds with fish and game, they have no difficulty in making a subsistence. In fact, the Corentyne coast is fast relapsing into a state of nature.'

"'Canje Creek was formerly considered a flourishing district of the county, and numbered on its east bank seven sugar and three coffee estates, and on its west bank eight estates, of which two were in sugar and six in coffee,

---

* The Corentyne.

making a total of eighteen plantations. The coffee cultivation has long since been entirely abandoned, and of the sugar estates but eight still now remain. They are suffering severely for want of labor, and being supported principally by African and Coolie immigrants, it is much to be feared that if the latter leave and claim their return passages to India, a great part of the district will become abandoned.'

" 'Under present circumstances, so gloomy is the condition of affairs here,* that the two gentlemen whom your commissioners have examined with respect to this district, both concur in predicting "its slow but sure approximation to the condition in which civilized man first found it." '

" 'A district† that in 1829 gave employment to 3635 registered slaves, but at the present moment there are not more than 600 laborers at work on the few estates still in cultivation, although it is estimated there are upward of 2000 people idling in villages of their own. The roads are in many parts several feet under

---

* East bank of the Berbice River.
† West bank of the Berbice River.

water and perfect swamps, while in some places the bridges are wanting altogether. In fact the whole district is fast becoming a total wilderness, with the exception of the one or two estates which yet continue to struggle on, and which are hardly accessible now but by water.'

" ' Except in some of the best villages,* they care not for back or front dams to keep off the water; their side-lines are disregarded, and consequently the drainage is gone, while in many instances the public road is so completely flooded that canoes have to be used as a means of transit. The Africans are unhappily following the example of the Creoles in this district, and buying land on which they settle in contented idleness; and your commissioners cannot view instances like these without the deepest alarm, for if this pernicious habit of squatting is allowed to extend to the immigrants also, there is no hope for the colony.' "†

We might fill a volume with extracts to the same effect. We might in like manner point to other regions, especially to Guatemala, to the British colony on the southern coast of

---

* West coast of Berbice River.
† Quoted in Carey's Slave Trade.

Africa, and to the island of Hayti, in all of which emancipation has been followed by precisely similar results. But we must hasten to consider how it is that emancipation has wrought all this ruin and desolation. In the mean time, we shall conclude this section in the ever-memorable words of Alison, the historian: "The negroes," says he, "who, in a state of slavery, were comfortable and prosperous beyond any peasantry in the world, and rapidly approaching the condition of the most opulent serfs of Europe, *have been by the act of emancipation irretrievably consigned to a state of barbarism.*"

§ III. *The manner in which emancipation has ruined the British Colonies.*

By the act of emancipation, Great Britain paralyzed the right arm of her colonial industry. The laborer would not work except occasionally, and the planter was ruined. The morals of the negro disappeared with his industry, and he speedily retraced his steps toward his original barbarism. All this had been clearly foretold. "Emancipation," says Dr. Channing in 1840, "was resisted on the ground that the slave, if restored to his rights, *would fall into idleness and vagrancy, and even relapse into bar-barism."*

This was predicted by the West Indian plant-ers, who certainly had a good opportunity to know something of the character of the negro, whether bond or free. But who could suppose for a moment that an enlightened abolitionist would listen to slaveholders? His response was, that "their unhappy position as slave-holders had robbed them of their reason and blunted their moral sense." Precisely the same thing had been foretold by the Calhouns and the Clays of this country. But they, too, were unfortunately slaveholders, and, consequently, so completely "sunk in moral darkness," that their testimony was not entitled to credit. The calmest, the profoundest, the wisest statesmen of Great Britain likewise forewarned the agi-tators of the desolation and the woes they were about to bring upon the West Indies. But the madness of the day would confide in no wisdom except its own, and listen to no testimony except to the clamor of fanatics. Hence the frightful experiment was made, and, as we have seen, the prediction of the anti-abolitionists has been fulfilled to the very letter.

The cause of this downward tendency in the British colonies is now perfectly apparent to all who have eyes to see. On this point, the two committees above referred to both concur in the same conclusion. The committee of 1842 declare, "that the principal causes of this diminished production, and consequent distress, are the great difficulty which has been experienced by the planters in obtaining *steady* and *continuous* labor, and the high rate of remuneration which they give for even the *broken* and *indifferent* work which they are able to procure."

The cry of the abolitionist has been changed. At first—even before the experiment was more than a year old—he insisted that the industry of the freed black was working wonders in the British colonies. In the West Indies, in particular, he assured us that the freed negro would do "an infinity of work for wages."* Though he had been on the islands, and had had an opportunity to see for himself, he boasted that "the old notion that the negro is, by constitution, a lazy creature, who will do no work at all except by compulsion, *is now forever ex-*

---

* Gurney's Letters on the West Indies.

ploded."[*]   He even declared, that the free
negro "understands his interest as well as a
Yankee."[†]   These confident statements, made
by an eye-witness, were hailed by the abolitionists as conclusive proof that the experiment
was working admirably.   "The great truth has
come out," says Dr. Channing, "that the hopes
of the most sanguine advocates of emancipation
have been realized—if not surpassed—by the
West Indies."   What! the negro become idle,
indeed!   "He is more likely," says the enchanted doctor, "to fall into the civilized man's
cupidity than into the filth and sloth of the
savage."   But all these magnificent boasts were
quite premature.   A few short years have suf-
ficed to demonstrate that the deluded authors
of them, who had so lamentably failed to
predict the future, could not even read the
present.

Their boasts are now exploded.   Their former
hopes are blasted; and their cry is changed.
The song now is,—"Well, suppose the negroes
will not work: they are FREE!   They can now
do as they list, and there is no man to hinder."
Ah, yes! they can now, at their own sweet will,

---

* Gurney's Letters on the West Indies.   † Ibid.

stretch themselves "under their gracefully-waving groves," and be lulled to sleep amid the sound of waterfalls and the song of birds.

Such, precisely, is the paradise for which the negro sighs, except that he does not care for the waterfalls and the birds. But it should be remarked, that when sinful man was driven from the only Paradise that earth has ever seen, he was doomed to eat his bread in the sweat of his brow. This doom he cannot reverse. Let him make of life—as the Haytian negroes do—"one long day of unprofitable ease,"* and he may dream of Paradise, or the abolitionists may dream for him. But while he dreams, the laws of nature are sternly at their work. Indolence benumbs his feeble intellect, and inflames his passions. Poverty and want are creeping on him. Temptation is surrounding him; and vice, with all her motley train, is winding fast her deadly coils around his very soul, and making him the devil's slave, to do his work upon the earth. Thus, the blossoms of his paradise are *fine words*, and its fruits are *death*.

"If but two hours' labor per day," says

---

* Dr. Channing.

Theodore Parker, "are necessary for the support of each colored man, I know not why he should toil longer." You know not, then, why the colored man should work more than two hours a day? Neither does the colored man himself. You know not why he should have any higher or nobler aim in life than to supply his few, pressing, animal wants? Neither does he. You know not why he should think of the future, or provide for the necessities of old age? Neither does he. You know not why he should take thought for seasons of sickness? Neither does he; and hence his child often dies under his own eyes, for the want of medical attendance. You know not that the colored man, who begins with working only two hours a day, will soon end with ceasing from all regular employment, and live, in the midst of filth, by stealing or other nefarious means? In one word, you know not why the colored man should not live like the brute, in and for the present merely—blotting out all the future from his plans of life? If, indeed, you really know none of these things, then we beg you will excuse us, if *we* do not know why you should assume to teach our senators wisdom;— if we do not know why the cobbler should not stick to his last, and all such preachers to their pulpits.*

Abolitionism is decidedly progressive. The time was when Dr. Channing thought that men should work, and that, if they would not labor from rational motives, they should be compelled to labor.† The time was, when even abolitionists looked upon labor with respect, and regarded it as merely an obedience to the

---

* We moot a higher question: Is he fit for the pulpit,—for that great conservative power by which religion, and morals, and freedom, must be maintained among us? "I do not believe," he declares, in one of his sermons, "the miraculous origin of the Hebrew church, or the Buddhist church, or of the Christian church, nor the miraculous character of Jesus. I take not the Bible for my master—nor yet the church—nor even Jesus of Nazareth for my master. . . . . He is my best historic ideal of human greatness; not without errors—not without the stain of his times, and I presume, of course, not without sins; for men without sins exist in the dreams of girls." Thus, the truth of all miracles is denied; and the faith of the Christian world, in regard to the sinless character of Jesus, is set down by this very modest *divine* as the dream of girls! Yet he believes that half a million of men were, by the British act of emancipation, turned from slaves into freemen! That is to say, he does not believe in the miracles of the gospel; he only believes in the miracles of abolitionism. Hence, we ask, is he fit for the pulpit,—for the sacred desk,—for any holy thing?

† See extract, p. 111.

very first law of nature, or merely a compliance with the very first condition of all economic, social, and moral well-being.   But the times are changed.   The exigencies of abolitionism now require that *manual labor, and the gross material wealth* it produces, should be sneeringly spoken of, and great swelling eulogies pronounced on the infinite value of the negro's freedom.   For this is all he has; and for this, all else has been sacrificed.   Thus, since abolitionists themselves have been made to see that the freed negro — the pet and idol of their hearts — will not work from rational motives, then the principles of political economy, and the affairs of the world, all must be adjusted to the course *he* may be pleased to take.

In this connection we shall notice a passage from Montesquieu, which is exactly in point. He is often quoted by the abolitionists, but seldom fairly.   It is true, he is exceedingly hostile to slavery *in general*, and very justly pours ridicule and contempt on some of the arguments used in favor of the institution.   But yet, with all his enthusiastic love of liberty,—nay, with his ardent passion for equality,—he saw far too deeply into the true "Spirit of Laws" not to perceive that slavery is, in certain cases, founded on the great principles of political justice. It is precisely in those cases in which a race or a people will not work without being compelled to do so, that he justifies the institution in question. Though warmly and zealously opposed to slavery, yet he was not bent on sacrificing the good of society to abstractions or to prejudice. Hence, he could say: "But as all men are born equal, slavery must be accounted unnatural, THOUGH IN SOME COUNTRIES IT BE FOUNDED ON NATURAL REASON; and a wide difference ought to be made betwixt such countries, and those in which natural reason rejects it, as in Europe, where it has been happily abolished."* Now, if we inquire in what countries, or under what circumstances, he considered slavery founded on natural reason, we may find his answer in a preceding portion of the same page. It is in those "countries," says he, "where the excess of heat enervates the body, and renders men so slothful and dispirited, that nothing but the fear of chastisement can oblige them to perform any laborious duty," &c. Such, as we have seen, is precisely the case with the African race in its present condition.

---

* Spirit of Laws, vol. i. book xv. chap. vii.

"Natural slavery, then," he continues, "is to be limited to some particular parts of the world."* And again: "Bad laws have made lazy men—they have been reduced to slavery because of their laziness." The first portion of this remark—that bad laws have made lazy men —is not applicable to the African race. For they were made lazy, not by bad laws, but by the depravity of human nature, in connection and in co-operation with long, long centuries of brutal ignorance and the most savage modes of life. But, be the cause of this laziness what it may, it is sufficient, according to the principles of this great advocate of human freedom and equality, to justify the servitude in which the providence of God has placed the African.

No doubt it is very hard on lazy men that they should be compelled to work. It is for this reason that Montesquieu calls such slavery "the most cruel that is to be found among men;" by which he evidently means that it is the most cruel, though necessary, because those on whom it is imposed are least inclined to work. If he had only had greater experience

---

* Spirit of Laws, vol. i. book xv. chap. viii.

of negro slavery, the hardship would have seemed far less to him. For though the negro is naturally lazy, and too improvident to work for himself, he will often labor for a master with a right good will, and with a loyal devotion to his interests. He is, indeed, often prepared, and made ready for labor, because he feels that, in his master, he has a protector and a friend.

But whether labor be a heavy burden or a light, it must be borne. The good of the lazy race, and the good of the society into which they have been thrown, both require them to bear this burden, which is, after all and at the worst, far lighter than that of a vagabond life. "Nature cries aloud," says the abolitionist, "for freedom." Nature, we reply, demands that man shall work, and her decree must be fulfilled. For ruin, as we have seen, is the bitter fruit of disobedience to her will.

It is now high time that we should notice some of the exalted eulogies bestowed by abolitionists upon freedom; and also *the kind of freedom* on which these high praises have been so eloquently lavished. This, accordingly, we shall proceed to do in the following section.

§ IV. *The great benefit supposed by American abolitionists to result to the freed negroes from the British act of emancipation.*

We have, in the preceding sections, abundantly seen that the freed colored subjects of the British crown are fast relapsing into the most irretrievable barbarism, while the once flourishing colonies themselves present the most appalling scenes of desolation and distress. Surely it is no wonder that the hurrahing of the English people has ceased. "At the present moment," says the London Times for December 1st, 1852, "if there is one thing in the world that the British public do not like to talk about, or *even to think about*, it is the condition of the race for whom this great effort was made." Not so with the abolitionists of this country. They still keep up the annual celebration of that great event, the act of emancipation, by which, in the language of one of their number, more than half a million of human beings were "turned from brutes into freemen!"

It is the freedom of the negro which they celebrate. Let us look, then, for a few moments, into the mysteries of this celebration, and see, if we may, the nature of the praises they pour forth in honor of freedom, and *the kind of freedom on which* they are so passionately bestowed.

We shall not quote from the more insane of the fraternity of abolitionists, for their wild, raving nonsense would, indeed, be unworthy of serious refutation. We shall simply notice the language of Dr. Channing, the scholar-like and the eloquent, though visionary, advocate of British emancipation. Even as early as 1842, in an address delivered on the anniversary of that event, he burst into the following strain of impassioned eulogy: "Emancipation works well, far better than could have been anticipated. *To me it could hardly have worked otherwise than well.* It banished *slavery*, that wrong and curse not to be borne. It gave *freedom*, the dear birthright of humanity; and had it done nothing more, I should have found in it cause for joy. Freedom, simple freedom, is 'in my estimation just, far prized above all price.' *I do not stop to ask if the emancipated are better fed and clothed than formerly.* THEY ARE FREE; AND THAT ONE WORD CONTAINS A WORLD OF GOOD,* unknown to the most pampered slave."

---

* The emphasis is ours.

And again, he says, "Nature cries aloud for freedom as our proper good, our birthright and our end, and resents nothing so much as its loss."

In these high-sounding praises, which hold up personal freedom as "our proper good," as "our end," it is assumed that man was made for liberty, and not liberty for man. It is, indeed, one of the fundamental errors of the abolitionist to regard freedom as a great substantive good, or as in itself a blessing, and not merely as a relative good. It may be, and indeed often is, an unspeakable benefit, but then it is so only as a means to an end. The end of our existence, the *proper good*, is the improvement of our intellectual and moral powers, the perfecting of our rational and immortal natures. When freedom subserves this end, it is a good; when it defeats this end, it is an evil. Hence there may be a world of evil as well as a world of good in "this one word."

The wise man adapts the means to the end. It were the very height of folly to sacrifice the end to the means. No man gives personal freedom to his child because he deems it always and in all cases a good. His heart teaches him a better doctrine when the highest good of his child is concerned. Should we not be permitted, then, to have something of the same feeling in regard to those whom Providence has placed under our care, especially since, having the passions of men, with only the intellects of children, they stand in utmost need of guidance and direction?

As it is their duty to labor, so the law which compels them to do so is not oppressive. It deprives them of the enjoyment of no right, unless, indeed, they may be supposed to have a right to violate their duty. Hence, in compelling the colored population of the South to work, the law does not deprive them of liberty, in the true sense of the word; that is, *it does not deprive them of the enjoyment of any natural right*. It merely requires them to perform a natural duty.

This cannot be denied. It has been, as we have shown, admitted both by Dr. Wayland and Dr. Channing.* But while the *end* is approved, the *means* are not liked. Few of the abolitionists are disposed to offer any substitute for our method. They are satisfied merely to pull down and destroy, without the least

* See pages 110 and 119.

thought or care in regard to consequences. Dr. Channing has, however, been pleased to propose another method, for securing the industry of the black and the prosperity of the State. Let us then, for a moment, look at this scheme.

The black man, says he, should not be owned. He should work, but not under the control of a master. His overseer should be appointed by the State, and be amenable to the State for the proper exercise of his authority. Now, if this learned and eloquent orator had only looked one inch beneath the surface of his own scheme, he would have seen that it is fraught with the most insuperable difficulties, and that its execution must needs be attended with the most ruinous consequences.

Emancipate the blacks, then, and let the State undertake to work them. In the first place, we must ignore every principle of political economy, and consent to the wildest and most reckless of experiments, ere we can agree that the State should superintend and carry on the agricultural interest of the country. But suppose this difficulty out of the way, on what land would the State cause *its slaves* to be worked? It would scarcely take possession of the plantations now under improvement; and, setting aside the owners, proceed to cultivate the land. But it must either do this, or else leave these plantations to become worthless for the want of laborers, and open new ones for the benefit of the State! In no point of view could a more utterly chimerical or foolish scheme be well conceived. If we may not be allowed to adhere to our own plan, we beg that some substitute may be proposed which is not fraught with such inevitable destruction to the whole South. Otherwise, we shall fear that these self-styled friends of humanity are more bent on carrying out their own designs than they are on promoting our good.

But what is meant by the freedom of the emancipated slaves, on which so many exalted eulogies have been pronounced? Its first element, it is plain, is a freedom from labor*— freedom from the very first law of nature. In one word, its sum and substance is a power on the part of the freed black to act pretty much as he pleases. Now, before we expend oceans of enthusiasm on such a freedom, would it not be well to see *how* he would be pleased to act?

---

* See chap. i. § 2.

S

Dr. Channing has told us, we are aware, of the "indomitable love of liberty," which had been infused into the breast of "fierce barbarians" by their native wildernesses.* But we are no great admirers of a liberty which knows no law except its own will, and seeks no end except the gratification of passion.† Hence, we have no very great respect for the liberty of fierce barbarians. It would make a hell on earth. "My maxim," exclaims Dr. Channing, "is any thing but slavery!" Even slavery, we cry, before a freedom such as his!

This kind of freedom, it should be remembered, was born in France and cradled in the revolution. May it never be forgotten that the "Friends of the Blacks" at Boston had their exact prototypes in "*les Amis des Noirs*" of Paris. Of this last society Robespierre was the ruling spirit, and Brissot the orator. By the dark machinations of the one,‡ and the fiery eloquence of the other, the French people— *la grande nation*—were induced, in 1791, to pro-

---

* Works, vol. v. p. 63. † See chap. i. § 2.

‡ We have in the above remark done Boston some injustice. For New York has furnished the Robespierre, and Massachusetts only the Brissot, of "les Amis des Noirs" in America.

claim the principle of equality to and for the free blacks of St. Domingo. This beautiful island, then the brightest and most precious jewel in the crown of France, thus became the first of the West Indies in which the dreadful experiment of a forced equality was tried. The authors of that experiment were solemnly warned of the horrors into which it would inevitably plunge both the whites and the blacks of the island. Yet, firm and immovable as death, Robespierre sternly replied, then "Perish the colonies rather than sacrifice one iota of our principles!"* The magnificent colony of St. Domingo did not quite perish, it is true; but yet, as every one, except the philanthropic "Ami des Noirs" of the present day, still remembers with a thrill of horror, the entire white population soon melted, like successive flakes of snow, in the furnace of that freedom which a Robespierre had kindled.

The atrocities of this awful massacre have had, as the historian has said,† no parallel in the

---

* This reply is sometimes attributed to Robespierre and sometimes to Brissot; it is probable that in substance it was made by both of these bloody compeers in the cause of abolitionism.

† See Alison's History of Europe, vol. ii. p. 241.

annals of human crime. "The negroes," says
Alison, "marched with spiked infants on their
spears instead of colors; they sawed asunder
the male prisoners, and violated the females on
the dead bodies of their husbands." The work
of death, thus completed with such outbursts
of unutterable brutality, constituted and closed
the first act in the grand drama of Haytian
freedom.

But equality was not yet established. The
colored men, or mulattoes, beheld, with an eye
burning with jealousy, the superior power and
ascendency of the blacks. Hence arose the
horrors of a civil war. Equality had been proclaimed, and anarchy produced. In this frightful
chaos, the ambitious mulattoes, whose insatiable
desire of equality had first disturbed the peace
of the island, perished miserably beneath the
vengeance of the very slaves whom they had
themselves roused from subjection and elevated
into irresistible power. Thus ended the second
act of the horrible drama.

This bloody discord, this wild chaos of disgusting brutalities, of course terminated not in
freedom, but in a military despotism. With
the subsequent wars and fearful destruction of
human life our present inquiry has nothing to

do. We must confine our attention to the point before us, namely, the kind of freedom achieved by the blacks of St. Domingo. We have witnessed the two great manifestations of that freedom; we shall now look at its closing scene. This we shall, for obvious reasons, present in the language of an English author.

"An independent negro state," says he, "was thus established in Hayti; but the people have not derived all the benefits which they sanguinely expected. Released from their compulsory toil, they have not yet learned to subject themselves to the restraints of regular industry. The first absolute rulers made the most extraordinary efforts to overcome the indolence which soon began to display itself. The *Code Rural* directed that the laborer should fix himself on a certain estate, which he was never afterward to quit without a passport from the government. His hours of labor and rest were fixed by statute. The whip, at first permitted, was ultimately prohibited; but as every military officer was allowed to chastise with a thick cane, and almost every proprietor held a commission, the laborer was not much relieved. By these means Mr. Mackenzie supposes that the produce of 1806 was raised to about a third of that of 1789. But such violent regulations could not continue to be enforced amid the succeeding agitations, and under a republican *régime*. Almost all traces of laborious culture were soon obliterated; large tracts, which had been one entire sugar garden, presented now only a few scattered plantations."*

Thus the lands were divided out among the officers of the army, while the privates were compelled to cultivate the soil under their former military commanders, clothed with more than "a little brief authority." No better could have been expected except by fools or fanatics. The blacks might preach equality, it is true, but yet, like the more enlightened ruffians of Paris, they would of course take good care not to practise what they had preached. Hence, by all the horrors of their bloody revolution, they only effected a change of masters. The white man had disappeared, and the black man, one of their own race and color, had assumed his place and his authority. And of all masters, it is well known, the naturally servile are the most cruel. "The earth," says Solo-

* Encyclopædia of Geo., vol. iii. pp. 302, 303.

mon, "cannot bear a servant when he reigneth."*

> "The sensual and the dark rebel in vain:
> Slaves by their own compulsion, in mad game
> They burst their manacles, to wear the *name*
> Of Freedom, graven on a heavier chain."
>
> COLERIDGE.

Thus "the world of good" they sought was found, most literally, in "the word;" for the word, the name of freedom, was all they had achieved—at least of good. Poverty, want, disease, and crime, were the substantial fruits of their boasted freedom.

In 1789, the sugar exported was 672,000,000 pounds; in 1806, it was 47,516,531 pounds; in 1825, it was 2020 pounds; in 1832, it was 0 pounds. If history had not spoken, we might have safely inferred, from this astounding decline of industry, that the morals of the people had suffered a fearful deterioration. But we are not left to inference. We are informed, by the best authorities,† that their "morals are exceedingly bad;" and that under the reign of

---

* Prov. xxx. 22.

† Encyc. of Geo., vol. iii. p. 303. Mackenzie's St. Domingo, vol. ii. pp. 260, 321.

liberty, as it is called, their condition has, in all respects, become far worse than it was before. "There appears every reason to apprehend," says James Franklin, "that it will recede into irrecoverable insignificance, poverty, and disorder."*

Mr. T. Babington Macaulay has, we are aware, put forth certain notions on the subject of liberty, which are exactly in accordance with the views and the spirit of the abolitionists, as well as with the cut-throat philosophy of the Parisian philanthropists of the revolution. As these notions are found in one of his juvenile productions, and illustrated by "a pretty story" out of Ariosto, we should not deem it worth while to notice them, if they had not been retained in the latest edition of his Miscellanies. But for this circumstance, we should pass them by as the rhetorical flourish of a young man who, in his most mature productions, is often more brilliant than profound.

"Ariosto," says he, "tells a pretty story of a fairy, who, by some mysterious law of her nature, was condemned to appear at certain seasons in the form of a foul and poisonous snake.

---

* Franklin's Present State of Hayti, &c., p. 265.

Those who injured her during the period of her disguise were forever excluded from participation in the blessings which she bestowed. But to those who, in spite of her loathsome aspect, pitied and protected her, she afterward revealed herself in the beautiful and celestial form which was natural to her, accompanied their steps, granted all their wishes, filled their houses with wealth, made them happy in love, and victorious in war. Such a spirit is Liberty. At times she takes the form of a hateful reptile. She grovels, she hisses, she stings. But wo to those who in disgust shall venture to crush her! And happy are those who, having dared to receive her in her degraded and frightful shape, shall at length be rewarded by her in the time of her beauty and her glory."

For aught we know, all this may be very fine poetry, and may deserve the place which it has found in some of our books on rhetoric. But yet this beautiful passage will—like the fairy whose charms it celebrates—be so surely transformed into a hateful snake or venomous toad, that it should not be swallowed without an antidote. Robespierre, Danton, Marat, Barrère, and the black Dessalines, took this hateful, hissing, stinging, maddening reptile to their bosoms, and they are welcome to its rewards. But they mistook the thing: it was not liberty transformed; it was tyranny unbound, the very scourge of hell, and Satan's chief instrument of torture to a guilty world. It was neither more nor less than Sin, despising God, and warring against his image on the earth.

We do not doubt—nay, we firmly believe— that in the veritable history of the universe, *analogous* changes have taken place. But then these awful changes were not mere fairy tales. They are recorded in the word of God. When Lucifer, the great bearer of light, himself was *free*, he sought equality with God, and thence became a hateful, hissing serpent in the dust. But he was not fully cursed, until " by devilish art" he reached " the organs of man's fancy," and with them forged the grand illusion that equality alone is freedom.

For even sinless, happy Eve was made to feel herself oppressed, until, with keen desire of equality with gods, " forth reaching to the fruit, she plucked, she ate:"—

> " Earth felt the wound, and Nature from her seat,
> Sighing through all her works, gave signs of wo,
> That all was lost."

How much easier, then, to effect the ruin of poor, fallen man, by stirring up this fierce desire of equality with discontented thoughts and vain hopes of unattainable good! It is this dark desire, and not liberty, which, in its rage, becomes the "poisonous snake;" and, though decked in fine, allegoric, glowing garb, it is still the loathsome thing, the "false worm," that turned God's Paradise itself into a blighted world.

If Mr. Macaulay had only distinguished between liberty and license, than which no two things in the universe are more diametrically opposed to each other, his passion for fine rhetoric would not have betrayed him into so absurd a conceit respecting the diverse forms of freedom. Liberty is — as we have seen — the bright emanation of reason in the form of law; license is the triumph of blind passion over all law and order. Hence, if we would have liberty, the great deep of human passion must be restrained. For this purpose, as Mr. Burke has said, there must be power somewhere; and if there be not moral power within, there must be physical power without. Otherwise, the restraints will be too weak; the safeguards of liberty will give way, and the passions of men will burst into anarchy, the most frightful of all the forms of tyranny. Shall we call this liberty? Shall we seek the secure enjoyment of natural rights in a wild reign of lawless terror? As well might we seek the pure light of heaven in the bottomless pit. It is, indeed, a most horrible desecration of the sacred name of liberty, to apply it either to the butcheries and brutalities of the French Revolution, or to the more diabolical massacres of St. Domingo. If such were freedom, it would, in sober truth, be more fitly symbolized by ten thousand hissing serpents than by a single poisonous snake; and by all on earth, as in heaven, it should be abhorred. Hence, those pretended friends and advocates of freedom, who would thus fain transmute her form divine into such horribly distorted shapes, are with her enemies confederate in dark misguided league.

§ V. *The consequences of abolition to the South.*

"We have had experience enough in our own colonies," says the *Prospective Review*, for November, 1852, "not to wish to see the experiment tried elsewhere on a larger scale." Now this, though it comes to us from across the Atlantic, really sounds like the voice of genuine philanthropy. Nor do we wish to see the experiment, which has brought down such widespread ruin on all the great interests of St. Domingo and the British colonies, tried in this prosperous and now beautiful land of ours. It requires no prophet to foresee the awful consequences of such an experiment on the lives, the liberties, the fortunes, and the morals, of the people of the Southern States. Let us briefly notice some of these consequences.

Consider, in the first place, the vast amount of property which would be destroyed by the madness of such an experiment. According to the estimate of Mr. Clay, "the total value of the slave property in the United States is twelve hundred millions of dollars," all of which the people of the South are expected to sacrifice on the altar of abolitionism. It only moves the indignation of the abolitionist that we should for one moment hesitate. "I see," he exclaims, "in the immenseness of the value of the slaves, the enormous amount of the robbery committed on them. I see 'twelve hundred millions of dollars' seized, extorted by unrighteous force."* But, unfortunately, his

* Dr. Channing's Works, vol. v. p. 47.

passions are so furious, that his mind no sooner comes into contact with any branch of the subject of slavery, than instantly, as if by a flash of lightning, his opinion is formed, and he begins to declaim and denounce as if reason should have nothing to do with the question. He does not even allow himself time for a single moment's serious reflection. Nay, resenting the opinion of the most sagacious of our statesmen as an insult to his understanding, he deems it beneath his dignity even to make an attempt to look beneath the surface of the great problem on which he condescends to pour the illuminations of his genius. Ere we accept his oracles as inspired, we beg leave to think a little, and consider their intrinsic value.

Twelve hundred millions of dollars extorted by unrighteous force! What enormous robbery! Now, let it be borne in mind, that this is the language of a man who, as we have seen, has—in one of his lucid intervals—admitted that *it is right to apply force* to compel those to work who will not labor from rational motives. Such is precisely the application of the force which now moves his righteous indignation! This force, so justly applied, has created this enormous value of twelve hundred millions of dollars. It has neither seized, nor extorted this vast amount from others; it has simply created it out of that which, but for such force, would have been utterly valueless. And if experience teaches any thing, then, no sooner shall this force be withdrawn, than the great value in question will disappear. It will not be restored; it will be annihilated. The slaves—now worth so many hundred millions of dollars—would become worthless to themselves, and nuisances to society. No free State in the Union would be willing to receive them—or a considerable portion of them—into her dominions. They would be regarded as pests, and, if possible, everywhere expelled from the empires of freemen.

Our lands, like those of the British West Indies, would become almost valueless for the want of laborers to cultivate them. The most beautiful garden-spots of the sunny South would, in the course of a few years, be turned into a jungle, with only here and there a forlorn plantation. Poverty and distress, bankruptcy and ruin, would everywhere be seen. In one word, the condition of the Southern States would, in all material respects, be like that of the once flourishing British colonies in which the fatal experiment of emancipation has been tried.

Such are some of the fearful consequences of emancipation. But these are not all. The ties that would be severed, and the sympathies crushed, by emancipation, are not at all understood by abolitionists. They are, indeed, utter strangers to the moral power which these ties and sympathies now exert for the good of the inferior race. "Our patriarchal scheme of domestic servitude," says Governor Hammond, "is indeed well calculated to awaken the higher and finer feelings of our nature. It is not wanting in its enthusiasm and its poetry. The relations of the most beloved and honored chiefs, and the most faithful and admiring subjects, which, from the time of Homer, have been the theme of song, are frigid and unfelt, compared with those existing between the master and his slaves; who served his father, and rocked his cradle, or have been born in his household, and look forward to serve his children; who have been through life the props of his fortune, and the objects of his care; who have partaken of his griefs, and looked to him for comfort in their own; whose sickness he has so frequently watched

over and relieved; whose holidays he has so
often made joyous by his bounties and his
presence; for whose welfare, when absent, his
anxious solicitude never ceases, and whose
hearty and affectionate greetings never fail to
welcome him home. In this cold, calculating,
ambitious world of ours, there are few ties more
heart-felt, or of more benignant influence, than
those which mutually bind the master and the
slave, under our ancient system, handed down
from the father of Israel."

Let the slaves be emancipated then, and, in
one or two generations, the white people of the
South would care as little for the freed blacks
among us, as the same class of persons are now
cared for by the white people of the North.
The prejudice of race would be restored with
unmitigated violence. The blacks are contented in servitude, so long as they find themselves excluded from none of the privileges of
the condition to which they belong; but let
them be delivered from the authority of their
masters, and they will feel their rigid exclusion
from the society of the whites and all participation in their government. They would become clamorous for "their inalienable rights."
Three millions of freed blacks, thus circum

stanced, would furnish the elements of the most horrible civil war the world has ever witnessed.

These elements would soon burst in fury on the land. There was no civil war in Jamaica, it is true, after the slaves were emancipated; but this was because the power of Great Britain was over the two parties, and held them in subjection. It would be far otherwise here. For here there would be no power to check—while there would be infernal agencies at work to promote—civil discord and strife. As Robespierre caused it to be proclaimed to the free blacks of St. Domingo that they were naturally entitled to all the rights and privileges of citizens; as Mr. Seward proclaimed the same doctrine to the free blacks of New York; so there would be kind benefactors enough to propagate the same sentiments among our colored population. They would be instigated, in every possible way, to claim their natural equality with the whites; and, by every diabolical art, their bad passions would be inflamed. If the object of such agitators were merely to stir up scenes of strife and blood, it might be easily attained; but if it were to force the blacks into a social and political equality with the whites, it would most certainly and forever fail. For the government of these Southern States was, by our fathers, founded on the VIRTUE and the INTELLIGENCE of the people, and there we intend it shall stand. The African has neither part nor lot in the matter.

We cannot suppose, for a moment, that abolitionists would be in the slightest degree moved by the awful consequences of emancipation. Poverty, ruin, death, are very small items with these sublime philanthropists. They scarcely enter into their calculations. The dangers of a civil war—though the most fearful the world has ever seen — lie quite beneath the range of their humanity.

Indeed, we should expect our argument from the consequences of emancipation to be met by a thorough-going abolitionist with the words, — "Perish the Southern States rather than sacrifice one iota of our principles!" We ask them not to sacrifice their principles to us; nor do we intend that they shall sacrifice us to their principles. For if perish we must, it shall be as a sacrifice to our own principles, and not to theirs.

NOTE. — It has not fallen within the scope of our design to consider the effects of emancipation, and of the consequent destruction of so large an amount of property, on the condition and prosperity of the world. Otherwise it might easily have been shown that every civilized portion of the globe would feel the shock. This point has been very happily, though briefly, illustrated by Governor Hammond, in his "Letters on Slavery."

Nor has it formed any part of our purpose, in the following section, to discuss the influence of American slavery on the future destiny and civilization of Africa. This subject has been ably discussed by various writers; and especially by an accomplished divine, the Rev. William N. Pendleton, in a discourse published in the "Virginia Colonizationist," for September, 1854.

§ VI. *Elevation of the Blacks by Southern slavery.*

The abolitionists, with the most singular unanimity, perseveringly assert that Southern slavery degrades its subjects "into brutes." This assertion fills us with amazement. If it were possible, we would suppose, in a judgment of charity, that its authors knew nothing of the history of Africa or of the condition of our slaves. But such ignorance is not possible. On the other hand, we find it equally impossible to believe that so many men and women—the very lights of abolitionism — could knowingly utter so palpable a falsehood. Thus we are forced to the conclusion, that the authors of this charge are so completely carried away by a blind hatred of slavery, that they do not care to

keep their words within the sacred bounds of
eternal truth. This seems to be the simple,
melancholy fact. The great question with them
seems to be, not what is true or what is false,
but what will most speedily effect the destruction
of Southern slavery. Any thing that seems to
answer this purpose is blindly and furiously
wielded by them. The Edinburgh Review, in a
high-wrought eulogy on an American authoress,
says that she assails slavery with arrows "poi-
soned by truth." Her words, it is true, are
dipped in flaming poison; but *that* poison is
not truth. The truth is never poison.

The native African could not be degraded.
Of the fifty millions of inhabitants of the continent of Africa, it is estimated that forty millions were slaves. The master had the power of
life and death over the slave; and, in fact, his
slaves were often fed, and killed, and eaten, just
as we do with oxen and sheep in this country.
Nay, the hind and fore-quarters of men, women,
and children, might there be seen hung on the
shambles and exposed for sale! Their women
were beasts of burden; and, when young, they
were regarded as a great delicacy by the palate
of their pampered masters. A warrior would
sometimes take a score of young females along

with him, in order to enrich his feasts and regale his appetite. He delighted in such delicacies. As to his religion, it was even worse than his morals; or rather, his religion was a mass of the most disgusting immoralities. His notion of a God, and the obscene acts by which that notion was worshipped, are too shocking to be mentioned. The vilest slave that ever breathed the air of a Christian land could not begin to conceive the horrid iniquities of such a life. And yet, in the face of all this, we are told—yea, we are perseveringly and eternally told—that "the African has been degraded into a brute" by American slavery! Indeed, if such creatures ever reach the level of simple brutality at all, is it not evident they must be elevated, and not degraded, to it?

The very persons who make the above charge know better. Their own writings furnish the most incontestable proof that they know better. A writer in the Edinburgh Review,* for example, has not only asserted that "slavery degrades its subjects into brutes," but he has the audacity to declare, in regard to slavery in the United States, that "we do not believe that

---

* April No., 1855.

such oppression is to be found in any other part of the world, civilized or uncivilized. We do not believe that such oppression ever existed before." Yet even this unprincipled writer has, in the very article containing this declaration, shown that he knows better. He has shown that he knows that the African has been elevated and improved by his servitude in the United States. We shall proceed to convict him out of his own mouth.

"The African slave-trade was frightful," says he; "but its prey were savages, accustomed to suffering and misery, and to endure them with patience almost amounting to apathy. The victims of the American slave-trade have been bred in a highly-cultivated community. Their dispositions have been softened, their intellects sharpened, and their sensibilities excited, by society, by Christianity, and by all the ameliorating but enervating influences of civilization. The savage submits to be enslaved himself, or have his wife or his child carried off by his enemies, as merely a calamity. His misery is not embittered by indignation. He suffers only what—if he could—he would inflict. He cannot imagine a state of society in which there shall not be masters and slaves,

kidnapping and man-selling, coffles and slave-
traders, or in which any class shall be exempt
from misfortunes which appear to him to be
incidental to humanity."

Thus, according to this very sagacious, honest, consistent writer, it matters little what
you do with the native African : he has no
moral sense ; he feels no wrong ; he suffers only
what he would inflict. But when you come to
deal with the American slave, or, as this writer
calls him, "the civilized Virginian," it is quite
another thing! His dispositions have been
softened, his intellect sharpened, and his sensibilities roused to a new life, by society and by
Christianity! And yet, according to this very
writer, this highly civilized Virginian is the
man who, by American slavery, has been degraded from the native African into a brute!
We dismiss his lawless savage, and his equally
lawless pen, from our further consideration.

We proceed, in like manner, to condemn
Dr. Channing out of his own mouth. He has
repeatedly asserted that slavery among us degrades its subjects into brutes. Now hear
him on the other side of this question

"The European race," says he, "have manifested more courage, enterprise, invention ; but

in the dispositions which Christianity particularly honors, how inferior are they to the African! When I cast my eyes over our Southern region,—the land of bowie-knives, lynch-law, and duels, of 'chivalry,' 'honor,' and revenge; and when I consider that Christianity is declared to be a spirit of charity, 'which seeketh not its own, is not easily provoked, thinketh no evil, and endureth all things,' and is also declared to be 'the wisdom from above, which is 'first pure, then peaceable, gentle, easy to be entreated, full of mercy and good fruits;' can I hesitate in deciding to which of the races in that land Christianity is most adapted, and in which its noblest disciples are most likely to be reared?"*

It was by casting his eyes over "our Southern region" that Dr. Channing concluded "that we are holding in bondage one of the best races of the human family." If he had cast them over the appallingly dark region of Africa, he would have been compelled, in spite of the wonder-working power of his imagination, to pronounce it one of the very worst and most degraded races upon earth. If, as he imagines,

* Dr. Channing's Works, vol. vi. p. 50, 51.

this race among us is now nearer to the kingdom of heaven than we ourselves are, how dare he assert—as he so often has done—that our slavery has "degraded them into brutes?" If, indeed, they had not been elevated—both physically and morally—by their servitude in America, it would have been beyond the power of even Dr. Channing to pronounce such a eulogy upon them. We say, then, that he knew better when he asserted that we have degraded them into brutes. He spoke, not from his better knowledge and his conscience, but from blind, unreflecting passion. For he knew—if he knew any thing—that the blacks have been elevated and improved by their contact with the whites of this enlightened portion of the globe.

The truth is, the abolitionist can make the slave a brute or a saint, just as it may happen to suit the exigency of his argument. If slavery degrades its subjects into brutes, then one would suppose that slaves are brutes. But the moment you speak of selling a slave, he is no longer a brute,—he is a civilized man, with all the most tender affections, with all the most generous emotions. If the object be to excite indignation against slavery, then it always transforms its subjects into brutes; but if it be to excite indignation against the slaveholder, then he holds, not brutes, but a George Harris—or an Eliza—or an Uncle Tom—in bondage. Any thing, and every thing, except fair and impartial statement, are the materials with which he works.

No fact is plainer than that the blacks have been elevated and improved by their servitude in this country. We cannot possibly conceive, indeed, how Divine Providence could have placed them in a better school of correction. If the abolitionists can conceive a better method for their enlightenment and religious improvement, we should rejoice to see them carry their plan into execution. They need not seek to rend asunder our Union, on account of the three millions of blacks among us, while there are fifty millions of the same race on the continent of Africa, calling aloud for their sympathy, and appealing to their Christian benevolence. Let them look to that continent. Let them rouse the real, active, self-sacrificing benevolence of the whole Christian world in behalf of that most degraded portion of the human family; and, after all, if they will show us on the continent of Africa, or elsewhere, three millions of blacks in as good a condition — physically and morally — as our slaves, then will we most cheerfully admit that all other Christian nations, combined, have accomplished as much for the African race, as has been done by the Southern States of the Union.

CHAPTER V.

THE FUGITIVE SLAVE LAW.

WE have, under our present Union, advanced in prosperity and greatness beyond all former example in the history of nations. We no sooner begin to reason from the past to the future, than we are lost in amazement at the prospect before us. We behold the United States, and that too at no very distant period, the first power among the nations of the earth. But such reasoning is not always to be relied on. Whether, in the present instance, it points to a reality, or to a magnificent dream merely, will of course depend on the wisdom, the integrity, and the moderation, of our rulers.

It cannot be disguised that the Union, with all its unspeakable advantages and blessings, is in danger. It is the Fugitive Slave Law against which the waves of abolitionism have dashed with their utmost force and raged with an almost boundless fury. On the other hand,

26

it is precisely the Fugitive Slave Law—that great constitutional guarantee of our rights— which the people of the South are, as one man, the most inflexibly determined to maintain. We are prepared, and we shall accordingly proceed, to show that, in this fearful conflict, the great leaders of abolitionism—the Chases, the Sewards, and the Sumners, of the day—are waging a fierce, bitter, and relentless warfare against the Constitution of their country.

§ I. *Mr. Seward's attack on the Constitution of his country.*

There is one thing which Mr. Seward's reasoning overlooks,—namely, that he has taken an oath to support the Constitution of the United States. We shall not lose sight of this fact, nor permit him to obscure it by his special pleadings and mystifications; since it serves to show that while, in the name of a "higher law," he denounces the Constitution of his country, he at the same time commits a most flagrant outrage against that higher law itself.

The clause of the Constitution which Mr. Seward denounces is as follows: "No person held to service or labor in one state, under the laws thereof, escaping into another, shall, in consequence of any law or regulation therein, be discharged from such service or labor, but shall be delivered up on claim of the party to whom such service or labor may be due." This clause, as Mr. Seward contemptuously says, is "from the Constitution of the United States in 1787." He knows of only one other compact like this "in diplomatic history;" and that was made between despotic powers "in the year of grace 902, in the period called the Dark Ages." But whether this compact made by the fathers of the Republic, or the sayings and doings of Mr. Seward in regard to it, are the more worthy of the Dark Ages, it is not for him alone to determine.

"The law of nature," says he, "disavows such compacts; the law of nature, written on the hearts and consciences of freemen, repudiates them." If this be so, then it certainly follows that in founding states no such compacts should be formed. For, as Mr. Seward says, "when we are founding states, all these laws must be brought to the standard of the laws of God, and must be tried by that standard, and must stand or fall by it." This is true, we repeat; but the Senator who uttered this truth was *not* founding states or forming a constitution. He was living and acting under a constitution already formed, and one which he had taken an oath to support. If, in the construction of this instrument, our fathers really followed "as precedents the abuses of tyrants and robbers," then the course of the Senator in question was plain: *he should have suffered martyrdom rather than take an oath to support it.* For the law of nature, it is clear, permits no man first to take an oath to support such compacts, and then repudiate them. If they are at war with his conscience, then, in the name of all that is sacred, let him repudiate them, but, by all means, without having first placed himself under the necessity of repudiating, at the same time, the obligation of his oath.

There is a question among casuists, whether an oath extorted by force can bind a man to act in opposition to his conscience. But this was not Mr. Seward's case. His oath was not extorted. If he had refused to take it, he would have lost nothing *except an office.*

"There was deep philosophy," says he, "in the confession of an eminent English judge. When he had condemned a young woman to death, under the late sanguinary code of his country, for her first theft, she fell down dead at his feet. 'I seem to myself,' said he, 'to have been pronouncing sentence, not against the prisoner, but against the law itself.'" Ay, there was something better than "deep philosophy" in that English judge; there was stern integrity; for, though he felt the law to be hard and cruel, yet, having taken an oath to support it, he hardly felt himself at liberty to dispense with the obligation of his oath. We commend his example to the Senator from New York.

But who is this Senator, or any other politician of the present day, that he should presume to pass so sweeping and so peremptory a sentence of condemnation on a compact made by the fathers of the Republic and ratified by the people of the United States? For our part, if we wished to find "the higher law," we should look neither into the Dark Ages nor into his conscience. We had infinitely rather look into the great souls of those by whom the Constitution was framed, and by every one of whom the very compact which Mr. Seward pronounces so infamous was cordially sanctioned.

"Your Constitution and laws," exclaims Mr. Seward, "convert hospitality to the refugee

U 26*

from the most degrading oppression on earth into a crime, but all mankind except you esteem that hospitality a virtue." Not content with thus denouncing the "Constitution and laws," he has elsewhere exhorted the people to an open resistance to their execution. "It is," says he, in a speech at a mass-meeting in Ohio, "written in the Constitution of the United States," and "in violation to divine law,* that we shall surrender the fugitive slave who takes refuge at our fireside from his relentless pursuer." He then and there exhorts the people to resist the execution of this clear, this unequivocal, this *acknowledged*, mandate of the Constitution! "Extend," says he, a "cordial welcome *to the fugitive who lays his weary limbs at your door*, and DEFEND HIM AS YOU WOULD YOUR HOUSEHOLD GODS."

We shall not trust ourselves to characterize such conduct. In the calm, judicial language of the Chancellor of his own State such proceeding of Mr. Seward will find its most fitting rebuke. "Independent, however," says Chancellor Walworth, "*of any legislation on this subject either by the individual States or by Congress,*

* On this point, see page 153.

if the person whose services are claimed is in fact a fugitive from servitude under the laws of another state, *the constitutional provision is imperative that he shall be delivered up to his master upon claim made.*" Thus far, Mr. Seward concurs with the chancellor in opinion; but the latter continues — "and any state officer or private citizen, who owes allegiance to the United States, and has taken the usual oath to support the Constitution thereof, cannot, WITHOUT INCURRING THE MORAL GUILT OF PERJURY, do any act to deprive the master of his right of recaption, when there is no real doubt that the person whose services are claimed is in fact the slave of the claimant."* Yet, regardless of the question whether the fugitive is a slave or not, the life and labors of Mr. Seward are, in a great measure, dedicated to a subversion of the constitutional clause and right under consideration. He counsels open resistance! Yea, he exhorts the people to protect and defend fugitive slaves *as such*, and though they had confessed themselves to have fled from servitude! But we doubt not that "the law of nature, written on the hearts and consciences

---

* XIV. Wendell, Jack *v.* Martin, p. 528.

of freemen," will reverse this advice of his, and reaffirm the decision of the chancellor of his own State. Nay, wherever there exists a freeman with a real heart and conscience, there that decision already stands affirmed.

As Mr. Seward's arguments are more fully elaborated by Mr. Sumner, of Massachusetts, so they will pass under review when we come to examine the speech of that Senator. In the mean time, we beg leave to lay before the reader a few living examples of the manner in which the law of nature, as written on the hearts and consciences of freemen, has expressed itself in regard to the points above considered.

"I recognise, indeed," says the Hon. R. C. Winthrop, of Boston, "a power above all human law-makers and a code above all earthly constitutions! And whenever I perceive a clear conflict of jurisdiction and authority between the Constitution of my country and the laws of my God, my course is clear. I shall resign my office, whatever it may be, and renounce all connection with public service of any sort. Never, never, sir, will I put myself under the necessity of calling upon God to witness my promise to support a constitution, any part of which I consider to be inconsistent with his commands.

"But it is a libel upon the Constitution of the United States—and, what is worse, sir, it is a libel upon the great and good men who framed, adopted, and ratified it; it is a libel upon Washington and Franklin, and Hamilton and Madison, upon John Adams, and John Jay, and Rufus King; it is a libel upon them all, and upon the whole American people of 1789, who sustained them in their noble work, and upon all who, from that time to this, generation after generation, in any capacity,—national, municipal, or state,—have lifted their hands to heaven in attestation of their allegiance to the government of their country;—it is a gross libel upon every one of them, to assert or insinuate that there is any such inconsistency! Let us not do such dishonor to the fathers of the Republic and the framers of the Constitution."

Mr. Ashmun, of Massachusetts, after reciting the clause in the Constitution which demands the restoration of fugitive slaves, proceeds as follows: "This reads very plainly, and admits of no doubt but that, so far as fugitive slaves are concerned, the Constitution fully recognises the right to reclaim them from within the limits of the free States. It is the Constitution which we have all sworn to support, and which I hope we all mean to support; and I have no mental reservation excluding any of its clauses from the sanction of that oath. It is too late now to complain that such a provision is there. Our fathers, who formed that entire instrument, placed it there, and left it to us as an inheritance; and nothing but an amendment of the Constitution, or a violation of our oaths, can tear it out. And, however much we may abhor slavery, there is no way for honorable, honest— nay, conscientious—men, who desire to live under our laws and our Constitution, but to abide by it in its spirit."

In like manner, the Hon. S. A. Douglas, of Illinois, declares: "All I have to say on that subject is this, that the Constitution provides that a fugitive from service in one State, escaping into another, 'shall be delivered up.' The Constitution also provides that no man shall be a Senator unless he takes an oath to support the Constitution. Then, I ask, how does a man acquire a right on this floor to speak, except by taking an oath to support and sustain the Constitution of the United States? And when he takes that oath, I do not understand that he has a right to have a mental reservation, or entertain any secret equivocation that he excepts that clause which relates to the surrender of fugitives from service. I know not how a man reconciles it to his conscience to take that oath to support the Constitution, when he believes that Constitution is in violation of the law of God. If a man thus believes, and takes the oath, he commits perfidy to his God in order that he may enjoy the temporary honors of a seat upon this floor. In this point of view, it is simply a question of whether Senators will be true to their oaths and true to the Constitution under which we live."

§ II. *The attack of Mr. Sumner on the Constitution of his country.*

If we have not noticed the arguments of Mr. Chase, of Ohio, it is because they are reproduced in the celebrated speech of Mr. Sumner, and because he has so fully endorsed the history and logic of this speech as to make it his own. Hence, in replying to the one of these Senators, we at the same time virtually reply to the other.

We select the speech of Mr. Sumner for examination, because it is generally considered the more powerful of the two. It is, indeed, the most elaborate speech ever made in the Senate of the United States, or elsewhere, on the subject of the Fugitive Slave Law. Even Mr. Weller found it "so handsomely embellished with poetry, both Latin and English, so full of classical allusions and rhetorical flourishes," as to make it more palatable than he supposed an abolition speech could possibly be made. As to the abolitionists themselves, they seem to know no bounds in their enthusiastic admiration of this sublime effort of their champion. We should not wonder, indeed, if many a female reformer had gone into hysterics over an oration which has received such violent bursts of applause from grave and dignified Senators. "By this effort," says Mr. Hale, he has placed "himself side by side with the first orators of antiquity, and as far ahead of any living American orator as freedom is ahead of slavery. I believe that he has formed to-day a new era in the history of the politics and of the eloquence of the country; and that in future generations the young men of this nation will be stimulated to effort by the record of what an American Senator has this day done," &c.

We have no doubt that young men may attempt to imitate the speech in question; but, as they grow older, it is to be hoped that their taste will improve. The speech in question will make a "new era" in the tactics of abolitionism, and that is all. We shall see this when we come to examine this wonderful oration, which so completely ravished *three Senators*, and called forth such wild shouts of applause from the whole empire of abolitionism.

Mr. Chase seems almost equally delighted with this marvellous effort. "I avow my conviction, now and here," says he, "that, logically and historically, his argument is impregnable—entirely impregnable." ...... "In my judgment," he continues, "the speech of my friend from Massachusetts will make a NEW ERA in American history." Indeed, Mr. Sumner himself does not seem altogether dissatisfied with this effort, if we may judge from the manner in which it is referred to in his other speeches. We do not blame him for this. We can see no reason why he should be the only abolitionist in the universe who is not enraptured with his oration. But when he so "fearlessly asserts" that his speech "has never been answered," we beg leave to assure him that it *may* be refuted

27

with the most perfect ease. For, indeed, its history is half fiction, and its logic wholly false: the first containing just enough of truth to deceive, and the last just enough of plausibility to convince those who are waiting, and watching, and longing to be convinced.

The first thing which strikes the mind, on reading the speech of Mr. Sumner, is the strange logical incoherency of its structure. Its parts are so loosely hung together, and appear so distressingly disjointed, that one is frequently at a loss to perceive the design of the oration. Its avowed object is to procure a repeal of the Fugitive Slave Law of 1850; but no one would ever imagine or suspect such a thing from the title of the speech, which is as follows: "Freedom, national; Slavery, sectional." It is difficult, at first view, to perceive what logical connection this title, or proposition, has with the repeal of the Fugitive Slave Law. But if there be little or no logical connection between these things, we shall soon see how the choice of such a title and topic of discourse opens the way for the rhetorician to make a most powerful appeal to the passions and to the prejudices of his readers. We say, of his readers, because it is evident that the speech was made for Buncombe, and not for the Senate of the United States.

Mr. Sumner deems it necessary to refute the position that slavery is a national institution, in order to set the world right with respect to the relations of the Federal Government to slavery. "The relations of the Government of the United States," says he,—"I speak of the National Government—to slavery, *though plain and obvious, are constantly misunderstood.*" Indeed, nothing in history seems more remarkable than the amount of ignorance and stupidity which prevailed in the world before the appearance of the abolitionists, except the wonderful illuminations which accompanied their advent. "A popular belief at this moment," continues Mr. Sumner, "makes slavery a national institution, and, of course, renders its support a national duty. The extravagance of this error can hardly be surpassed." In truth, it is so exceedingly extravagant, that we doubt if it really exists. It is certain, that we have no acquaintance, either historically or personally, with those who have fallen into so wild an absurdity.

It is true, there is "a popular belief"—nay, there is a deep-rooted national conviction—that

the Government of the United States is bound
to protect the institution of slavery, in so far as
this may be done by the passage of a Fugitive Slave Law. This national conviction has
spoken out in the laws of Congress; it has been
ratified and confirmed by the judicial opinion
of the Supreme Court of the United States, as
well as by the decisions of the Supreme Courts
of the three great non-slaveholding States of
Massachusetts, New York, and Pennsylvania.
But no one, so far as we know, has ever deduced
this obligation to protect slavery, in this respect,
from the absurd notion that "it is a national
institution." No such deduction is to be found
in any of the arguments of counsel before the
courts above-mentioned, nor in the opinions of
the courts themselves. We shrewdly suspect
that it is to be found nowhere except in the fertile imagination of Mr. Sumner.

We concede that slavery is *not* "a national
institution." In combatting this position, Mr.
Sumner is merely beating the air. We know
that slavery is not national; it is local, being
confined to certain States, and exclusively established by local or State laws. Hence, Mr.
Sumner may fire off as much splendid rhetoric
as he pleases at his men of straw. "Slavery

national!" he indignantly exclaims: "Sir, this is all a mistake and absurdity, fit to take a place in some new collection of 'Vulgar Errors' by some other Sir Thomas Browne, with the ancient but exploded stories that the toad has a stone in its head and that ostriches digest iron." These may be very fine embellishments; they certainly have nothing to do with the point in controversy. The question is not whether slavery is a national institution, but whether the National Government does not recognise slavery as a local institution, and is not pledged to protect the master's right to reclaim the fugitive from his service. This is the question, and by its relevancy to this question the rhetoric of Mr. Sumner must be tried.

We do not say it has no such relevancy. Mr. Sumner beats the air, it is true, but he does not beat the air in vain. His declamation may have no logical bearing on the point in dispute, but, if you watch it closely, you will always find that it is most skilfully adapted to bring the prejudices and passions of the reader to bear on that point. Though he may not be much of a logician, yet, it must be admitted, he is "skilful of fence." We should do him great injustice as an antagonist, at least before the tribunal of

27*

human passion, if we should suppose that it is merely for the abstract glory of setting up a man of straw, and then knocking it down, that he has mustered all the powers of his logic and unfurled all the splendors of his rhetoric. He has a design in all this, which we shall now proceed to expose.

Here are two distinct questions. First, Is slavery a national institution? Secondly, Has Congress the power to pass a Fugitive Slave Law? These two questions are, we repeat, perfectly distinct; and hence, if Mr. Sumner wished to discuss them fairly and honestly, he should have argued each one by itself. We agree with him in regard to the first; we dissent *toto cœlo* from him in regard to the last. But he has not chosen to keep them separate, or to discuss each one by itself. On the contrary, he has, as we have seen, connected them together as premiss and conclusion, and he keeps them together through the first portion of his speech. Most assuredly Mr. Sumner knows that one of the very best ways in the world to cause a truth or proposition to be rejected is to bind it up with a manifest error or absurdity. Yet the proposition for which we contend—that Congress has the power to support slavery by the passage of a Fugitive Slave Law —is bound up by him with the monstrous absurdity that "slavery is a national institution;" and both are denounced together as if both were equally absurd. One instance, out of many, of this unfair mode of proceeding, we shall now lay before our readers.

"The Constitution contains no power," says he, "to make a king or to support kingly rule. With similar reason it may be said that it contains no power to make a slave, or to support a system of slavery. The absence of all such power is hardly more clear in one case than in the other. But, if there be no such power, all national legislation upholding slavery must be unconstitutional and void."

Thus covertly, and in company with the supposed power of Congress to make slaves or to institute slavery, Mr. Sumner denounces the power of Congress to enact a Fugitive Slave Law! He not only denounces it, but treats it as absurd in the extreme; just as absurd, indeed, as it would be to assert that Congress had power "to support kingly rule!" We can listen to the arguments of Mr. Sumner; but we cannot accept his mere opinion as authority that the power of Congress to enact such a law is so glaringly unconstitutional, is so monstrously absurd; for, however passionately that opinion may be declaimed, we cannot forget that a Fugitive Slave Law was passed by the Congress of 1793, received the signature of George Washington, and, finally, the judicial sanction of the Supreme Court of the United States. Mr. Sumner is but a man.

— This advantage of mixing up with a glaring falsehood the idea he wishes to be rejected is not the only one which Mr. Sumner derives from his man of straw. By combatting the position— "the popular belief," as he calls it—that "slavery is a national institution," he lays open a wide field for his peculiar powers of declamation. He calls up all the fathers—North and South— to bear witness against slavery, in order to show that it is not a national institution. He quotes colleges, and churches, and patriots, against slavery. Not content with this, he pours down furious invectives of his own, with a view to render slavery as odious as possible. But, since the simple question is, *What saith the Constitution*—why this fierce crusade against slavery? In deciding this very question, namely, the constitutionality of the Fugitive Slave Law of 1793, a high judicial authority has said that "the abstract proposition of the justice or injustice of slavery is wholly irrelevant here, and, I apprehend, ought not to have the slightest influence upon any member of this court."*

It ought not to have—and it did not have—the slightest influence on the highest judicial tribunal of New York, in which the above opinion was delivered. Much as the author of that opinion (Mr. Senator Bishop) abhorred slavery, he did not permit such an influence to reach his judgment. It would have contaminated his judicial integrity. But although before a judicial tribunal, about to decide on the constitutionality of a Fugitive Slave Law, the abstract proposition of the justice or injustice of slavery is out of place, yet at the bar of passion and prejudice it is well calculated, as Mr. Sumner must know, to exert a tremendous influence. Hence, if he can only get up the horror of his readers against slavery before he comes to the real question, namely, the constitutionality of the Fugitive Slave Law, he knows that his victory will be more than half gained. But we admonish him that passion and prejudice can only give a temporary éclat to his argument.

---

* XIV. Wendell's Reports, Jack v. Martin.

So much for the unfairness of Mr. Sumner. If we should notice all such instances of artful design in his speech, we should have no space for his logic. To this we would now invite the attention of the reader, in order to see if it be really "impregnable."

As we have already intimated, Mr. Sumner does not, like Mr. Seward, openly denounce the Constitution of his country. On the contrary, he professes the most profound respect for every part of that instrument, not even excepting the clause which demands the restoration of the fugitive from labor. But an examination of his argument, both *historical* and *logical*, will enable us, we trust, to estimate this profession at its real intrinsic worth.

We shall begin with his argument from history. In the examination of this argument, we beg to excuse ourselves from any further notice of all that vast array of historical proofs to show that "freedom is national and slavery sectional."* We shall consider those proofs alone

---

* In asserting that freedom is national, Mr. Sumner may perhaps mean that it is the duty of the National Government to exclude slavery from all its territories, and to admit no new state in which there are slaves. If this be his meaning, we should reply, that it is as foreign from the merits of the Fugi-

which relate to the real point in controversy, namely, Has Congress the power to pass a Fugitive Slave Law?

Mr. Sumner argues, from the well-known sentiments of the framers of the Constitution with respect to slavery, that they intended to confer no such power on Congress. Thus, after quoting the sentiments of Gouverneur Morris, of Elbridge Gerry, of Roger Sherman, and James Madison, he adds: "In the face of these unequivocal statements, it is absurd to suppose that they consented *unanimously* to any provision by which the National Government, the work of their own hands, could be made the most offensive instrument of slavery." Such

---

tive Slave Law, which he proposed to discuss, as it is from the truth. The National Government has, indeed, no more power to exclude, than it has to ordain, slavery; for slavery or no slavery is a question which belongs wholly and exclusively to the sovereign people of each and every state or territory. With our whole hearts we respond to the inspiring words of the President's Message: "If the friends of the Constitution are to have another struggle, its enemies could not present a more acceptable issue than that of a state, whose Constitution clearly embraces a republican form of government, being excluded from the Union because its domestic institutions may not, in all respects, comport with the ideas of what is wise and expedient entertained in some other state."

is the historical argument of Mr. Sumner. Let us see what it is worth.

Elbridge Gerry had said: "We ought to be careful NOT *to give any sanction to slavery;*"—language repeatedly quoted, and underscored as above, by Mr. Sumner. It is absurd, he concludes, to suppose that a man who could use such language had the least intention to confer a power on Congress to support slavery by the passage of a Fugitive Slave Law. This is one branch of his historical argument. It may appear perfectly conclusive to Mr. Sumner, and "entirely impregnable" to Mr. Chase; but, after all, it is not quite so invulnerable as they imagine. Mr. Sumner stopped his historical researches at a most convenient point for his argument. If he had only read a little further, he would have discovered that this same identical Elbridge Gerry was in the Congress of 1793, and VOTED FOR the Fugitive Slave Law then passed!

It fares no better with the historical argument to prove the opinion or intention of Roger Sherman. He had declared, it is true, that he was opposed to any clause in the Constitution "acknowledging men to be property." But we should not, with Mr. Sumner, infer from this that he never intended that Congress should possess a power to legislate in reference to slavery. For, unfortunately for such a conclusion, however confidently it may be drawn, or however dogmatically asserted, Roger Sherman himself was in the Senate of 1793, and was actually on the committee which reported the Fugitive Slave Law of that session! Thus, although the premiss of Mr. Sumner's argument is a historical fact, yet its conclusion comes directly into conflict with another historical fact!

We cannot, in the same way, refute the argument from the language of Gouverneur Morris, who said "that he never would concur in upholding domestic slavery," because he was not in the Congress of 1793. But Robert Morris was there, and, although he helped to frame the Constitution in 1787, he uttered not a syllable against the constitutionality of the Fugitive Slave Law. Indeed, this law passed the Senate by resolution simply, *the yeas and nays not having been called for!*

The words of Mr. Madison, who "thought it wrong to admit in the Constitution the idea that there could be property in man," are four or five times quoted in Mr. Sumner's speech.

28

As we have already seen,* there cannot be, in the strict sense of the terms, "property in man;" for the soul is the man, and no one, except God, can own the soul. Hence Mr. Madison acted wisely, we think, in wishing to exclude such an expression from the Constitution, inasmuch as it would have been misunderstood by Northern men, and only shocked their feelings without answering any good purpose.

When we say that slaves are property, we merely mean that their masters have a right to their service or labor. This idea is recognised in the Constitution, and *this right is secured.* We ask no more. As Mr. Madison, and the whole South, had the *thing*, he did not care to wrangle about the *name*. We are told, again and again, that the word *slave* does not appear in the Constitution. Be it so. We care not, since our slaves are there recognised as "persons held to service" by those to whom "such service is due." It is repeated without end that the "Constitution acts on slaves as *persons*, and not as property." Granted; and if Northern men will, according to the mandate of the Constitution, only deliver up our fugitive servants,

---

* Chap. ii. § x.

we care not whether they restore them as persons or as property. If we may only reclaim them as persons, and regain their service, we are perfectly satisfied. We utterly despise all such verbal quibbling.

Mr. Madison was above it. He acted wisely, we repeat, in refusing to shock the mind of any one, by insisting upon a mere word, and upon a word, too, which might not have conveyed a correct idea of his own views. But that Mr. Madison could, as he understood the terms, regard slaves as property, we have the most incontestable evidence. For in the Convention of Virginia, called to ratify the Constitution of the United States, he said, "Another clause secures us that *property* which we now possess. At present, if any slave elopes to any of those States where slaves are free, he becomes emancipated by their laws, for the laws of the States are uncharitable to one another in this respect." He then quotes the provision from the Constitution relative to fugitives from labor, and adds: "This clause was expressly inserted to enable *owners* of slaves to reclaim them." So much for Mr. Sumner's main argument from the language of the members of the Convention of 1787.

Arguing from the sentiments of that convention with respect to slavery, he concludes that nothing could have been further from their intention than to confer upon Congress the power to pass a uniform Fugitive Slave Law. He boldly asserts, that if a proposition to confer such a power upon Congress had "been distinctly made it would have been distinctly denied." "But no person in the convention," he says, "*not one of the reckless partisans of slavery, was so audacious as to make the proposition.*" Now we shall show that the above statement of his is diametrically opposed to the truth. We shall show that the members of the convention in question were perfectly willing to confer such a power upon Congress.

The reason why they were so is obvious to any one who has a real knowledge of the times about whose history Mr. Sumner so confidently declaims. This reason is well stated in the language of the Chancellor of New York whom we have already quoted. "The provision," says he, "as to persons escaping from servitude in one State into another, appears by their journal to have been adopted by a unanimous vote of the convention. At that time the existence of involuntary servitude, or the relation of master and servant, was known to and recognised by the laws of every State in the Union except Massachusetts, and *the legal right of recaption by the master existed in all*, AS A PART OF THE CUSTOMARY OR COMMON LAW OF THE WHOLE CONFEDERACY." Hence, instead of shocking the convention, a clause recognising such right would have been merely declaratory of the "customary or common law" which then universally prevailed. The "history of the times" confirms this view, and furnishes no evidence against it.

Mr. Sumner tries to make a different impression. He lays great stress on the fact that it was not until late in the convention that the first clause relative to the surrender of fugitive slaves was introduced. But this fact agrees more perfectly with our view than with his. There was no haste about the introduction of such a provision, because it was well known that, whenever it should be introduced, it would pass in the affirmative without difficulty. And, in fact, when it was introduced, it "WAS UNANIMOUSLY ADOPTED." This single fact speaks volumes.

Let us now attend, for a moment, to Mr. Sumner's historical proofs. He quotes the fol-

28*

lowing passage from the Madison Papers:—
"Gen. (Charles Cotesworth) Pinckney was not
satisfied with it. He seemed to wish some provision should be included in favor of property
in slaves." "But," by way of comment, Mr.
Sumner adds, "he made no proposition. Un-
willing to shock the convention, and uncertain
in his own mind, he only *seemed* to wish such a
provision." Now, a bare abstract proposition to
recognise property in men is one thing, and a
clause to secure the return of fugitive slaves is
quite another. The first, it is probable, would
have been rejected by the convention; the last
was actually and unanimously adopted by it.

Mr. Sumner's next proof is decidedly against
him. Here it is. "Mr. Butler and Mr. Charles
Pinckney, both from South Carolina, now
moved openly to require 'fugitive slaves and
servants to be delivered up like criminals.' . . . . .
Mr. Wilson, of Pennsylvania, at once objected: 'This would oblige the executive of the
State to do it at the public expense.' Mr.
Sherman, of Connecticut, saw no more pro-
priety in the public seizing and surrendering a
slave or servant than a horse! Under the pressure of these objections the offensive proposition
was quietly withdrawn."

Now mark the character of these objections. It is objected, not that it is wrong to deliver up fugitive slaves, but only that they should not be "delivered up like criminals;" that is, by a demand on the executive of the State to which they may have fled. And this objection is based on the ground that such a requisition would oblige the public to deliver them up at its own expense. Mr. Sherman insists, not that it is wrong to surrender fugitive slaves or fugitive horses, but only that the executive, or public, should not be called upon to surrender them. Surely, if these gentlemen had been so violently opposed to the restoration of fugitive slaves, here was a fair occasion for them to speak out; and as honest, out-spoken men they would, no doubt, have made their sentiments known. But there is, in fact, not a syllable of such a sentiment uttered. There is not the slightest symptom of the existence of any such feeling in their minds. If any such existed, we must insist that Mr. Sumner has discovered it by instinct, and not by his researches in history.

The statement that "under the pressure of these objections the offensive proposition was *quietly withdrawn*" is not true. It was not quietly withdrawn; on the contrary, it was withdrawn with the assurance that it would be again introduced. "Mr. Butler withdrew his proposition," says Mr. Madison, "*in order that some particular provision might be made*, apart from this article."* Accordingly, the very next day he introduced a provision, which, as Mr. Madison declares, "was expressly inserted to enable owners of slaves to reclaim them."

These glosses of Mr. Sumner on the history of the times will appear important, if we view them in connection with his design. This design is to bring into doubt the idea that slaves are embraced in the clause of the Constitution which requires fugitives from service or labor to be delivered up. We should not suspect this design from the hints here thrown out, if it were not afterward more fully disclosed. "On the next day," says Mr. Sumner, "August 29th, profiting by the suggestions already made, Mr. Butler moved a proposition, substantially like that now found in the Constitution, *not directly for the surrender of 'fugitive slaves*,' as originally proposed, but as 'fugitives from service or labor,' which, without debate or opposition of

---

* Madison Papers, p. 1448.

any kind, was unanimously adopted." Was it then unanimously adopted because it was a clause for the surrender of "fugitives from service or labor" only, and not for the surrender of fugitive slaves?

Such appears to be the insinuation of Mr. Sumner. Be this as it may, it is certain that he has afterward said that it may be questioned whether "the language employed" in this clause "can be judicially regarded as justly applicable to fugitive slaves, *which is often and earnestly denied.*" . . . "*Still further,*" he says, in italics, "*to the courts of each State must belong the determination of the question, to which class of persons, according to just rules of interpretation, the phrase 'persons held to service or labor' is strictly applicable.*"

Mr. Sumner doubts, then, whether this provision, after all, refers to "fugitive slaves." Now, although he has said much in regard to "the effrontery of the Southern members of the convention" that formed the Constitution, we may safely defy him, or any other man, to point to any thing in their conduct which approximates to such audacity. What! the clause in question not designed to embrace fugitive slaves? Mr. Butler, even before he introduced the clause, declared, as we have seen, that such would be its design. It was so understood by every member of the convention; for there was not a man there who possessed the capacity to misunderstand so plain a matter; and it has been so understood by every man, of all parties and all factions, from that day down to the present. Not one of the hired advocates who have been employed, in different States, to argue against the constitutionality of the Fugitive Slave Law, has ever had the unblushing effrontery to contend that the clause in question is not applicable to fugitive slaves. Nay, more, until Mr. Sumner appeared, the frantic zeal of no abolitionist had ever so completely besotted his intellect as to permit him to take such ground. By Dr. Channing, by Mr. Seward, and by Mr. Chase, such application of the words in question is unhesitatingly admitted; and hence we dismiss Mr. Sumner's discovery with the contempt it deserves.

But to return. "The provision," says Mr. Sumner, "which showed itself thus tardily, and was so slightly noticed in the National Convention, was neglected in most of the contemporaneous discussions before the people." No wonder; for it was merely declaratory of the "customary or common law" of that day. "In the Conventions of South Carolina, North Carolina, and Virginia," he admits, "it was commended as securing important rights, though on this point there was a difference of opinion. In the Virginia Convention, an eminent character,—Mr. George Mason,—with others, expressly declared that there was 'no security of property coming within this section.'"

Now, we shall not stickle about the fact that Mr. Sumner has not given the very words of Mr. Mason, since he has given them in substance. But yet he has given them in such a way, and in such a connection, as to make a false impression. The words of Mr. Mason, taken in their proper connection, are as follows: "We have no security for the property of that kind (slaves) which we already have. There is no clause in this Constitution to secure it, *for they may lay such a tax as will amount to manumission.*" This shows his position, not as it is misrepresented by Mr. Sumner, but as it stands in his own words. If slave property may be rendered worthless by the taxation of Congress, how could it be secured by a clause which enables the owner to reclaim it? It would not be worth reclaiming. Such was the argument and true position of Mr. George Mason.

"Massachusetts," continues Mr. Sumner, "while exhibiting peculiar sensitiveness at any responsibility for slavery, seemed to view it with unconcern." If Massachusetts had only believed that the clause was intended to confer on Congress the power to pass a Fugitive Slave Law, into what flames of indignation would her sensitiveness have burst! So Mr. Sumner would have us to believe. But let us listen, for a moment, to the sober voice of history.

It was only about four years after the government went into operation that Congress actually exercised the power in question, and *passed a Fugitive Slave Law*. Where was Massachusetts then? Did she burst into flames of indignation? Her only voice, in reply, was as distinctly and as emphatically pronounced in favor of that law as was the voice of Virginia itself. With a single exception, her whole delegation in Congress,* with Fisher Ames at their head, voted for the Fugitive Slave Law of 1793! Not a whisper of disapprobation was heard from their constituents. As Mr. Sumner himself says, the passage of that act "drew little attention." Hence he would have us to believe that Massa-

---

* One member seems to have been absent from the House.

chusetts would have been stirred from her depths if the convention had conferred such a power upon Congress, and yet that she was not moved at all when Congress proceeded, as he maintains, to *usurp* and exercise that power!

This is not all. Every member from the free States, with the exception of five, recorded his vote in favor of the same law.* In the Senate, as we have already said, it was passed by resolution, and not by a recorded vote. No one, in either branch of Congress, uttered a syllable against the constitutionality of the law, though many of the most distinguished members of the very convention which framed the Constitution itself were there. Not to mention others, there were James Madison, and Roger Sherman, and Elbridge Gerry, and Rufus King, and Caleb Strong, and Robert Morris, and Oliver Elsworth; and yet from not one of these illustrious framers of the Constitution was a syllable uttered against the constitutionality of the law in question. Nay, the law was supported and enacted by themselves. What, then, in the face of these indubitable facts, becomes of all Mr. Sumner's far-fetched arguments from "the lite-

---

* Annals of Congress; 2d Congress, 1791–1793, p. 861.

rature of the age" and from his multitudinous
voices against slavery? It is absurd, says Mr.
Sumner, to suppose that such men intended to
confer any power upon Congress to pass a Fugitive Slave Law. It is a *fact*, we reply, that as
members of Congress they proceeded, without
hesitation or doubt, to exercise that very
power. It "dishonors the memory of the
fathers," says Mr. Sumner, to suppose they
intended that Congress should possess such a
power. How, then, will he vindicate the
memory of the fathers against the imputation
of his own doctrine that they, as members of
Congress, must have knowingly usurped the
power which, as members of the convention,
they had intended not to confer?

One more of Mr. Sumner's historical arguments, and we are done with this branch of the
subject. He deems it the most conclusive of
all. It is founded on the arrangement of certain clauses of the Constitution, and is, we believe, perfectly original. We must refer the
reader to the speech itself if he desire to see
this very curious argument, since we cannot
spare the room to give it a full and fair statement.

Nor is this at all necessary to our purpose,

inasmuch as we intend to notice only one thing about this argument, namely, the wonderful effect it produces on the mind of its inventor. "The framers of the Constitution," says he, "were wise and careful men, who had a reason for what they did, and who understood the language which they employed." We can readily believe all this. Nor can we doubt that they "had a design in the peculiar arrangement" of the clauses adopted by them. That design, however, we feel quite sure, is different from the one attributed to them by Mr. Sumner. But let us suppose he is right, and then see what would follow.

The design attributed to them by Mr. Sumner was to make every one see, beyond the possibility of a mistake, that the Constitution confers no power on Congress to pass a Fugitive Slave Law. "They not only decline all addition of any such power to the compact," says he, "but, *to render misapprehension impossible,—to make assurance doubly sure,—to exclude any contrary conclusion*, they punctiliously arrange," &c. Now, if such were the case, then we ask if design of so easy accomplishment were ever followed by failure so wonderful?

They failed, in the first place, "to exclude a

contrary conclusion" from the Supreme Courts of Massachusetts, of New York, and of Pennsylvania, all of which tribunals have decided that they *did* confer such a power upon Congress. In the second place, although those wise men labored to make "misapprehension impossible," yet, according to Mr. Sumner, the Supreme Court of the United States has entirely misapprehended them. So far from seeing that the power in question is not granted to Congress, this high tribunal decides that it is clearly and unquestionably granted. This is not all. The most marvellous failure is yet to come. For, after all their pains to make the whole world see their meaning, these wise men did not see it themselves, but went away, many of them, and, in the Congress of 1793, helped to pass a Fugitive Slave Law!

It is to be feared, indeed, that the failure would have been absolutely total but for the wonderful sagacity of a few abolitionists. For the design imputed to the framers of the Constitution, and which they took so much pains to disclose, had remained profoundly concealed from nearly all men, not excepting themselves, until it was detected by Messrs. Sumner, Chase, and company. But these have, at last, discovered it, and now see it as in a flood of light. Indeed, they see it with such transcendent clearness, with such marvellous perspicacity of vision, as to atone for the stupidity and blindness of the rest of mankind.

So much for Mr. Sumner's historical argument. His logical argument is, if possible, still more illogical than his historical. In regard to this, however, we shall be exceedingly brief, as we are sick of his sophisms, and long to be delivered from the pursuit of them.

He encounters, at the outset, "a difficulty" in the legislation of the Congress of 1793 and in the decision of the Supreme Court of the United States." But "on examination," says he, "this difficulty will disappear." Perhaps difficulty so great never vanished so suddenly from before any other man.

The authority of the Congress of 1793, though it contained so many of the most distinguished framers of the Constitution, is annihilated by a few bold strokes of Mr. Sumner's pen. One short paragraph, containing two ineffably weak arguments, does the business.

The first of these arguments is as follows: "The act of 1793 proceeded from a Congress that had already recognised the United States Bank, chartered by a previous Congress, which, though sanctioned by the Supreme Court, has been since in high quarters pronounced unconstitutional. If it erred as to the bank, it may have erred also as to fugitives from labor." We cannot conceive why such an argument should have been propounded, unless it were to excite a prejudice against the Congress of 1793 in the minds of those who may be opposed to a National Bank. For if we look at its conclusion we shall see that it merely aims to establish a point which no one would deny. It merely aims to prove that, as the Congress of 1793 was composed of fallible men, "so it may have erred!" We admit the conclusion, and therefore pass by the inherent weaknesses in the structure of the argument.

His second argument is this: " But the very act contains a capital error* on this very subject, so declared by the Supreme Court, in pretending to vest a portion of the judicial power of the nation in state officers. *This error takes from the act all authority as an interpretation of the Constitution.* I DISMISS IT." This passage, considered as an argument, is simply ridiculous. How

---

* This error was by no means a capital one.

many of the best laws ever enacted by man have, in the midst of much that is as clear as noonday, been found to contain an error! Should all, therefore, have been blindly rejected? As soon as the error has been detected, has any enlightened tribunal on earth ever said, "I dismiss" the whole?

By such a process we might have made as short work with Mr. Sumner's speech. If, after pointing out one error therein, we had dismissed the whole speech as worthless, we should have imitated his reasoning, and in our conclusion have come much nearer to the truth. If we should say, indeed, that because the sun has a spot on its surface it is therefore a great ball of darkness, our argument would be exactly like that of Mr. Sumner. But that great luminary would not refuse to shine in obedience to our contemptible logic. In like manner, the authority of the illustrious Congress of 1793, in which there were so many profound statesmen and pure patriots, will not be the less resplendent because Mr. Charles Sumner has, with Titanic audacity and Lilliputian weakness, assailed it with one of the most pitiful of all the pitiful sophisms that ever were invented by man.

In regard to the decision of the Supreme

Court he says: "Whatever may be the influence of this judgment as a rule to the judiciary, it cannot arrest our duty as legislators. And here I adopt, with entire assent, the language of President Jackson, in his memorable veto, in 1832, of the Bank of the United States." He then quotes this language, in which he italicizes the following sentence: "*Each public officer, who takes an oath to support the Constitution, swears that he will support it as he understands it, and not as it is understood by others.*" "With these authoritative words of Andrew Jackson," says he, "I dismiss this topic. The early legislation of Congress and the decisions of the Supreme Court cannot stand in our way. I advance to the argument." We shall let him advance.

But we must say a few words in conclusion. Mr. Sumner swears to support the Constitution as he understands it; but how is it supported by him? Is it supported by him at all or in any way? Let us see. The clause respecting "persons held to service or labor," says he, imposes an obligation, not upon "the National Government, but upon the States." Is he then in favor of the States passing any law, or doing any act, by which fugitive slaves may be delivered up? "Never," he replies. Massachusetts will never do any such thing by his advice or consent. Surely, then, he will speak a kind word to the good people of Massachusetts, and advise them to do nothing in violation of this solemn compact of the Constitution. If he will do nothing to support the compact, surely he will do nothing to break it down. He will not permit us to indulge any such charitable hope. For it is his *avowed* object, by speech-making and by agitation, to create such a "public opinion" as "shall blast with contempt, indignation, and abhorrence, all who, *in whatever form*, or *under whatever name*, undertake to be agents"* in reclaiming fugitive slaves. Yea, upon the very officers of the law themselves, who, for this purpose, act under and by authority of the supreme laws of the land, he pours down scorn and derision. Even these, though in the discharge of an official duty, are—if it be in the power of Mr. Sumner—to be blasted with abhorrence, indignation, and contempt!

The Constitution declares that the fugitive slave "shall be delivered up." He shall NOT "be delivered up," says Mr. Sumner; and, in order to make his words good, he means to

---

* Speech in the Senate, in 1855.

create a "public opinion," which no Southern master dare encounter. Nay, he rejoices to believe that such public opinion is, in some localities, already created and prepared for open resistance to the Constitution of the United States. "There are many," says he, "who will never shrink at any cost, and, notwithstanding all the atrocious penalties of this bill, from efforts to save a wandering fellow-man from bondage. They will offer him the shelter of their houses, and, IF NEED BE, WILL PROTECT HIS LIBERTY BY FORCE."* Horrible words! Words tending directly to a conflict in which the brightest hopes of humanity must perish, and the glory of the Republic be extinguished in oceans of blood.

In the face of such things, we are imperiously constrained to doubt Mr. Sumner's regard for the obligation of the oath which binds him to support the Constitution of his country. It is certain that he can rejoice in the breach of this obligation by others. A certain judge in Vermont, who, like every other State officer, had taken an oath to support the Constitution of the United States, just set Constitution, laws, evi-

---

* Speech in Boston, October 3d, 1850.

dence, all at defiance, and boldly declared that the fugitive should *not* be delivered up, "*unless the master could show a bill of sale from the Almighty.*" This deed, which, in the language of Chancellor Walworth, is stamped with "the moral guilt of perjury," appears heroic to Mr. Sumner, by whom it is related with evident delight. It would seem, indeed, as if the moral sensibility of an abolitionist of his stamp is all drawn to a single point of his conscience, so that it can feel absolutely nothing except slavery. It seems dead to the obligation of an oath, to the moral guilt of perjury. Nay, it seems to rejoice in the very bravery of its perpetration, provided it only enables a fugitive slave to effect his escape.

Perhaps Mr. Sumner would seek to justify himself by declaring that the language *fugitives from service* does not include fugitive slaves. If so, we reply that the Vermont judge, whose infamous decision he approves, had no such fine pretext. It is Mr. Sumner, as we have seen, who first suggested this most excellent method of reconciling conscience with treachery to the Constitution. Though he professes the most profound respect for that instrument, he deliberately sets to work to undermine one of its most clear and unequivocal mandates. He does not, like Mr. Seward, openly smite the Constitution with his hand, or contemptuously kick it with his foot. *He betrays it with a kiss.*

Mr. Sumner admires the conduct of the Vermont judge; but he can heap the most frantic abuse on the acts of the best men America has produced. Though they be the deliberate public acts of a Clay, or a Calhoun, or a Webster, or a GEORGE WASHINGTON, his language is not the less violent, nor his raving vituperation the less malignant. In regard to the Fugitive Slave Law of 1850, he says: "And still further, as if to do a deed which should 'make heaven weep, all earth amazed,' this same Congress, in disregard of all the cherished safeguards of freedom, has passed a most cruel, unchristian, devilish act." The great difficulty under which Mr. Sumner labors, and which all the energy of his soul struggles to surmount, is to find language violent enough in which to denounce this "foul enactment," this "detestable and heaven-defying bill," this "monster act," which "sets at naught the best principles of the Constitution and the very laws of God!"

Now, this bill, let it be remembered, is liable to no objection which may not be urged against the Fugitive Slave Law of 1793. It will not be denied, indeed, that if the one of these laws be unconstitutional so also is the other, and that both must stand or fall together. Let it also be borne in mind that, as the one received the support of a Clay, and a Calhoun, and a Webster, so the other received the sanction and the signature of George Washington. Yet, in the face of these facts, Mr. Sumner does not moderate his rage. They only seem to increase the intensity and the fury of his wrath. "The soul sickens," he cries, "in the contemplation of this legalized outrage. In the dreary annals of the past there are many acts of shame—there are many ordinances of monarchs, and laws which have become a byword and a hissing to the nations. But when we consider the country and the age, I ask fearlessly, what act of shame, what ordinance of monarch, what law, can compare in atrocity with this enactment of an American Congress?"

Not content with pouring floods of abuse on the law itself, Mr. Sumner proceeds to consign to infamy its authors and all who have given it their support. For, after furnishing examples of what he deems among the most atrocious transactions of the past, he adds: "I would not exag-

30

gerate.   I wish to keep within bounds; but
I think no person can doubt that the condemnation affixed to all these transactions and to their
authors must be the lot hereafter of the Fugitive Slave Bill, and of every one, according to
the measure of his influence, who gave it his
support.   Into the immortal catalogue of national crimes this has now passed, drawing with
it, by an inexorable necessity, its authors also,
and chiefly him who, as President of the United
States, set his name to the bill, and breathed into
it that final breath without which it would have
no life.   Other Presidents may be forgotten,
but the name signed to the Fugitive Slave Bill
can never be forgotten.   There are depths of
infamy, as there are heights of fame.   I regret
to say what I must, but truth compels me.
Better far for him had he never been born;
better for his memory, and for the name of his
children, had he never been President!''

If neither Mr. Fillmore nor George Washington swore to support the Constitution as Mr.
Sumner understands it, we beg him to consider
that *his opinion was not known* when they took the
oath of office.   Mr. Fillmore had, at that time,
no better guide to go by than the decisions of
the most enlightened judicial tribunals of his

country, with the Supreme Court of the United
States at their head. He was not so far raised
above other men, nor possessed of so wonderful
an insight into the Constitution, as Mr. Sumner;
for he could understand it no better than its
framers. Hence he was, no doubt, so conscious
of his own fallibility that he could hardly look
upon modesty as a crime, or upon a deference
to the judicial tribunals of his country as infamous. We trust, therefore, that his good
name will survive, and that his children will
not blush to own it. It is certain that the
American people will never believe, on the bare
authority of Mr. Sumner, that, in his course re-
garding the Fugitive Slave Law, he planted his
feet in the very "depths of infamy," when they
can so clearly see that he merely trod in the
footsteps of George Washington.

If what a man lacks in reason he could only
make up in rage, then, after all, it would have
to be concluded that Mr. Sumner is a very respectable Senator; for, surely, the violence of
his denunciations is almost as remarkable as
the weakness of his logic. Fortunately, however, it can hurt no one except himself or those
whom he represents. Certainly, the brightest
names in the galaxy of American statesmen are

not to be swept away by the filthy torrent of his invectives. The Clays, the Calhouns, the Websters, and the Washingtons of America, are, indeed, as far above the impotent rage of this Senator as the very stars of heaven are beyond his arm.*

---

* Mr. Sumner has a great deal to say, in his speech, about "the memory of the fathers." When their sentiments agree with his own, or only seem to him to do so, then they are "the demi-gods of history." But only let these demi-gods cross his path or come into contact with his fanatical notions, and instantly they sink into sordid knaves. The framers of the Constitution of the United States, says he, made "a compromise, which *cannot be mentioned without shame.* It was that *hateful bargain* by which Congress was restrained until 1808 from the prohibition of the foreign slave trade, thus securing, down to that period, *toleration for crime.*" . . . . "The effrontery of slaveholders was matched by *the sordidness of the Eastern members.*" . . . . "The bargain was struck, and at this price the Southern States gained the detestable indulgence. At a subsequent day, Congress branded the slave trade as piracy, and thus, by solemn legislative act, adjudged this compromise to be *felonious and wicked.*"

But for this compromise, as every one who has read the history of the times perfectly well knows, no union could have been formed, and the slave trade might have been carried on to the present day. By this compromise, then, the Convention did not tolerate crime nor the slave trade; they merely formed the Union, and, in forming it, *gained the power to abolish the slave trade in twenty years.* The gain of this power, which Congress

§ III. *The right of Trial by Jury not impaired by the Fugitive Slave Law.*

It is alleged that the power to enact such a law does not reside in Congress, because no such power has been "expressly delegated," and because it is not "necessary and proper" to carry any expressly delegated authority into effect. We should have replied to this argument; but it has been urged before every tri-

---

had not before possessed, was considered by them as a great gain to the cause of humanity. If the Eastern members, from a blind and frantic hatred of slavery, had blasted all prospects of a union, and at the same time put the slave trade beyond their power forever, they would have imitated the wisdom of the abolitionists, who always promote the cause they seek to demolish.

If any one will read the history of the times, he will see that "the fathers," the framers of the Constitution, were, in making this very compromise, governed by the purest, the most patriotic, and the most humane, of motives. He who accuses them of corruption shows himself corrupt; especially if, like Mr. Sumner, he can laud them on one page as demi-gods, and on the very next denounce them as sordid knaves, who, for the sake of filthy lucre, could enter into a "felonious and wicked" bargain. Yet the very man who accuses them of having made so infamous and corrupt a bargain in regard to the slave trade can and does most eloquently declaim against the monstrous injustice of supposing them capable of the least act in favor of slavery!

X   30*

bunal in which the great question under consideration has been tried, and everywhere refuted. By Mr. Justice Nelson, in the Supreme Court of New York,* by Mr. Senator Bishop, in the Court of Errors in the same State,† and by Mr. Justice Story, in the Supreme Court of the United States, it has been so clearly, so powerfully, and so triumphantly demolished as to leave nothing more to be desired on the subject. And besides, it has been our object not so much to refute arguments against the law in question, or to establish that which has been so long established,‡ as to show on what slender grounds, and yet with what unbounded confidence, the greatest champions of abolitionism are accustomed to oppose the Constitution, the laws, the judicial decisions, and the uniform practice, of the whole government under which we live.

In pursuance of this design, there is another sophism of theirs, which it now devolves upon us to examine. We allude to the argument

---

* XII. Wendell, p. 314.

† XIV. Wendell, p. 530; XVI. Peters, p. 608.

‡ Indeed, if we had produced all the arguments in favor of the constitutionality of the Fugitive Slave Law, it would have carried us far beyond our limits, and swelled this single chapter into a volume.

that the Fugitive Slave Law is unconstitutional, because it denies the right of trial by jury.

Is this still an open question? In the biography of Mr. Justice Story, published by his son, it is said: "The argument that the Act of 1793 was unconstitutional, because it did not provide for a trial by jury according to the requisitions of the sixth article in the amendment to the Constitution, having been suggested to my father on his return from Washington, he replied that this question was not argued by counsel nor considered by the court, and that he should still consider it an open one." Mr. Sumner adduces this "distinct statement that the necessity of trial by jury was not before the court;" and adds, "So that, in the estimation of the judge himself, it was still an open question."

In the case here referred to—Prigg v. The Commonwealth of Pennsylvania, reported in XVI. Peters—it is true that the question of trial by jury was not argued by counsel nor considered by the court. But if the greater includes the less, then this question was embraced in the decision; for, in that case, Prigg had seized the fugitive slave without process, and carried her away without any certificate from magistrate or judge in the State of Pennsylvania. The court declared that he had a right to do so under and by virtue of the Constitution of the United States. Most assuredly, if he had a constitutional right to such proceeding, then, in such cases, the Constitution dispenses with the necessity of trial by jury.

It was urged by counsel that such summary method of reclaiming fugitive slaves was unconstitutional; but the court decided otherwise. It was insisted by Mr. Hambly, just as it is now insisted by Mr. Sumner and others, that such arrest was unconstitutional, because it was made by the mere will of the party, and not, as the Constitution requires, "by due process of law." Thus the point was presented by the record, argued by the counsel, and overruled by the court.

In overruling this argument the court says: "The owner must, therefore, have the right to seize and repossess the slave which the local laws of his own State confer upon him as property; and we all know that this right of seizure and recaption is universally acknowledged in all the slave-holding States. Indeed, this is no more than a mere affirmance of the principles of the common law applicable to this very subject." Then, after a quotation from Blackstone, the court adds: "Upon this ground, we have not the slightest hesitation in holding that, under and in virtue of the Constitution, the owner of a slave is clothed with entire authority in every State in the Union to seize and recapture his slave whenever he can do it without any breach of the peace or any illegal violence."

In accordance with this opinion of the court—delivered by Mr. Justice Story—Mr. Chief Justice Taney says: the master "has a right, peaceably, to take possession of him, and carry him away, without any certificate or warrant from a judge of the District or Circuit Court of the United States, or from any magistrate of the State; and whosoever resists or obstructs him is a wrong-doer; and every State law which proposes, directly or indirectly, to authorize such resistance or obstruction, is null and void, and affords no justification to the individual or the officer of the State who acts under it. This right of the master being given by the Constitution of the United States, neither Congress nor a State Legislature can by any law or regulation impair it or restrict it."*

---

* This decision of the Supreme Court, which authorizes the master to seize his fugitive slave *without process*, (see his speech,

Hence it would have been well if Mr. Sumner and the son of Judge Story had looked into this decision again before they proclaimed the opinion that the right of trial by jury is, in such cases, still an open question. Mr. Justice Story himself must, on reflection, have seen that the off-hand expression attributed to him was erroneous. His more deliberate opinion is recorded, not only in the case of Prigg, but also

---

Appendix to Congressional Globe, vol. xxii., part 2, p. 1587,) is exceedingly offensive to Mr. Chase, of Ohio; and no wonder, since the legislature of his own State has passed a law, making it a penitentiary offence in the master who should thus prosecute his constitutional right as declared by this decision. But, in regard to this point, the Supreme Court of the United States does not stand alone. The Supreme Court of New York, in the case of Jack *v.* Martin, had previously said: "Whether the owner or agent might have made the arrest in the first instance without any process, we will not stop to examine; authorities of deserved respectability and weight have held the affirmative. 2 Pick. 11, 5 Serg. & Rawle, 62, and the case of Glen *v.* Hodges, in this court, before referred to, (in 9 Johnson,) seem to countenance the same conclusion. It would indeed appear to follow as a necessary consequence, from *the undoubted position, that under this clause of the Constitution the right and title of the owner to the service of the slave is as entire and perfect within the jurisdiction of the State to which he has fled as it was in the one from which he escaped. Such seizure would be at the peril of the party; AND IF A FREEMAN WAS TAKEN, HE WOULD BE ANSWERABLE LIKE ANY OTHER TRESPASSER OR KIDNAPPER.*"

in his "Commentaries on the Constitution of the United States." "It is obvious," says he, "that these provisions for the arrest and removal of fugitives of both classes contemplate summary ministerial proceedings, and not the ordinary course of judicial investigations to ascertain whether the complaint be well-founded or the claim of ownership be established beyond all legal controversy. In cases of suspected crimes the guilt or innocence of the party is to be made out at his trial, and not upon the preliminary inquiry whether he shall be delivered up. All that would seem in such cases to be necessary is that there should be *primâ facie* evidence before the executive authority to satisfy its judgment that there is probable cause to believe the party guilty, such as, upon an ordinary warrant, would justify his commitment for trial. And in the cases of fugitive slaves there would seem to be the same necessity of requiring only *primâ facie* proofs of ownership, without putting the party to a formal assertion of his rights by a suit at the common law."*

But, since the abolitionists will discuss this point, then let it be considered an open ques-

---

* Story on Constitution, vol. iii., book iii., chap. xl.

tion, and let them produce their arguments. The first we shall notice is from Mr. Sumner, who again reasons from the sentiments of the fathers. "At the close of the National Convention," says he, "Elbridge Gerry refused to sign the Constitution, because, among other things, it established 'a tribunal *without juries*, a Star Chamber as to civil cases.' Many united in his opposition, and, on the recommendation of the First Congress, this additional safeguard was adopted as an amendment." Thus, according to Mr. Sumner, Elbridge Gerry was the father of the clause in the Constitution which guarantees the right of trial by jury. Yet Elbridge Gerry never dreamed of applying this clause to the case of fugitive slaves; for, as we have already seen, he voted for the Fugitive Slave Law of 1793, in which such application of it is denied. Nor did any other member of that Congress propose the right of trial by jury in such cases.

No doubt there would have been opposition to the act of 1793 if any member of Congress had supposed, for a moment, that it denied the right of trial by jury to the fugitive slave. It does no such thing. It leaves that right unimpaired; and if any slave in the Union, whether fugitive

or otherwise, desire such trial, it is secured to
him by the Constitution and laws of the country. But he cannot have such trial where or
in what State he chooses. If he lives in Richmond, he may have a trial by jury there; but he
cannot escape to Boston, and there demand this
as a right. The fugitive from labor, like the
fugitive from justice, has a right to a trial by
jury, but neither can claim to have this trial in
any part of the world he pleases. The latter
must be tried in "the vicinage" where the offence is alleged to have been committed, because there the witnesses are to be found. He
has no right to flee from these and require
them to follow him with their testimony. As
he has a constitutional right to be tried in the
vicinage of the alleged offence, so has the commonwealth a right to insist on his trial there.
In like manner, and for a similar reason, if the
colored man wish to assert his freedom under
the law, he may appeal to a jury of the country;
but this must be done in the State under whose
laws he is claimed as a slave and where the
witnesses reside. He cannot fly to a distant
State, and there demand a kind of trial which
neither the Constitution, nor the laws, nor public
expediency, secures to him. If he assert this

right at all, he must assert it in conformity with the *undoubted right of the other party*, which is to be sued in this, as in all other personal actions, in the place where he resides.

In the face of these considerations, it is no wonder that the Congress of 1793 were so unanimous in regard to the Fugitive Slave Law. Though this law did not provide for a jury trial, yet its authors all knew that such trial was not denied to the fugitive slave, if he had a mind to claim it. Hence the law was passed by that Congress, without even an allusion to this modern abolition objection to its constitutionality. Among all the members of that body who had taken part in framing the Constitution of the United States,* not one was found to hint

---

* The framers of the Constitution in that Congress were:—
"John Langdon and Nicholas Gilmer, of New Hampshire; Caleb Strong and Elbridge Gerry, of Massachusetts; Roger Sherman and Oliver Ellsworth, of Connecticut; Rufus King, of New York; Robert Morris and Thomas Fitzsimmons, of Pennsylvania; George Reid and Richard Basset, of Delaware; Jonathan Dayton, of New Jersey; Pierce Butler, of South Carolina; Hugh Williamson, of North Carolina; William Few and Abraham Baldwin, of Georgia; and last, but not least, James Madison, of Virginia." Yet from not one of these framers of the Constitution—from not one of these illustrious guardians of freedom—was a syllable heard in regard to the right of trial by

at such an objection. This objection is of more recent origin, if not of less respectable parentage.

An amendment to the law in question, allowing a trial by jury to the fugitive slave in a distant State, would indeed be a virtual denial of the constitutional right of the master. Either because the jury could not agree, or because distant testimony might be demanded, the trial would probably be continued, and put off, until the expense, the loss of time, and the worriment of vexatious proceedings, would be more than the slave is worth. The language of Mr. Chief Justice Taney, in relation to an action for damages by the master, is peculiarly applicable to such a trial by jury. The master "*would be compelled*," says he, "*to encounter the costs and expenses of a suit, prosecuted at a distance from his own home, and to sacrifice perhaps the value of his property in endeavoring* to obtain compensation." This is not the kind of remedy, says he, the Constitu-

jury in connection with the Fugitive Slave Law then passed. The more pity it is, no doubt, the abolitionist will think, that neither Mr. Chase, nor Mr. Sumner, nor Mr. Seward, was there to enlighten them on the subject of trial by jury and to save the country from the infamy of such an Act. Alas! for the poor, blind fathers!

tion "intended to give. The delivery of the property itself—its PROMPT AND IMMEDIATE DELIVERY—*is plainly required, and was intended to be secured.*" Such prompt and immediate delivery was a part of "the customary or common law" at the time the Constitution was adopted, and its framers, no doubt, intended that this practice should be enforced by the clause in question, as appears from the fact that so many of them concurred in the Act of 1793.

But if such right to a prompt and immediate delivery be guaranteed by the Constitution itself, then, with all due submission, we would ask, what power has Congress to limit or abridge this right? If under and by virtue of the Constitution this right to a prompt and immediate delivery be secured, then what power has Congress to say there shall *not* be a prompt or immediate delivery? "This right of the master," says Mr. Chief Justice Taney, "being given by the Constitution of the United States, NEITHER CONGRESS NOR A STATE LEGISLATURE CAN BY ANY LAW OR REGULATION IMPAIR IT OR RESTRICT IT." If this be sound doctrine,—and such we hold it to be,—then Congress has no constitutional power to impair or restrict the right in question, by giving the fugitive slave a trial by jury in the

State to which he may have fled. This would not be to give a "prompt and immediate delivery," such as the Supreme Court declares the master is entitled to by the Constitution itself; it would be either to give no delivery at all, or else one attended with such delays, vexations, and costs, as would materially impair, if not wholly annihilate, the right in question.

It is right and proper, we think, that questions arising exclusively under our own laws should be tried in our own States and by our own tribunals. Hence we shall never consent, unless constrained by the judicial decision of the Supreme Court of the Union, to have such questions tried in States whose people and whose juries may, perhaps, be hostile to our interests and to our domestic institutions. For we are SOVEREIGN as well as they.

Only conceive such a trial by jury in a Northern State, with such an advocate for the fugitive slave as Mr. Chase, or Mr. Sumner, or some other flaming abolitionist! There sits the fugitive slave,—"one of the heroes of the age," as Mr. Sumner calls him, and the very embodiment of persecuted innocence. On the other hand is the master,—the vile "Slave-hunter," as Mr. Sumner delights to represent him, and

31*

whom, if possible, he is determined "to blast with contempt, indignation, and abhorrence." The trial begins. The advocate appeals to the prejudices and the passions of the jury. He denounces slavery—about which neither he nor the jury know any thing—as the epitome of all earthly wrongs, as the sum and substance of all human woes. Now, suppose that on the jury there is *only one man*, who, like the Vermont judge, requires "a bill of sale from the Almighty" before he will deliver up a fugitive slave; or who, like Mr. Seward, sets his own private opinion above the Constitution of his country; or who, like Mr. Sumner, has merely sworn to support the supreme law as he understands it; and who, at the same time, possesses his capacity to understand it just exactly as he pleases: then what chance would the master have for a verdict? Just none at all. For that one man, however clear the master's evidence, would hang the jury, and the cause would have to be tried over again.

But suppose the whole twelve jurors should decide according to the law and the evidence, and give a verdict in favor of the claimant; would his rights then be secured? Very far from it. For there is the eager crowd, which never fails to flock to such trials, and which the inflammatory eloquence of the advocate has now wrought into a frenzy. Cannot such crowd, think you, furnish a mob to effect by force what every member of the jury had refused to accomplish by falsehood? If the master—if the abhorred "slave-hunter"—should escape from such a crowd with a sound body only, and without his property, he ought, we think, to deem himself exceedingly fortunate.

Mr. Winthrop, of Massachusetts, has advocated a trial by jury in such cases. He was, no doubt, perfectly sincere in the belief expressed by him, that under such a provision more fugitive slaves would be reclaimed than under the law as it now stands. But it is equally certain that neither Mr. Seward nor Mr. Chase was of this opinion when the one proposed, and the other voted for, a trial by jury in such cases. Neither of these Senators, we think we may confidently affirm, intended to aid the master in reclaiming his fugitive slaves.

"At any rate, sir," says Mr. Winthrop, "I shall vote for the amendment offered by the Senator from New Jersey, as right and just in itself, whatever may be its effects." That is to say, whatever may be the effect of a jury trial in such cases, he means to vote for it *as right and just in itself!* Whether this were a burst of passion merely, or the deliberate conviction of the author of it, we are not able to determine, but we shall trust it was the former. For surely such an opinion, if deliberately entertained, is creditable neither to a Senator nor to a jurist. Neither this, nor any other mode of trial, is "right in itself;" and when right at all, it is only so as a means to an end. It is only right when it subserves the great end of justice; and if it fail to answer this end it is then worse than worthless. Hence the statesman who declares that, "*whatever may be the effects*" of a particular mode of trial, he will nevertheless support it "as right and just in itself," thereby announces that he is prepared to sacrifice the end to the means,—a sentiment which, we venture to affirm, is more worthy of a fanatical declaimer than of the high-minded and accomplished Senator by whom it was uttered.

The great objection urged against the Fugitive Slave Law is that under it a freeman may be seized and reduced to slavery. This law, as well as every other, may, no doubt, be grossly abused, and made a cover for evil deeds. But is there no remedy for such evil deeds? Is there no protection for the free blacks of the North, except by a denial of the clear and unquestionable constitutional rights of the South? If not, then we should be willing to submit; but there is a remedy against such foul abuse of the law of Congress in question, and, as we conceive, a most ample remedy.

The master may recapture his fugitive slave. This is his constitutional right. But, in the language of the Supreme Court of New York, already quoted, if a villain, under cover of a pretended right, proceeds to carry off a freeman, he does so *"at his peril, and would be answerable like any other trespasser or kidnapper."* He must be caught, however, before he can be punished. Let him be caught, let the crime be proved upon him, and we would most heartily concur in the law by which he should himself be doomed to slavery for life in the penitentiary.

The Fugitive Slave Law is not the only one liable to abuse. The innocent may be, and often have been, arrested for crime; but this is no reason why the law of arrest should be abolished, or even impaired in its operation. Nay, innocent persons have often been mali-

Y

ciously prosecuted; yet no one, on this account, ever dreamed of throwing obstacles in the way of prosecution for crime. The innocent have been made the victims of perjury; but who imagines that all swearing in courts of justice should therefore be abolished? Such evils and such crimes are sought to be remedied by separate legislation, and not by undermining the laws of which they are the abuses. In like manner, though we wish to see the free blacks of the North protected, and would most cheerfully lend a helping hand for that purpose, yet, at the same time, we would maintain our own constitutional rights inviolate. The villain who, under cover of the law made for the protection of our rights, should seek to invade the rights of Northern freemen, is as much abhorred by us as by any abolitionists on earth. Nor, on the other hand, have we any sympathy with those who, under cover of a law *to be made* for the protection of the free blacks of the North, seek to invade the rights of the South. We have no sympathy with either class of kidnappers.

Is it not wonderful that, while the abolitionists of the North create and keep up so great a clamor about the danger their free blacks are in, they do so little, and ask so little, either by legislation or otherwise, in order to protect them, except in such manner, or by such legislation, as shall aim a deadly blow at the rights and interests of the South? If they really wish to protect their free blacks, and if the laws are not already sufficient for that purpose, we are more than willing to assist in the passage of more efficient ones. But we are not willing to abandon the great right which the Constitution spreads, like an impenetrable shield, over Southern property to the amount of sixteen hundred millions of dollars.

The complaint in regard to the want of protection for the free blacks of the North is without just foundation. In the case of Jack *v.* Martin, decided in the Court of Errors of New York, we find the following language, which is here exactly in point:—"It was contended on the argument of this cause, with great zeal and earnestness, that, under the law of the United States, a freeman might be dragged from his family and home into captivity. This is supposing an extreme case, as I believe it is not pretended any such ever has occurred, or that any complaint of that character has ever been made; at all events, I cannot regard it as a very potent argument. The same position might as well be taken in the case of a fugitive from justice. It might be assumed that he was an innocent man, and entitled to be tried by a jury of the State where he was arrested, to ascertain whether he had violated the laws of the State from which he fled; whereas the fact is, the executive of this State would feel bound to deliver up the most exalted individual in this State, (however well satisfied he might be of his innocence,) if a requisition was made upon him by the executive of another State."

In the same case, when before the Supreme Court of New York, the court said: "In the case under review, the proceedings are before a magistrate of our own State, presumed to possess a sympathy with his fellow-citizens, and *where, upon the supposition that a freeman is arrested, he may readily procure the evidence of his freedom.* If the magistrate should finally err in granting the certificate, *the party can still resort to the protection of the national judiciary. The proceedings by which his rights have been invaded being under a law of Congress, the remedy for error or injustice belongs peculiarly to that high tribunal.* UNDER THEIR AMPLE SHIELD, THE AP-

PREHENSION OF CAPTIVITY AND OPPRESSION CANNOT
BE ALARMING."

It is evident that when this opinion was pronounced by the Supreme Court of New York, it
had not fathomed the depths of some men's
capacity of being alarmed by apprehensions of
captivity and oppression. The abolitionists will,
whether or no, be most dreadfully alarmed.
But the danger consists, not in the want of laws
and courts to punish the kidnapper, but in the
want of somebody to catch him. If he does all
the mischief ascribed to him by the abolitionists,
is it not wonderful that he is not caught by
them? Rumor, with her thousand tongues, is
clamorous about his evil deeds; and fanatical
credulity, with her ten thousand ears, gives heed
to the reports of rumor. But yet, somehow or
other, the abolitionists, with all their fiery, restless zeal, never succeed in laying their hands
on the offender himself. He must, indeed, be a
most adroit, a most cunning, a most wonderful
rogue. He boldly goes into a community in
which so many are all eye, all ear, and all
tongue, in regard to the black man's rights; he
there steals a free negro, who himself has the
power to tell when, where, and how, he became
free; and yet, in open day, and amid ten thou-

sand flaming guardians of freedom,* he escapes with perfect impunity! Is he not a most marvellous proper rogue? But perhaps the reason the abolitionists do not lay hands on him is that he is an imaginary being, who, though intangible and invisible, will yet serve just as well to create an alarm and keep up a great excitement as if he were a real personage.

§ IV. *The Duty of the Citizen in regard to the Constitution of the United States.*

The Constitution, it is agreed on all sides, is "the supreme law of the land,"—of every State in the Union. The first duty of the citizen in regard to the Constitution is, then, to respect and obey each and every one of its provisions. If he repudiates or sets at naught this or that provision thereof, because it does not happen to agree with his own views or feelings, he does not respect the Constitution at all; he makes his own will and pleasure the supreme law. The true principle of loyalty resides not in his bosom. We may apply to him, and to the supreme law of the land, the language of an in-

---

* This crime of kidnapping, says Mr. Chase, of Ohio, is "not unfrequent" in his section of country; that is, about Cincinnati.

spired apostle, that "whosoever shall keep the whole law, and yet offend in one point, he is guilty of all." He is guilty of all, because, by his wilful disobedience in the one instance, he sets at naught the authority by which the whole was ordained and established.

In opposing the Fugitive Slave Law, it is forgotten by the abolitionists that, if no such law existed, the master would have, under the Constitution itself, the same right to reclaim his fugitive from labor, and to reclaim him in the same summary manner; for, as we have seen, the Supreme Court of the United States has decided that by virtue of the Constitution alone the master has a right to pursue and reclaim his fugitive slave, without even a writ or legal process. Hence, in opposing the Fugitive Slave Law because it allows a summary proceeding in such cases, the abolitionists really make war on the Constitution. The battery which they open against the Constitution is merely masked behind the Fugitive Slave Law; and thus the nature of their attack is concealed from the eyes of their non-legal followers.

But, says Mr. Chase, of Ohio, I do not agree with the Supreme Court of the United States. I oppose not the Constitution, but the decision of the Supreme Court. "A decision of the Supreme Court," says he, "cannot alter the Constitution." This is very true; but then, on the other hand, it is equally true that neither can his opinion alter the Constitution. But here the question arises, which is the rule of conduct for the true and loyal citizen,—the decision of the Supreme Court of the United States, or the opinion of Governor Chase? We decidedly prefer the former. "Sir," says Mr. Chase, "when gentlemen from the slave States ask us to support the Constitution, I fear they mean only their *construction* of the Constitution." We mean not so. We mean neither *our* nor *his* construction of the Constitution, but that construction only which has been given to it by the highest judicial tribunal in the land, by the supreme and final arbiter in all such conflicts of opinion.

But Mr. Chase opposes argument as well as opinion to the decision of the Supreme Court in regard to slavery. "What more natural," says he, "than that gentlemen from the slave States, in view of the questions likely to come before the Supreme Court, should desire that a majority of its members might have interests like those which they would desire to maintain!

Certain it is that some care has been taken to secure such a constitution of the court, and not without success." If Mr. Chase, or any other abolitionist, should insinuate that the decision in question is owing to such an unfair constitution of the Supreme Court, the answer is as easy and triumphant as the accusation would be infamous and vile; for, as is well known, the very decision which is so obnoxious to his sentiments was delivered by the great jurist of Massachusetts, Mr. Justice Story, and was concurred in by the other Northern members of the Court. This is not all. How did it happen that substantially the same decision has been rendered by the Supreme Courts of New York, Massachusetts, and Pennsylvania? Were these high tribunals also constituted with reference to the peculiar interests of the South?

The question is not whether the decision of the Supreme Court, or the opinion of Mr. Chase, the more perfectly reflects the Constitution. Even if he were infallible, as the Supreme Court certainly is not, we, the people of the United States, have not agreed that he shall decide such questions for us. And besides, it would be difficult, perhaps, to persuade the people that he is, for the determination of such questions, any

more happily constituted than the Supreme
Court itself, with all the manifold imperfections
of its Southern members. But, however this
may be, it is certain that until the people shall
be so persuaded, and shall agree to abide by his
opinions, it is the duty of the good citizen to
follow the decisions of the great judicial tribunal provided by the Constitution of his
country.

If you, good citizen of the North, have a right
to set up your opinion in opposition to such decisions, then I have the same right, and so has
every other member of the commonwealth.
Thus, as many constructions of the Constitution
would necessarily result as there are individual
opinions in the land. Law and order would be
at an end; a chaos of conflicting elements
would prevail, and every man would do that
which seemed right in his own eyes. The only
escape from such anarchy is a just and loyal
confidence in the judicial tribunals of the land—
is a subjection of the intense egotism of the individual to the will of the nation, as expressed
in the Constitution and expounded by the constitutional authorities. Hence, we mean to support the Constitution, not as *we* understand it
nor as *you* understand it, but as it is understood

by the Supreme Court of the United States. Such, it seems to us, is the only wise course— nay, is the imperative duty—of every citizen who does not intend to disorganize the fundamental law and revolutionize the government of his country.

It may be supposed, perhaps, by those who have reflected little on the subject, that the controversy respecting the Fugitive Slave Law is merely about the value of a few slaves. It is, in our opinion, far otherwise; it is a great constitutional question; and hence the deep interest which it has excited throughout the nation, as well as in the Senate of the United States. It is a question, as it appears to us, whether the Constitution or the abolitionists shall rule the country. The Fugitive Slave Law is, as we have seen, surrounded by the strongest possible evidences of its constitutionality; and hence, if this may be swept away as unconstitutional by the passions of a mad faction, then may every other legal defence be levelled before like storms, and all security annihilated. Hence, as the friends of law and order, we intend to take our stand right here, and defend this Act, which, although despised and abhorred by a faction, has received the sanction of the fathers, as well as of the great judicial tribunals, of the land.

We are asked to repeal this law—ay, by the most violent agitator of the North we are asked to repeal this law—for "*the sake of tranquillity and peace!*" But how can this bring peace? Suppose this law were repealed; would tranquillity be restored? We have not forgotten—nor can we be so easily made to forget—that this very agitator himself has declared, that slavery is "a wrong so transcendent" that no truce is to be allowed to it so long as it occupies a single foot of ground in the United States. Is it not, then, a delusive prospect of peace which is offered to us in exchange for the law in question?

Nor can we forget what other agitators have uttered respecting the abolition of slavery in the Southern States. "Slavery," said Mr. Seward, at a mass-meeting in Ohio, "can be limited to its present bounds; it can be ameliorated. It can be—and it *must* be—ABOLISHED, and you and I can and *must* do it." Does this look like peace, if the Fugitive Slave Law were only out of the way? Mr. Seward, from his place in the Senate of the United States, tells us how we must act among the people of the North, if, in reclaiming our fugitive slaves, we would not disturb their peace. But he had already exhorted the people of the North to "extend a cordial welcome" to our fugitive slaves, and to "defend them as they would their household gods." What, then, does he mean by peace?

This outcry, indeed, that the peace of the country is disturbed by the Fugitive Slave Law, is as great a delusion as ever was attempted to be palmed off on any people. If this law were repealed to-morrow, would agitation cease? Would the abolitionists of the North cease to proclaim that their doors are open, and their hospitality is ready, to receive the poor benighted blacks? (the blacks of the South, we mean; for we have never heard of their open doors, or cordial hospitality, for the poor free blacks of their own neighborhood.) But we have heard—from Dr. Channing himself—of "a convention at the North, of highly respected men, preparing and publishing an address to the slaves, in which they are exhorted to fly from bondage, and to *feel no scruple in seizing and using horse or boat which may facilitate their escape.*" Now, if the Fugitive Slave Law were repealed, would all such proceedings cease? Or if, under the Constitution as expounded by the

Supreme Courts of the Union and of New York, and without any such law to back him, the master should seek to reclaim his property, would he be welcomed, or hooted and resisted, by the defenders of the fugitive from his service? Let these things be considered, and it will be evident, we think, that the repeal of the law in question would only invite further aggressions, and from this prostrate outpost the real enemies of the peace of the country would march, if possible, over every other defence of the Constitution.

Hence, although we most ardently desire harmony and concord for the States of the Union, we shall never seek it by a surrender of the Constitution or the decisions of the Supreme Court. If it cannot be found under these, it cannot be found at all. Mr. Chase assures us, indeed, that just so long as the rule laid down by the Supreme Court in the case of Prigg prevails, we must "encounter difficulties, and serious difficulties."* If it must be so, then so be it. If the question be whether the decisions of the Supreme Court, or the dictation of demagogues,

---

* Appendix to Congressional Globe, vol. xxii., part ii., p. 1587.

shall rule our destinies, then is our stand taken and our purpose immovably fixed.

We have a right to peace under the decisions of that august tribunal. It is neither right nor proper—it is contrary to every principle of natural justice—that either party to this great controversy should decide for itself. Hence, if the abolitionists will not submit to the decisions of the Supreme Court, we shall most assuredly refuse submission to their arrogant dictation. We can, from our inmost hearts, respect the feelings of those of our Northern brethren who may choose to remain passive in this matter, and leave us—by such aid as the law may afford—to reclaim our own fugitives from labor. For such we have only words of kindness and feelings of fraternal love. But as for those—and especially for those in high places—who counsel resistance to the laws and to the Constitution of the Republic, we hold them guilty of a high misdemeanor, and we shall ever treat them as disturbers of the public peace, nay, as enemies of the independence, the perpetuity, the greatness, and the glory of the Union under which, by the blessing of Almighty God, we have hitherto so wonderfully prospered.

THE END.